Reflective Teaching,
Reflective Learning

Reflective Teaching, *Reflective Learning*

How to Develop Critically Engaged Readers, Writers, and Speakers

EDITED BY
THOMAS M. MCCANN
LARRY R. JOHANNESSEN
ELIZABETH KAHN
PETER SMAGORINSKY
AND MICHAEL W. SMITH

HEINEMANN
PORTSMOUTH, NH

Heinemann

A division of Reed Elsevier Inc.

361 Hanover Street

Portsmouth, NH 03801–3912

www.heinemann.com

Offices and agents throughout the world

Library of Congress Cataloging-in-Publication Data

Reflective teaching, reflective learning : how to develop critically engaged readers, writers, and speakers / edited by Thomas M. McCann ... [et al.] ; foreword by Jeffrey D. Wilhelm.

     p. cm.

    Includes bibliographical references.

    ISBN 0-325-00852-3 (alk. paper)

  1. Language arts. I. McCann, Thomas M.

    LB1631.R34 2005

    428'.0071'2—dc22   2005020766

Editor: *Lisa Luedeke*

Production: *Patricia Adams*

Typesetter: *Gina Poirier Design*

Cover design: *Night & Day Design*

Cover photograph: *Getty/Photodisc;* Photographer: *GeoStock*

Manufacturing: *Jamie Carter*

Printed in the United States of America on acid-free paper

09 08 07 06 05 RRD 1 2 3 4 5

CONTENTS

FOREWORD

JEFFREY D. WILHELM
Boise State University
Boise, Idaho

I *almost* became George Hillocks' Master of Arts in Teaching (MAT) student at the University of Chicago.

It's one of my many George Hillocks stories, from a repertoire that is continually growing. You see, as an undergraduate I took two introductory education courses, and they were so insipid, boring, and uninspiring that I dropped out of education altogether in favor of a double major in English and German. But as I neared the end of my undergraduate career (the five-year plan, including a one-year Rotary scholarship to Germany), I continued to want to teach. I wanted a program that would focus on what I considered to be the substantive challenge of teaching, instead of the mindless minutiae I had been exposed to in my first education courses. I spoke to several professors at Ohio universities about my options: Every one of them recommended that I pursue my MAT degree and that I do so at the University of Chicago. Every one of them invoked the name George Hillocks. At least one of them remembered George as an outstanding teacher of seventh-grade English from Euclid, Ohio.

I applied to the program at the University of Chicago and the MAT program at Brown University. In April, my girlfriend, Peggy (now my wife), and I planned a trip to Chicago for an open house offered by UC's MAT program. But the day before we were to depart, a Friday in early April, both Peggy and I received scholarship offers: I from Brown and Peg from Boston University. We agreed that we both would accept these offers and canceled our trip to Chicago.

But I quickly learned, and have been learning ever since, that if you are serious about English education, George Hillocks is not an easy person to escape.

In fact, while a student in what continues to be the very fine MAT program at Brown, one of our first readings was about George's questioning hierarchy to promote skills in interpreting literature. We later looked at his review of written composition. He became a character in our discussions and debates, as we asked, "But what would Hillocks say?" It seemed to me that George was everywhere, particularly when we were tempted to accept a simplistic answer to a teaching problem or to let ourselves off the hook in terms of our responsibility as teachers.

After my first few years of teaching, my desire to be a better teacher led me to immerse myself in professional reading. I remember my excitement with the Theory and Research Into Practice (TRIP) books put out by the National Council of Teachers of English (NCTE). *Writing About Literature* by Elizabeth Kahn, Larry Johannessen, and Carolyn Calhoun Walter made me think for the first time about how to sequence instructional activities; *Designing and Sequencing Prewriting Activities*, also by Kahn, Johannessen, and Walter, taught me about the demands placed on readers by different kinds of texts like extended definition. I devoured *Reducing Writing Apprehension* by Michael Smith and *Explorations: Introductory Activities for Literature and Composition, 7–12* by Peter Smagorinsky, Tom McCann, and Steve Kern—and with big utensils. What I didn't realize at the time was that the texts I found most useful and transformative were almost all by George's students. I found out later that these teachers' public careers began on a famous weekend when George invited his students to his home, locked them in, and said, "It's time to give something back to the profession. You don't leave until you write a proposal for the next NCTE convention."

Eight years into my teaching career I was struggling with my teaching of eighth-grade remedial reading. In the midst of this struggle I heard Michael Smith speak at the Wisconsin Council of Teachers of English conference in Stevens Point. He was presenting about how to develop new interests and abilities by building on kids' existing interests and strengths. He then launched into a talk about how to teach conventions of writing that would help kids understand how to read and write particular texts, like argument. I remember being electrified: This is what I had been looking for. I had been confronted with the fact that I didn't know how to motivate kids who were unmotivated readers and writers or how to use students' existing resources to develop new ones. I felt I had underarticulated the complexity of reading and writing. Michael, a student of George's, was helping me fill in the gaps. Afterward, I rushed up to him and said, "I want to study with you!" And he responded, "That would be great. Do you want to tell me your name?"

I went on to enter the doctoral program at the University of Wisconsin with Michael as my major professor. Michael is the best teacher I've ever had. He liked to say that he wanted to be perched on his students' shoulders, whispering in our ears to think from certain angles. This has certainly become the case for me. I don't think I read or teach or write anything without hearing Michael's voice. And I know that it is the case that George is perched on Michael's shoulder whispering to him who whispers to me, reminding me how to pay attention. Perhaps my greatest debt to George is that he gave me Michael. I know that doctoral students around the country feel the same way about Peter Smagorinsky, Larry Johannessen, Carol Lee, and many other of George's students.

Doctoral students are part of a peculiar genealogy. There are many folks in the profession like Miles Myers, the former executive director of NCTE, who can trace the lineages of figures in the profession. By this method, Michael is George's student and I am Michael's student, which makes me a "grandstudent" of George's. Likewise my students are George's "great-grandstudents." Given the number of George's former students now teaching in the university ranks, he has a big family of grandstudents and great-grandstudents indeed. At a recent Maine Writing Project meeting, one of our fellows declaimed, "I am a Hillocksian!" He was greeted by a chorus of us, chanting, "We are ALL Hillocksians!" It was a great moment.

Another great benefit of being one of George's grandstudents is that one is welcomed into a clan of folks who are among those who are thinking the hardest of anybody about the most challenging problems of teaching the English language arts. Some academic groups are insular. Not George's former students. They are wonderful colleagues in their own rights, but one can't help but think that they inherited and learned from George some of his legendary generosity of spirit. In turn, his students revere George for his selfless sharing and great-hearted sense of caring. This past fall, at the Illinois Association of Teachers of English conference (where the idea for this book was born), more than thirty of George's former students made presentations dedicated to him and founded on what he had taught them. After George received a distinguished service award, his students gathered to pay him homage: Literally dozens of students who still teach on the front lines—editors, writers, university professors, and many others like me—had come to thank George for his salutary influences. It was like an Acadian family reunion. George was presented with two thick scrapbooks containing letters and photos and thank-yous from nearly all of the MAT and doctoral students he had taught during his tenure at the University of Chicago.

There's much more I could say about this gentle giant of literacy education. He has won numerous awards, including the most distinguished awards of our profession; written seminal articles, reviews, and books; led one of the most successful teacher preparation programs in the country; and been a national leader in professional service. But George is proudest of being a teacher, so I will move toward my conclusion by identifying one of the many things he has taught me: how to inquire. His idea of "frame experiments" moved me into the realm of teacher research. He taught me that reading and writing are forms of inquiry and are best taught as inquiry in contexts of inquiry. And George taught me how to think about, theorize, and do this kind of work that has ever since undergirded my career as a teacher, researcher, and writer.

A few nights ago, I was in Chicago to work with the Chicago Public Schools and the Chicago Teachers Center. As soon as George found out I was scheduled to be in town, he shot me an email. He asked if he could attend a session I was leading with teachers at the Marie Curie High School, where he had worked for many years, and if he could invite me to his home for dinner afterward. The email was a nice summary of why George inspires me so much. He is always learning, always in school, always working with kids, and always generous.

During dinner that night, conversation turned to a new book of mine that had just been released. George said to me, "I taught you something that you used in that book."

"I cited you, I hope," I said, already worried about how I could possibly remember and acknowledge everything George has taught me.

"No, you somehow neglected to," he replied, then gave a hearty laugh. I was ready to blurt out that he should identify the omission and I would add the appropriate acknowledgment in the next reprint, but he beat me to the punch. "Listen," he said, leaning over the kitchen table, "When I teach anybody anything, I'm not what is important. If I teach something it's because I want you to use it and I want you to make it your own and spread the word. That's how teaching makes a difference."

I've come to expect this kind of generosity from George. Nonetheless, it is important to me that any reader of any of my work knows how grateful I am to George; and I want George himself to know that I am aware of at least some of the debt I owe him. Though he waves off that kind of talk, I think it is important that George's manifold contributions to our professional understanding be acknowledged and celebrated. This book has come about because there are many of the most influential English educators in this country who feel the same way as I do. The contributions are a testimony both to what George has taught all of us individually and to what he has contributed to our field as a whole.

In the final analysis, I suppose, I *could* say that I *almost* became George Hillocks' MAT student. But in the end, I have to admit that I *did* become his student. This is something for which I am extremely grateful. Sometimes we find our teachers, and sometimes our teachers find us. I'm grateful that George found me in so many ways: through his writing, his students and their writing, through Michael Smith, and through a valued personal relationship. There is no question that without George's contributions to my own thinking and to the profession, I would not have found teaching to be the exciting, complex, fulfilling, worthwhile pursuit of possibility that I have found it to be.

George's influence has transformed all of us who write here. If you do not know George and his work, then this volume will help make *you* his student in ways that will certainly be transformative for you as well. You'll enjoy the journey. I know that I have.

PREFACE

What I Have Tried to Teach My Students

GEORGE HILLOCKS, JR.
University of Chicago
Chicago, Illlinois

I have been asked to write about what I tried to teach my students in the Master of Arts in Teaching program at the University of Chicago, a program that I directed for thirty-one years. That adventure largely defined my life for the years between 1971 and 2002 and probably still does. When I began teaching in 1956, I knew almost nothing about teaching English. I covered the grammar we were supposed to cover; assigned the literature and led recitations about it, not knowing the difference between recitation and discussion; assigned the writing and book reports; and wrote comments on papers telling students what they should have done after they had done the writing. After teaching a year at the junior high and another at the high school, I left to do a year of graduate study at the University of Edinburgh. In 1959, I returned to find that the principal did not want me at the high school. (In a faculty meeting, I had strongly argued against part of the criteria for evaluating teachers that he asked the faculty to approve. He wanted no more of that.) I could go back to the junior high. To my mind, at the time, it was a demotion, and I was quite upset.

However, when I was back at the junior high, one of the first people I sought out was Bernie McCabe, the teacher who had supported my request to buy copies of *Pygmalion* for my ninth-grade class during my first year. By this time, he was a visiting teacher, a floating consultant whose job was to work with interested language arts teachers in the three junior highs, helping them develop their teaching skills and the curriculum. I confessed to him that I did not know how to teach writing. (I thought I knew something about teaching literature but, of course, was mistaken.) He said that he had one lesson, on haiku, that had always worked for him. He said he would be a happy to show me the lesson, but that first I needed to know something about haiku. He reached into his briefcase and withdrew a little anthology of haiku by Basho and several other Japanese poets and some Americans. He told me to read them to see what they're like. We arranged a meeting for a day the following week. In 1959 haiku was not commonly taught in schools. I had never even heard of the form.

Bernie began our discussion using the following poem by one of his seventh graders to illustrate the structure and content.

Someone lights a moon.
Then angels with silver chalk
Draw on their blackboard.

The book that Bernie had given me to read said that a haiku has three lines with a total of seventeen syllables (which in English imitate the Japanese structure), with five syllables in the first line, seven in the second, and five in the third. (Nowadays, writers argue about whether it must have that exact structure.) Bernie pointed out that haiku also have a stable element, a changing element, an allusion to time, and figurative language. He emphasized that students had to have had experience with figurative language for the lesson to proceed. We examined several haiku in the anthology to determine whether they really had that structure. They did.

Bernie said that the problem would be how to teach that knowledge to students and how to help them proceed with getting ideas and generating their own poems. The lesson he showed me begins with a brief introduction to haiku and to Japanese culture and a reading of the preceding poem. It proceeds with an analysis of the features of the poem, admittedly with leading questions.

Then students receive a sheet of eight haiku, several of which break the rules. They read and analyze them for the characteristics. Then in order to focus on the theme, students give titles to each with their answers converging, as one would expect. Next, students write a haiku using a first line supplied in the lesson, "Winter trees are hands." Students have five to ten minutes to finish this poem and to read examples aloud. Most students do very well with this as the given line does a lot of the work. That is okay at this point, Bernie told me, because what we want is student confidence.

Students next brainstorm for possible topics—real brainstorming with two students to write on the blackboard and the teacher pointing to one student after another for topic suggestions. At the end of the class, students begin homework, which is to write four haiku. We discussed all elements of the lesson with Bernie emphasizing the need to prepare the students carefully so that they would not be frustrated. I agreed to try the lesson with Bernie watching. I was excited. I had never thought out a lesson so carefully.

A few days later, I taught the lesson to my best ninth-grade class. They were wonderful and seemed excited themselves. When we finished the brainstorming, we had five sections of blackboard covered with suggestions. The homework was to write four original haiku. I could hardly wait to see what they wrote. To my surprise, all my students had written at least four haiku. I set them to work in small groups, another new activity for me. They were to read each other's haiku to determine if they had followed the rules, to decide if the topics were good ones, and to make recommendations for improvement. This activity was followed with time to revise and with students' using the remaining class time to read haiku in small groups and to nominate some for reading aloud to the whole class.

When I read the poems, I loved the results. Perhaps I would learn to teach English after all. All my ninth-grade classes did this lesson, and all of them produced a little pamphlet of haiku. Only one student never produced a haiku, but Sam produced a picture of a peacock for the cover of his class's pamphlet using three colors of ditto backing on deep yellow paper. And he was very proud of it. The pamphlets went to all parents.

This lesson became a model for me in my thinking and planning and marked the beginning of my love affair with teaching English. I began planning all my work this way, beginning with a concrete student objective (e.g., to write a haiku) and a detailed analysis of the task involved, including the necessary knowledge of the form, knowledge of the kinds of content, and the procedures involved in actually producing one. I began to plan in terms of the prerequisite knowledge for a task and to delay teaching until that was in place. I began inventing activities that would make initial approaches to learning tasks simpler (e.g., providing the first line of the poem) and sequencing learning activities from easy to difficult. Underneath all this planning lay the concept of inquiry, the focus of this book. That is, I worked to set up lessons so that students could derive and test rules, generalizations, and interpretations for themselves. Most important, I learned that what and how much students learned was dependent on my planning and my care in bringing those plans to fruition in the classroom. I would never be able to view teaching as a hit-or-miss operation again, one that was subject to the vagaries of the weather, students' moods, and other random factors out of my control. I learned that if students did not learn, on any given day, I should look for the cause in my assumptions about the learning tasks, my planning, my teaching, or all three. I suddenly was more excited about teaching English to junior high students than about my graduate work. As I look back on it now, what I had considered a disgraceful demotion was one of the most important events in my life.

The first literature unit I worked on using inquiry focused on satire. *Inquiry* is the process of developing what Dewey called "warrantable assertions" about some phenomena about which we have questions. The following example illustrates the process. I had overheard one little boy telling a friend that he had read Orwell's *Animal Farm* for his book report. The friend asked him what that book was about. I still remember his reply: "It's a stupid story about animals taking over a farm." He hadn't liked it. I had seen several book reports on satiric works into which students had no insight. (In those days, it was common for school systems to require book reports every six weeks.) It occurred to me that it might be possible to develop a unit on satire so that students would recognize it and be able to interpret it. I took that idea to Bernie. He took the idea to teachers at the two other junior highs, and they agreed to meet with me and Bernie to discuss the possibility of teaching such a unit to our ninth-grade honors classes.

In late 1959 in preparation for the meeting, I began a search for material that would provide an explanation of satire and how it worked. I had access to the best library in northern Ohio at Case Western Reserve University, but I found nothing. Kernan's *The Cankered Muse* was published by Yale in 1959 but eluded my search. Elliott's *The Power of Satire* was published by Princeton in 1960, and Highet's *The Anatomy of Satire* was published by Princeton in 1962. Wayne C. Booth's *A Rhetoric of Irony* would not be published until 1974. Having come up empty, we knew that we would have to buckle down and make the analysis ourselves.

We began by making a list of many satiric poems, short prose works such as fables, and novels. Our question was, How does satire work? It was obvious that some of the poetry made use of what we called direct attack, Juvenal's *Satires*, for example. Such works usually announce the object of ridicule and proceed to attack the target, explicating, in no uncertain terms, what the writer objected to. It required little or no inference-making to identify the targets of attack or to understand the reasons for the attack. Later, I learned to call this satire *diatribe*. It was also obvious that many satires, such as *Animal Farm*, and other works with satiric content, such as *Huckleberry Finn*, required, sometimes, a very high level of inference-making. Although, as a boy, I had read *Huckleberry Finn* nearly every summer (it was my vacation on the Mississippi River!), it never occurred to me that Huck's decision to help Jim, and thereby, go to hell, was in any way critical of anything. A college professor had to point that out to me.

I recall this analysis as being very hard work, but I knew that if I wanted to teach students how to read satire, I would have to do it. Bernie had taught me that. Eventually, we agreed that satirists employ three primary techniques that require readers to make complex inferences: symbolism, exaggeration, and irony. That, of course, was not enough. The most important questions remained: How does a reader recognize and interpret any of those? How could we teach such inference-making to our students?

We thought that exaggeration was easiest of all to recognize, especially in cartoons and certain written satires. Characteristics, habits, and ideas are exaggerated to such an extreme that we recognize that the satirist is drawing special attention to the target so that we recognize it as undesirable. Eventually, with enough clues, we see it as pernicious or even evil. The artist draws our attention to the target because the exaggeration of it does not accord with our expectations of the normal. Pap's extreme rantings and ravings about Blacks early in *Huckleberry Finn* condemn him as a thorough bigot. Symbols are a bit more subtle, but the artist draws attention to them as something more than they appear by their appearance, their actions, their language, or simply their repetitive appearances. The animals in fables, for example, are obviously more than simply beasts because they have human attributes. Usually their actions are human. With the clues provided, it is a relatively easy matter to infer that the rabbit lost the race to the tortoise through overconfidence. In fact, that is the only characteristic he has other than his natural speed. We have, first, to recognize that the hare is not simply a hare, that his human characteristics make him something more. We infer those qualities from what he does and what he says.

Irony is more subtle still. It lies in the language. Take the opening lines of Sassoon's (1918) poem, "Base Details":

> If I were fierce, and bald, and short of breath,
> I'd live with scarlet Majors at the Base,
> And speed glum heroes up the line to death.

Even on a first reading of the opening line, we see that something is amiss. There is a contrast that is unexpected; the word *fierce* does not accord with *bald, and short of breath*. We do not think of heroes as being *glum*. We infer that they are glum because they know their fate as they "speed...up the line." The larger contrast with our expectations is that we tend to think of officers as leading men into battle, not speeding them "up the line to death." In this kind of irony, what Booth (1974) calls "stable irony," such verbal contrasts alert the reader that there may be more to the text than the surface meanings, that there is a need to reject the surface meanings and reconstruct the meaning from the contradictions. The final lines of the poem read,

> And when the war is done and youth stone dead,
> I'd toddle safely home and die in bed.

Clearly, this is not really a poem about an officer who is fiercely brave, leading young men into battle, but is rather a poem about an officer who is fiercely devoted to his own safety back at the base, all the while sending young men to die in the trenches of World War I.

For adults who are experienced readers, the meanings of this poem may be transparent. But for inexperienced readers, they are not. More often than not, when inexperienced readers encounter irony, they make literal interpretations ("*Animal Farm* is a stupid story about animals who take over a farm."). Even when they recognize some of the contradictions in irony, more often than not they conclude that the work makes no sense or not very good sense. ("Why would anyone write a poem about an officer who only stays at the base and sends young men to die? That does not make any sense.")

It was clear to us that reading and interpreting any book-length satire would very likely involve responding to all these problems. Complex satires such as Huxley's *Brave New World* and Orwell's *1984*, or even Mark Twain's *Pudd'nhead Wilson* would require students to make sense of complex combinations of exaggeration, symbolism, and irony. Our analysis of the underlying tasks seemed crucial to the success of the unit. When we had arrived at this point, we realized that we still had even more difficult work to do. We had to find a way to teach students to recognize and interpret these satiric strategies.

From the outset, we rejected teacher explanations as the way to introduce our students to the strategies. We knew, for example, that if we simply lectured on exaggeration, symbolism, or irony and explained what those meant in literary works, our students might accept what we said, but would entertain it with skepticism because we would have deprived them of the opportunity of coming to their own conclusions about the use of the strategies.

We had to begin with something simple enough for students to recognize with some help. Nowadays, we might have said that we had to envisage a "zone of proximal development," but in 1959, we knew nothing of Vygotsky, whose work wasn't widely available in this country until 1962. Bernie McCabe suggested cartoons from newspaper editorial pages. Another teacher suggested *Mad* magazine cartoons. I suggested that we might start irony with a discussion of sarcasm, which our ninth graders used pretty frequently in their conversations. Someone suggested caricature to begin our work on exaggeration. Work on each satiric strategy (exaggeration, symbolism, and irony) began with the simplest examples we could find and moved through increasingly complex examples.

The sequence on irony, for example, began with spoken sarcasm. We'd say to students something like the following: "A teacher distributes a graded test with many failing grades and says with a sneer on his face, 'What a wonderful job you all did on this test.'" We ask, "What does he really mean? How do you know?" Our expectation was, at this stage in planning, that students would soon see the contrast between the literal meaning of the words and the context of failing papers and the sneer in the teacher's voice. We devised other examples for students to examine and then the plan was to have them devise their own sarcastic remarks, which proved to be no problem at all.

As soon as they appeared to understand the principle of the tone of voice and the context contrasting with and undercutting the literal meanings of words used, we moved to simple cartoons. One of our first cartoons showed a long, sandy beach fading into the distance with nothing on it except a very long row of large garbage cans, each with a sign reading, "Keep our beaches beautiful." We hoped that it would not be difficult for students to infer that the cartoonist's point was that the garbage cans were themselves the primary source of uglification on the beach.

From cartoons we moved to poems. The first we planned to use was a poem by Sarah Cleghorn (1917):

> The golf links lie so near the mill
> That almost every day,
> The laboring children can look out
> And see the men at play.

Our plan was to begin with a general question to see if students could interpret the poem without further help. We thought that they might not understand the words *links* or *mill*. We planned to ask if anyone knew the words and, if no one did, to explain them. If no one offered an interpretation of the poem after the explanation of the words, we would ask if anyone saw any unusual contrasts in the poem. In the actual teaching, my students immediately saw the contrast between the children working and the men playing but did not conclude anything about it.

I had to ask, "So what?" It did not take long for someone to say, "Well you don't expect kids to be working inside while men are playing outside." "No," said another student, "it is supposed to be the other way around."

"So what do you make of that?" I asked. "This was before child labor laws," said one boy. I asked him what he could tell us about child labor and the laws that went into effect. "We studied this a little bit in social studies," he said. "During the Industrial Revolution, it was common for children to work in factories, especially in textile mills. They worked twelve to sixteen hours a day. They were cheap. They did not have to be paid much." A girl added more details about children being small and having nimble fingers to work with the threads. "And they did not have to go to school," she added. There was a little laughter and a general murmur of approval. "So you all think that it was good for young children to work in factories twelve to sixteen hours a day?" I asked. The class went silent. "Not really," said the boy who had first mentioned child labor. "It was bad for their health and they never had a chance to learn anything except their jobs." "Given all that knowledge you have of child labor," I said, "what do you make of the poem?" I had one of the students reread the poem. Some smiled at the last line. One girl summed up the discussion: "It's sort of like sarcasm. You know she does not mean that last line as a good thing—that the men are playing while the children are working. And they work almost every day. So the first lines undercut the final line. You could read it like sarcasm." And she proceeded to read it sarcastically, the first three lines in a high, light, almost merry voice, but the last line in a lower tone, mustering as much contempt in her voice as she could for the final three words, "men at play." I reminded students that this was an example of irony used to make a cutting indictment.

We then moved on to a series of increasingly complex poems, from the relatively simple "Base Details" to some poems of cummings and Eliot's "The Hollow Men." Often in this sequence, students worked on poems in small groups to identify the targets, the reasons for the attack, and the means of attack, subsequently presenting ideas to the whole class for general discussion. The final poem uses all the satiric strategies we had examined, and it prepared us for the longer works to come, including *Animal Farm*, *Huckleberry Finn*, and Moliére's *The Physician in Spite of Himself*, which the class produced in a slightly bowdlerized version for an evening audience made up of parents and friends. As we worked on the production, the class began their independent reading, selecting one title from a list of more than a hundred satiric works by Swift, Mark Twain, Orwell, Huxley, Bernard Shaw, Jane Austen, Moliére, Thurber, Will Cuppy, Dickens, and many other writers. Some works on the list were satiric only in part, such as Dickens' *Hard Times*, but could still serve as a means of assessing our students' ability at identifying and interpreting satire independently. At the time, although we did not use the word, we thought of this activity as a more *authentic* assessment than a simple paper-and-pencil test would have been. Simple tests about the content of the works read in class would not have allowed evaluation of the major unit objectives; that is, to read and interpret satire effectively. And the independent reading fulfilled the district requirement for a book report every six weeks and was more useful, we thought.

By my third year in teaching, then, I had learned some important strategies in planning that I would pass on to my students in English education:

- doing task analysis,

- sequencing from the simple to complex in a cumulative fashion (so that the purpose of any activity in the sequence was to prepare for the next),

- sequencing from teacher-led to small peer group to independent activity,

- inventing activities that would introduce students to underlying concepts in a way that would be accessible to them (what I have come to call gateway activities),

- using small-group discussions consistently so that students became the authorities on the interpretation of works, and

- devising means of evaluation that would provide insight into students' ability to meet the major objectives of the lessons.

Underlying all these principles is the idea that when students interpret data for themselves, they learn strategies that they can apply to a wide variety of materials that become more and more complex. Learning the strategies requires real discussions during which students debate their ideas with each other. For the units to work well, students have to become the source of interpretations in the classroom. I realized that if I explained works to them, I only deprived them of opportunities for learning the needed strategies. My scholarly life for the past thirty-odd years has been devoted to articulating these principles and the theories that ground them and to studying the impact that instruction informed by those principles has on kids' reading and writing.

These were the major ideas I had acquired when I came to teach methods of teaching English at Case Western Reserve University and later for several years at Bowling Green State University. There was much more involved in these apparently simple teaching strategies, including setting meaningful goals for lessons and units; evaluating teaching in light of those goals; deciding which concepts were worth teaching; analyzing the relative complexity of tasks; using inventories to help decide what students needed to learn; and, perhaps most important, inventing new materials and activities to introduce difficult concepts.

For most of these formative years, my interests had been primarily in the teaching of literature. Literature, after all, was the focus of nearly all my graduate work. My oral comprehensives focused on the periods of Old English through the eighteenth century. When Bernie and another colleague, Jim McCampbell, and I began work on our first book, *The Dynamics of English Instruction*, in about 1966, we decided that I would do the lit section, Bernie the comp, and Jim the language. We shared the section on general processes in the teaching of English, such as the use of inventories, classroom discussion, and so forth. Bernie and I knew that we would always work together on various projects, but we decided that I would focus on literature and he would continue his focus on composition. My work at Bowling

Green State University pulled me more and more to writing, and when I became director of first-year English in 1969, I became heavily committed to writing.

At Case Western Reserve and at Bowling Green, the methods classes in English stood alone. There was only one course, and it was isolated from any work in classrooms. I could not deal effectively with classroom management, leading discussions, setting up and monitoring small-group discussions, evaluating teaching in progress, deciding when and how to modify lessons and materials in progress, or even how to recognize an effective lesson.

But when I came to the University of Chicago, I came as director of the Master of Arts in Teaching English program, and no one told me what to do. I remember going to Dean Thomas, who served as dean of the Graduate School of Education and as chair of the Department of Education, to ask what courses I was expected to teach. He told me that I was the expert in this field and that I should make those decisions for myself. I was pleasantly amazed and realized immediately, with some level of trepidation, that I would have the opportunity to help develop the very best teachers I could.

I began teaching at Chicago in the fall of 1971. For the following year I decided to begin the program in the summer with a course on teaching writing coupled with a four-week workshop that would begin after the first four weeks of class. The workshop recruited about forty young people between the ages of eleven and fifteen for a summer program in writing that included special-interest projects for which the attending students could volunteer to work with two or three MAT students. The projects included making a two-minute movie, writing and producing a puppet play, making a slide show accompanied by music and spoken-word literature, producing a cookbook, and so forth. Kids worked on the special projects for two or three hours, one day per week. On the other four days, the workshop focused on a conventional form, such as fables or trickster tales, and personal narrative writing. I hoped that the workshop would provide each MAT student with some real experience in class—opportunities to see the effects of the planning they were doing, to learn how to divide a large class into small collaborative groups and gain experience in running them smoothly, and especially to learn how to observe instruction and reflect on its impact.

The workshop, in conjunction with the course on teaching writing, had the effect of becoming a laboratory for me to develop ideas, with the help of my students, on teaching writing. After the tragic death of Bernie McCabe in 1975, I made the conscious decision to fulfill his work in composition. It was a move that I see in retrospect as an attempt to relieve the sense of utter devastation I felt at the loss of the man who had been my best friend and colleague for more than fifteen years. A few years later, I decided to move the workshop to the fall quarter so that it followed the course on teaching writing. We moved to a Chicago school down the street from the Department of Education where we taught the "low-level seventh-grade class in language arts" (so designated by the Chicago Board of Education) for about fifteen years. The methods of planning and teaching remained parallel to those I have already described in teaching literature. I have described the teaching of writing we did in those workshops in a book called *Teaching Writing as Reflective Practice* (1995).

Even though I had been thinking about what constituted outstanding teaching in English for more than ten years before I arrived at Chicago, my ideas continued to evolve and to be refined for the next thirty-one, thanks to the terrific students who came to the program. From the beginning of my work with the MAT program, I wanted my students to be effective planners of curriculum, from forty-minute lessons to yearlong sequences. I hoped they would become inventors of effective lessons and new curricular materials. I wanted them to develop materials and lessons such that their classrooms would be effective environments for active learning with most students on task most of the time and with most contributing to discussions and engaged in the processes of inquiry on any given day, thereby constructing knowledge for themselves and not simply listening to the teacher talk. Even from the beginning, I wanted my MAT students to be able to evaluate the effects of their own teaching in the moment of teaching, making their teaching open to revision immediately in class and later in the quiet of their own thinking and planning. Finally, I hoped that this kind of thinking would allow my students to be teacher-researchers who would continually invent, test, and revise their materials, curricular ideas, and teaching strategies.

At the beginning of my work with the program, I assumed, without making the assumption explicit, that outstanding teachers cared deeply about the moral, personal, and academic development of their students. I suspect that most professors working in English education would have a comparable goal. Hundreds of teachers I have observed in a wide variety of research projects and in my capacity as a supervisor of teachers have made such statements. Indeed, the myth is that all teachers share such caring or they would not be teaching. Certainly, no teacher in my long experience has ever flat out denied such caring.

Saying that we care is easy and trivial. Making such caring manifest consistently in every class is neither easy nor trivial. I believe that consistent manifestations of caring can take place only if the teacher has first a deep understanding of her students as developing people and learners, a thorough understanding of the subject matter taught, and a consistent willingness to depart from the tried and trite to explore better ways of teaching so that the subject matter becomes the vehicle for the student-teacher interactions that lead to the personal, moral, and academic development of young people. Success in the latter entails not only critical inquiry into what passes as a curriculum in the subject matter area, but critical inquiry into ideas that will serve the purpose of teaching more adequately. It entails not only the ability to analyze conventional teaching materials and strategies critically, but also to invent new ones and subject those to rigorous evaluation. Finally, it entails the willingness and ability to reject what is ineffective and to build consistently on what does work. This is a continuous, reflective project enhanced by formal and informal research.

By my second year at Chicago, I had in place the basic program that I hoped would do all these things, that would bring my MAT students to this level of caring. In addition to four or five English courses and three general education courses (educational psychology, philosophy, and special education), the program included five courses in English education that made up an integrated sequence of preparation for teaching. This sequence began with the course in teaching writing I mentioned earlier. The crucial concern of this course is learning to create environments, including materials and activities, that enable students to learn the complex strategies involved in various writing tasks. In many respects this course was the cornerstone of the program, and prepared students for the fall composition workshop and for a fall-quarter course focusing on creating instructional units that integrate literature, language, composition, and critical thinking.

In the fall-quarter composition workshop, groups of four or five MAT students with an advisor taught a sixth-, seventh-, eighth-, or ninth-grade class for approximately five weeks. Each day one of the group taught while everyone else observed. Following the actual class, we reviewed the teaching, deciding what went well and what did not, and planning for the coming days of the workshop. Each day we spent four hours on these teaching, reflecting, and planning activities. We had plenty of data to work with: the observational notes from four or five observers and the products of student work. We examined everything: how well the materials and activities had worked, the extent to which students were on task or engaged in discussions, how we might have been more efficient, and so forth.

These daily sessions both provided the grist for our planning and introduced my students to the kind of teacher research that is so important to being a reflective teacher. At the end of the workshop, as a group (I taught too), we evaluated our own teaching in part by examining what our students had learned by evaluating pre- and post-test writing samples. Each MAT student researched and wrote about some question related to the workshop; for example, whether our efforts in teaching revision paid off over the long run, the extent to which a particular model for organization worked, how well students learned to use and deal with counterarguments, the impact of our work with figurative language on writing, and so forth. These papers were exciting and often had an impact on the way a workshop developed the following year. For example, two papers argued that it would have been stronger in teaching narrative to introduce the use of dialogue earlier in the workshop. The next year we did, and it was.

One goal of the workshop was to learn to work collaboratively with other teachers to improve teaching. It had that effect and more. Many MAT students formed close bonds with each other that have been maintained many years after leaving the program. They continue to discuss their ideas with those who were their earliest colleagues; witness, for example, the editors of this book.

The state of Illinois requires that all prospective teachers engage in preliminary observations and work with classes prior to student teaching. In part, the composition workshop met this requirement. But I wanted students to see other teaching as well. MAT students were required to make a range of observations in the fall quarter, collect observational notes, and make analyses of the teaching they observed. During these observations, students also located a mentor teacher with whom they would like to work, usually in the Chicago schools, but often in suburban schools as well. It was the MAT students' responsibility to ask that teacher if she were willing to act as a mentor. Once an agreement was reached, they observed the mentor teacher's classes with a view to planning a unit of instruction for those classes.

In the fall quarter, students also took a course in teaching literature in which they created units that integrate literature, composition, and critical thinking that they taught to at least two classes during their winter-quarter student teaching. Prior to dealing with the unit strategies discussed earlier, we focused on choosing unit concepts, which could be generic (satire, protest, tragedy, etc.), authorial (Twain, Dickens, etc.), thematic (love, coming of age, etc.), opus-oriented (*To Kill a Mockingbird, Julius Caesar*, etc.), or period, or movement-oriented (Harlem Renaissance, Medieval Iconography, Augustan satire, etc.). However, the concept had to be defined and arguably generative. One might decide to develop a unit on war and find many works about war, but if there is no concept of war underlying the unit, then reading one work will provide no insight into reading another. Further, the concept my students chose had to be powerful enough to be applicable to the many works that students might encounter in the future. The concept had to be the object of inquiry itself (Does the concept hold up? Does it really work that way?) and the basis for inquiry into many other related problems.

Finally, the English-education sequence concluded with the MAT paper, required for completion of the degree. It was an inquiry, research usually devoted to the analysis and evaluation of some aspect of what the MAT student taught in student teaching. Perhaps this project, above all, represents what I wanted my students to be and to be able to do: highly skilled planners and enthusiastic, reflective teachers who have the courage and knowledge to evaluate their work against rigorous standards. I like to think that the chapters in this book present some evidence that those goals were met.

References

BOOTH, W. C. 1974. *A Rhetoric of Irony.* Chicago: University of Chicago Press.

CLEGHORN, SARAH N. 1917. "The Golf Links Lie So Near the Mill." In *Portraits and Protests.* New York: Holt and Company.

ELLIOTT, R. C. 1960. *The Power of Satire: Magic, Ritual, Art.* Princeton, NJ: Princeton University Press.

HIGHET, G. 1962. *The Anatomy of Satire.* Princeton, NJ: Princeton University Press.

HILLOCKS, G., JR. 1995. *Teaching Writing as Reflective Practice.* New York: Teachers College Press.

HILLOCKS, G., JR., B. MCCABE, AND J. MCCAMPBELL. 1971. *The Dynamics of English Instruction, Grades 1–12.* New York: Random House.

KERNAN, A. B. 1959. *The Cankered Muse: Satire of the English Renaissance.* New Haven, CT: Yale University Press.

SASSOON. S. 1918. "Base Details." In *Counterattack and Other Poems.* New York: E.P. Dutton.

INTRODUCTION

THOMAS M. MCCANN
LARRY R. JOHANNESSEN
ELIZABETH KAHN
PETER SMAGORINSKY
MICHAEL W. SMITH

The preamble of the *Standards for the English Language Arts* (1996), sponsored by the National Council of Teachers of English (NCTE) and the International Reading Association (IRA), begins with the following statement: "The vision guiding these standards is that all students must have the opportunities and resources to develop the language skills they need to pursue life's goals and to participate fully as informed, productive members of society." That vision has suggested standards that call for students to be critically engaged in their reading, writing, and speaking.

If teachers are to enact that vision, they have to devise instruction that departs from teacher-dominated discussion of discrete works of literature or of repetitive practice on the kind of writing prompts that appear on state tests. Easier said than done, especially for teachers facing unprecedented public scrutiny and pressure.

The purpose of this book is to help teachers enact the standards' vision of critically engaged students and teachers by sharing a coherent model of instruction and a wide range of applications of that model. The approach that this book explores is grounded in the work of George Hillocks, Jr.

In 1997, the National Council of Teachers of English honored George Hillocks with the David H. Russell Award, recognizing his significant contributions to research in the teaching of English language arts. NCTE cited in particular Professor Hillocks' *Teaching Writing as Reflective Practice* (1995), a synthesis of theory and practice for the reflective teaching of writing. Although the award focuses on one publication in particular, it also recognizes the impact that the body of Hillocks' work, both in the teaching of writing and in the teaching of literature, has had on the field. Then, in 2004, NCTE awarded Hillocks its Distinguished

Service Award. Among several letters of nomination, one was signed by 155 of his former students and said, in part:

> We can't imagine a more worthy recipient of this great award. In responding to the request for signatures to this letter, many expressed a variation on the following sentiment: "I would love to sign this letter. Every day in the classroom I draw on something that I learned from George." Just as impressively, the list of signatories that follows demonstrates George's influence beyond the classroom. A number of George's former students are now working in educational causes associated with social justice. One of those listed below remarked that his students' involvement in such efforts illustrates "one of the most powerful aspects of George's legacy—the fact that he connected teaching English to a larger vision of ethical leadership and as a result, so do his students."

Beginning with his work at the Euclid Demonstration Center in the 1960s, continuing through his many studies of teaching writing and his comprehensive analyses of composition research, and culminating in his recent analyses of the impact of high-stakes testing on teaching and learning, Hillocks has been a powerful voice for how teachers can help students be more engaged and critical readers, writers, and speakers. His approach is rooted in teachers' analyzing the demands of the reading, writing, and speaking their students will do and then preparing students to meet those demands by engaging them in meaningful social activity. In short, Hillocks sees teaching as an enterprise that prepares students for success rather than one that corrects students after they have failed.

This book is designed for the readers who care about instructional practices that are carefully planned; rely on inquiry processes; require frequent, meaningful peer interaction; and lend themselves to reflection. In the preface Hillocks summarizes the principles of practice in the teaching of English that he has promoted with his Master of Arts in Teaching (MAT) students. The principles include attention to the scaffolding that will connect students' prior knowledge to subsequent learning, and the strategic planning of units of instruction that promote a depth of understanding of concepts and procedures. The subsequent chapters offer a variety of examples to illustrate the principles in practice in the teaching of reading, writing, and critical thinking. The contributors also share insights into the planning process so that it is possible to plan beyond the models and not rely on the examples alone.

Some readers will recognize that this book has some features in common with the NCTE Theory and Research Into Practice (TRIP) books that have been produced by some of the contributors to the current book. They provide not just teaching ideas, but also an account of how to design them. Many teachers of English language arts have turned to the TRIP books by Hillocks (1975); Johannessen, Kahn, and Walter (1982); Kahn, Walter, and Johannessen (1984); Johannessen (1992); Smith (1984, 1991); Smagorinsky (1991); and Smagorinsky, McCann, and Kern (1987) for examples of instructional activities and the thinking processes that led to their design. After almost twenty years, some of these texts continue as mainstays in the English methods class.

The instructional practices that the authors of this book promote emphasize active inquiry as a key to learning. The action necessarily involves meaningful interaction with peers. Many of the book's chapters describe activities that engage learners in inquiry procedures that transfer from one learning occasion to another. The essential peer interactions that characterize the activities emphasize learning as a social experience. The models for lessons and for units of instruction contained in these chapters recommend that each learning episode be embedded in a larger sequence of related learning episodes, advancing the idea that coherence and transfer are vital elements in an instructional plan.

We hope that many readers find the book useful. We can imagine it being a valuable resource for beginning teachers who look for models and guidance in planning instruction. We expect also that veteran teachers of English will appreciate this book as a portfolio of teaching ideas and as a means for initiating dialogue with their peers about how to teach English.

For us, the most valuable books on our shelves have been the titles that have challenged us to reflect on our assumptions and to question our current practices. These books have opened up rich dialogues with our colleagues. We hope that the chapters of this text will serve the same valuable function and become frames of reference for renewing thinking and for generating further inquiry.

References

HILLOCKS, G., JR. 1975. *Observing and Writing.* Urbana, IL: NCTE.

———. 1984. "What Works in Teaching Composition: A Meta-analysis of Experimental Treatment Studies." *American Journal of Education* 93 (1) 133–70.

———. 1986. *Research on Written Composition: New Directions for Teaching.* Urbana, IL: ERIC/NCRE.

———. 1995. *Teaching Writing as Reflective Practice.* New York: Teachers College Press.

———. 1999. *Ways of Thinking, Ways of Teaching.* New York: Teachers College Press.

JOHANNESSEN, L. R. 1992. *Illumination Rounds: Teaching the Literature of the Vietnam War.* Urbana, IL: ERIC/NCTE.

JOHANNESSEN, L. R., E. KAHN, AND C. C. WALTER. 1982. *Designing and Sequencing Prewriting Activities.* Urbana, IL: NCTE.

KAHN, E., C. C. WALTER, AND L. R. JOHANNESSEN. 1984. *Writing About Literature.* Urbana, IL: NCTE.

SMAGORINSKY, P. 1991. *Expressions: Multiple Intelligences in the English Class.* Urbana, IL: NCTE.

SMAGORINSKY, P., T. MCCANN, AND S. KERN. 1987. *Explorations: Introductory Activities for Literature and Composition, 7–12.* Urbana, IL: NCTE.

SMITH, M. W. 1984. *Reducing Writing Apprehension.* Urbana, IL: NCTE.

———. 1991. *Understanding Unreliable Narrators: Treading Between the Lines in the Literature Classroom.* Urbana, IL: NCTE.

Standards for the Englich Language Arts. 1996. Urbana, IL: NCTE/IRA.

ACKNOWLEDGMENTS

This entire book is an expression of gratitude to George Hillocks, Jr., and an acknowledgment of his profound influence on our intellectual, professional, and personal lives.

The contributors to this book have all been connected in one way or another with the University of Chicago. We have spent innumerable hours together at the U of C: debating in classes, collaborating on projects, fretting over exams, and conjecturing about our futures. One of the great joys of all of our work at the U of C was the chance to work with so many great colleagues. Sixteen of George's students are represented here and we're all indebted to the hundreds of others with whom we shared ideas in classes, at George's famous parties, and at conferences over the years.

The 2003 Fall Conference of the Illinois Association of Teachers of English (IATE) brought many of us together to celebrate George Hillocks, Jr., on the occasion of his retirement from the University of Chicago. As we attended the many conference sessions presented by George's former students, we saw the opportunity to collaborate once again by developing conference presentations into chapters and by soliciting other chapters from our colleagues not in attendance that eventually grew into this book. We wish to thank the conference planners who provided the forum for George and for many of his former students. These conference leaders included Teri Knight, Mary Lou Flemal, and Janice Neulieb. We are also indebted to other important contributors to the IATE conference, especially Martha Frieberg, Marjorie Hillocks, and Vera Wallace.

We greatly appreciate the support, guidance, and encouragement that we have enjoyed from our editors Lisa Luedeke and Patty Adams from Heinemann. We are grateful to Lisa Luedeke for seeing merit in this project from the beginning, and for guiding us in molding the diverse contributions into a unified structure. We have benefited greatly from the tireless work and fine judgment of Patty Adams, whose attention to detail and quality have helped us to shape an uneven manuscript into a readable text.

We also acknowledge the help that our students have given, and continue to give us, in learning about language, teaching, and learning.

PART

1

AN INTRODUCTION TO INQUIRY

1

Taking Risks
Reflecting on At-Risk Teaching

JULIANNA CUCCI
Maine West High School
Des Plaines, Illinois

JAMIE A. KOWALCZYK
University of Wisconsin–Madison
Madison, Wisconsin

At-risk, struggling, reluctant, unmotivated, challenged—so many ways to describe some teachers. That's right, teachers. Imagine Melissa. Melissa has been teaching for three years in a high school just outside of a major metropolis. Because she is one of the more inexperienced teachers in the school, administrators assign Melissa to the lowest-tracked students in the school, exposing their philosophy that teachers must work their way up in rank to average or accelerated courses. Melissa, however, dives into the school year ready to show the school, the students, and herself that she can teach in a challenging environment, she can teach all students. It is not long, however, before Melissa meets with frustrations:

- Melissa teaches five classes of thirty students. Each of the five class periods meets in a different classroom, so administrators give Melissa a cart to transport the teaching supplies she has purchased with her own money from classroom to classroom, floor to floor. She shares an "office," what used to be a supply closet, with three other teachers in a remote corner of the basement of the school, adjacent to the malodorous trash dumpsters, down just a bit from the school cafeteria.

- When Melissa sits down to prepare for the week, she prepares for four different courses: Remedial Freshman English, Remedial Freshman Reading, Remedial Junior English, and Remedial Senior Composition. Curriculum guides direct teachers to focus on units such as "the comma"...this leads Melissa to ask the key question, *why the comma?* with no idea as to why to accomplish this task, let alone how. There are no curriculum guides for Freshman Reading or Senior Composition.

- On any given day, Melissa can expect 10 to 25 percent of the thirty students in her class to be gone. At first, it seemed a blessing to make the class size more manageable, to give students more one-on-one attention. However, each time a student is absent, she must fill out paperwork that adds to her workload. When students return, they are behind and find it difficult to participate in classroom activities. Consequently, she spends a great deal of time going over the previous day's lesson, which substantially slows down the pace of the class, not to mention fatiguing students who do attend regularly with excessive repetition. The chronic absenteeism means that on any given day she will have students ready for three or four different lessons in a unit of instruction.

- Students are accustomed to a teacher-centered classroom, as this is the mode of instruction used by the vast majority of teachers in the school. When Melissa allows for cooperative learning, some students are unable to handle the freedom and become disruptive and off task. In addition, students respond to her new teaching techniques by suggesting she is not "really teaching" because she is not "like the other teachers."

- When Melissa calls the homes of absent or disruptive students, she meets with varied responses. Some parents are eager to support her but have their own difficulties communicating with their teenagers. Some are uninterested in the "teacher's problem" and suggest the teacher do her job and they will do theirs. Some respond with promises to discipline their teenagers, either explicitly or implicitly suggesting corporeal punishment. Some parents defend their teenagers no matter what. Some just dismiss Melissa completely. And some are working the third shift—or third jobs—and are not available to talk.

- Melissa often comes up with teaching ideas that make use of the school's library and computer labs, but finds that she has to sign up weeks in advance to get a slot. If she's reserved a space at the lab, but it appears her students need to review or practice something, she cannot alter the plan because she will lose her spot. She cannot respond spontaneously to a teachable moment if that teachable moment involves any technology. Instead, when she brings her students, she finds herself contriving a lesson in order to "do something" just because she has access.

Melissa would like to be able to discuss her frustrations with an administrator, but finds that most discussions and almost all meetings are spent discussing how to meet state standards and raise test scores. The administrators do not veil their message to teachers: You are failing to teach. In response, some of Melissa's colleagues place the onus of the challenge on the students—they don't want to learn. Others refer sympathetically to the barriers in these students' lives that impede learning. Some teachers read "barriers" that are not there, relying on the deeply entrenched stereotypes that are perpetuated about students who do not succeed. These stereotypes often conflate "unsuccessful students," in a classist and racist manner with the labels "low socioeconomic status," "nonnative English speaker," "urban student," and "students of color." Melissa, however, does not abandon her belief that all students can learn and that all students want to learn. Instead, she has begun to lose faith in *her* ability to teach.

Do you know Melissa? Have you experienced what Melissa has experienced? Have you been the at-risk teacher? We use this highly contested term—*at risk*—not to insult Melissa or the teaching profession. Instead, we are suggesting two things:

1. Saddling students with labels such as "at risk" or "reluctant," thus mobilizing all the requisite narratives that accompany these labels, fixes our students in particular spaces.

2. It may be more productive to think of ourselves as sometimes "at risk" or "reluctant," "struggling," and "challenged."

It's nothing to be ashamed of, and it's how many of us have felt at one point or another during our teaching careers. Melissa's story is the composite of our years of "at-risk teaching" at various schools in the Chicago area—more than fifteen years of teaching at five different schools. Throughout these years, we have fought the forces that work against the at-risk teacher to construct meaningful, effective lessons for our students, sometimes with limited success. Rather than offer you a set of golden inquiry-based activities, we share the story of Melissa to demonstrate a way of thinking that is especially important to maintain with all students, including those in an at-risk setting. Indeed, if we rethink who or what is the object of immediate change in the student-teacher relation/context, and once again take on the onus of innovative, reflective instruction for all our students, we open up the possibilities for vision and change.

Just as teachers and students in the United States today must respond to external assessments, Melissa's school reality involves testing at both the state and national levels, whether she agrees with it or not. Many of the teachers at her school realize that the kinds of knowledge typically captured in these standardized tests are easily divorced from students' input, process, and construction of knowledge and learning. However, when students fail statewide assessments, these same teachers may "prescribe" ill-conceived remedies: more phonics, more memorization, more rote practice, or "skill and drill." They seem resigned to the fact that this testing is a way of life, something to which teachers and students alike must acclimate. Melissa admits that she, too, feels the pressure to help students succeed, if only because she wants her students to be able to attend college and she realizes the impact that high test scores can have in making that happen. But she is less convinced that the basic skills instruction that some of her colleagues have adopted can help the students learn anything, including how to master national tests like the SAT and ACT. She cannot help but wonder: Do these tests truly define and assess what it means to be educated? Is this "effective teaching"? Can students who score well on these tests think critically, employ creative stylistics to express their ideas, organize a cogent argument? Do they enjoy learning?

George Hillocks, Jr. (1995, 1999) suggests that learning is not just something we pour (or hammer) into the heads of kids so that they can ventriloquize the textbook or the teacher. Rather, education is a process of discovery of the self and of the world. Students' engagement in school, and thus teachers' efficacy, go beyond mere compliance and regurgitation. It makes sense that concerns over student engagement are highlighted the most when it appears students *aren't* engaged. What we want to suggest is this: It is helpful, when considering these disengaged students, to consider the possibility that perhaps their failures with school curriculum and teachers' teaching provide us with the opportunity to rethink our teaching of all students. How might we better encourage success for all our students? Hillocks (1995) cautions in *Teaching Writing as Reflective Practice*, "[Teachers] Holding strong to a belief that students would like to and can succeed is necessary but is *not in itself sufficient* for effecting change in learning..." (22).

In *Ways of Thinking, Ways of Teaching*, Hillocks (1999) presents two different epistemologies for teaching, objectivist and constructivist. Most of Melissa's colleagues see teaching as objective. In other words, to them "teaching is an act of telling, as though they are able to transfuse their ideas directly into the minds of students. And when the ideas do not hold, it is simply that students have not applied themselves to the task of learning what was put forward for them to learn" (93). Melissa embraces a constructivist understanding of teaching and learning, believing that "to be successful, learners must construct or reconstruct, for themselves, what is to be learned." However, given the restraints listed at the beginning of the chapter, Melissa has found designing units of instruction that embrace this philosophy easier said than done. When Melissa attends a session at the National Council of Teachers of English annual convention, she becomes excited about a unit of narrative writing based of the work of George Hillocks, Jr. in *Observing and Writing* (1975). In it she finds a collection of activities that engage students in observing and recording various sensory experiences that construct their knowledge of descriptive and narrative writing. Melissa finds a unit that not only helps students construct procedural knowledge, but also addresses the state standards for narrative writing. Melissa cannot wait to begin.

Activity One: Introduction of Unit and Pretest

Melissa prepares for the first day of her new unit by gathering samples of narratives for the students to read. She finds two student narratives: one talks about a ski trip devoid of any specific detail; another describes signing the yearbook of a former friend with great attention to the emotional detail. She also brings an excerpt from Richard Wright's (1945) *Black Boy*, "The Night I Won the Right to the Streets of Memphis."

She begins by asking, "What makes a great story?" As she anticipated, students respond by telling her that a great story has adventure and action in it. She writes these suggestions on the board and asks students to read the two sample student narratives to decide which is better. The students uniformly choose the narrative describing signing a yearbook. Melissa challenges, "Really? But the ski trip has more action in it. Why, then is the other story better?" The students respond to this question by changing their criteria: it needs description; it needs to tell what it was like. She writes their additions on the board. Next, she guides them in applying their criteria to Richard Wright's piece and asks them to underline the details they like as she reads them the story. Afterward, students share the details they like with the class. For each comment, she asks students to consider what makes it a great detail, until the class has a board full of criteria of what constitutes a great story: specific details about what a person sees, hears, smells, tastes, and feels; details about the emotions of the writer and other people; comparisons about what things were like; dialogue between people; adventure or action, either through plot or feelings; story is moments that are important; logic—it makes sense.

After the students finish their discussion about great stories, she asks them to write a personal experience narrative of their own as a pretest so that she can determine what they know and can do and what narrative writing skills she will need to teach them. She hands students the following pretest prompt:

> Write about an event (real or imaginary) and its consequences that concerned you or someone you know. Be as specific as you can in describing the event and its consequences. Try to write so that a reader of your composition will see what you saw and feel how you felt.

Melissa leaves that day excited about looking at the samples of what her students are capable of producing. They have been given the chance to read good narratives and break down the elements that made them good, so she feels that she can count on the writing being their best. She locates what she thinks is the best pretest, written by Bernardo, and the weakest, written by Leo.

"First Ride" by Bernardo

It was a hot, and windy summer day. I was ready to ride my bike, but I didn't know how to. I saw my brother riding his bike in the distance. I was so jealous because he was enjoying his bike. I started walking towards the shine red bike. I felt the sweat dripping down my fingers/I got up on my bike, and my feet were barely touching the ground. I started pelting hard but I fell in the first two yards. My elbow slammed onto the bumpy concrete floor. I felt pain, and wen I looked at my elbow it looked outrageous because blood was coming out of my arm. I was yelling at my mom, and she took me inside the house. She washed my arm and put some rubbing alcohol on my elbow. It felt like someone burning my elbow. The very next day I was afraid to get on my bike. My mom said, "If you want to ride a bike you have to practice." I never even wanted to see that bike again. My mother encouraged me to give it another try, so I went outside. I went outside. I went on the bike and was grabbing the handlebars tight. I started to move the bike with my leg then the other. I was riding my bike like a pro. I felt like I was on the top of the mountain. I will never forget leaning to ride my bike.

The following is Leo's untitled pretest.

by Leo

I was 9 I was with my cousin and brother. We were in Mexico. It was a hot and humid day in Mexico. My cousin was taking a very very nice big yellow horse to a water whole to give the horse water so my brother me my cousin and his horse were going to take the horse to the water whole. It was a long way to the water whole. I think it was one hour but it felt like 4 hours. On the way to the water whole we saw a lot of animals, bugs and plants. So we were there now. The horse was getting water and eating some grass. The my cousin side to stay away from the horse but I did not. The the horse just kicked me into some buch and it was stinging and I was bleing. So we were going home rining and fell one time or two times. The was home felt like days. Now we were in my cousin home. Then I was all right. I still love horses and all animals but now I do what my cousin says.

These representative samples with the lack of specific details illustrate that these students could benefit from instruction on narrative/descriptive writing.

Activity Two: Figurative Language Through the Shell Game

Basing her ideas on the shell games from Hillocks' *Observing and Writing* (1975), Melissa brings in a large conch shell to class and holds it up in front of the students to inspect. She challenges, "We need to describe this shell to the math class down the hall so that if they came into this room and had to pick it out of a group of shells, they would know exactly which shell we are talking about." A student volunteer records students' responses on the board. Students begin with obvious comments—the shell is small or it is bumpy or you can hear the ocean in it. But she reminds them that a lot of shells are like that and that they have to find a way to describe this specific shell. Soon a student throws out a comment that the shell looks like a little animal. Another says that it looks like a tornado. Melissa asks what else the shell looks *like*. The figurative language starts to pour in. Other students become involved in pointing out the minutiae of the shell—"There are seventeen ridges that stick out as much as your little finger." All of the responses go on the board.

After discussing the big shell and recording student responses, Melissa tells them that they are going to play a game using their skills of description. In small groups, students choose one of two shells and write a description so that another group will be able to read the description and pick out the correct shell. As she circulates around the room to remind students to continue their use of similes and specific sensory detail, she finds her suggestions are more disruptive than helpful to the collaborative work happening with the partners. She witnesses students huddled over their desks in intense concentration as they describe their shells. As she reads the descriptions of each of the groups, students listen carefully and are able to isolate the best details from the descriptions.

Next, students take a "shell quiz" to test their newfound powers of observation and description. Students write short descriptions of a shell so that another student can spot their shell in a lineup of all of the shells in the class. Most of the students are able to spot the shell in the description that they read. All the descriptions have figurative language and attention to specific detail. While she could have read any number of the papers aloud, she chooses Kenny's to read to the class:

Describing the Shell by Kenny

This shell is rough. But smooth. It has many indents like the moon. One of the indents is missing a side and the color of it is like a very light swiss chocolate. One indent goes all the way through the shell like a tunnel. Another indent is as black as the night sky. If you looks close enough it looks like a peanut butter color in some parts. It doesn't even look like a shell. It looks like a rock. Near the bottom of it there are many tiny indents as if someone has poked it with a toothpick. The shell smells like dirt. The shell fits in the palm of your hand.

The composition represents substantial improvement from the pretests. Notice the student's use of figurative language to specifically describe the shell, such as describing the color as "very light swiss chocolate."

Reflecting on Activity Two: Accounting for Student Growth

Student growth also provides teachers with moments for reflection: Why did this activity work? What accounts for the growth? How do we build on this growth? In fact, Hillocks turns to the work of Csikszentmihalyi and Larson in order to pose these questions using the idea of "flow," the experience one has when fully engaged in something stimulating and demanding.

But it is not just the educational underclass that is alienated by schools. It appears to include most students in even the best schools, most of the time. Csikszentmihalyi and Larson (1984) have examined the affective states of adolescents extensively as they go about their daily routines. The authors conclude that "the average student is usually bored, apathetic, and unfriendly" (205) in school situations. In fact, Csikszentmihalyi and Larson state that "schools are essentially machines for providing negative feedback. They are supposed to reduce deviance, to constrain the behavior and the minds of adolescents within straight and narrow channels" (198–199). Hillocks (1995) points out that these authors argue that schools do not provide "flow" experience, "the kind of experience that results in high levels of pleasure, confidence, and absorption by the tasks at hand" (19).

So how to scaffold "flow" experiences for our students? Hillocks (1995) points to a few key ingredients that students must have: (1) clear goals, (2) immediate feedback, and (3) the "ability to act and [the] opportunity to act" (21). In particular, Hillocks recommends that teachers build the proper environment for student growth through teacher-led and small-group work in order to support students as they acquire individual competency with a new concept or skill. In addition, he endorses inquiry as the primary method of instruction in class, a means by which students work to construct their own knowledge, thus offering them the "ability to act and [the] opportunity to act." The endorsement of inquiry speaks directly to one particular word in the Csikszentmihalyi passage: "constrain." One of the ill effects of objectivist pedagogy, as opposed to a constructivist approach, is the effect this type of teaching has on students and teachers; it constrains and narrows the opportunities for education and growth.

Students who are labeled "unsuccessful" and their teachers—teachers like Melissa—acutely feel this constraint. Many teachers might feel comfortable allowing for student choice and input, group work, and class projects that emphasize students' construction of knowledge through critical thinking and student presentation of findings—for their more advanced or "successful" students. But when a student is not succeeding? Typically, the response is to constrain the curriculum, the expectations, the pedagogy, and, thus, the students. And, lest we ignore their experience in the class-room—the teacher is constrained as well. But why constrain? Apparently the logic is this: Struggling students cannot be expected to commandeer a number of different variables at once, and if they are to grasp anything, let it be the basics. But to "do" school in this constrained fashion is to surely squash any attempt at all to allow students to experience "flow"—that is, what Hillocks (1995) describes as having "pleasure, confidence, and absorption of the tasks at hand" in their school work. The question is, how can teachers like Melissa break away from the constraints and help their students experience the kind of flow that Csikszentmihalyi and Larson (1984) say is important to learning in school?

Activity Three: Idea Sheets

Melissa tells the students that they did an excellent job describing shells, thinking to herself that this is evidence that these students, too, are capable of experiencing "flow" in the English classroom. She goes on to tell them that the ultimate goal of the unit, however, is for them to be able to write about their own experiences with specific and creative details. She reminds them of the narrator, Esperanza, in Sandra Cisneros' *The House on Mango Street* (1989). Just as Esperanza writes about her observations and experiences as she begins to come of age, the students should start to think of experiences that they could write about from their own lives. Together they make lists of the things that Esperanza writes about: people who made a strong impression on her, important places, conflicts, learning experiences, strong emotions, first experiences. She instructs students to brainstorm ten ideas that might fit into one of these categories. To help them remain focused on a single incident, she tells them to make sure that they start their idea with, "The time that..." She gives them a list of stories that she could tell to further model the brainstorming.

The students think and write for twenty minutes as she circulates around the room watching their progress. After they are done, she allows them time to share their ideas with each other and asks them to star the ideas they are most interested in seeing turned into stories by their peers. The enthusiasm with which the students approach thinking of stories alleviates any doubts Melissa had about taking the time out to teach this type of narrative writing unit rather than focusing, like her colleagues, on punctuation and grammar exercises and editing skills as preparation for the state writing assessment. She loves hearing the excitement in the students' voices as they talk about stories from their own lives. Again, the students appear to be in the writer's "flow." She drives home that day from school feeling like the energetic teacher she was during her student teaching days. This is working.

Activity Four: Describing People/Pictures

The next day in class she tells the students that they will return to their idea sheet soon enough, but that they are going to practice description some more. The students are going to examine portraits from a *Life* magazine publication today. Melissa begins by showing the students a photo taken by Dorothea Lange of a woman from the Depression era and asks them to think of words that describe the picture. Students reply, "very old," "sad," "about to cry," "poor," and "tired." Then she asks them to tell her what details in the picture make them think of these words. They come up with: "wrinkles all over her face like an elephant's trunk," "eyes open and teary like black marbles," "bags under her eyes," "holes in her clothes held together by pins," "wobbly skin like a turkey," and "her mouth is frowning like a half moon on her face." Melissa smiles and nods; she is encouraged that the students are able to share highly imaginative and descriptive observations.

She asks the class to break into their prearranged small groups. Next, students choose photos from a bunch Melissa has on a table at the front of the room. The groups repeat the same procedure of listing a few words that describe the person and then come up with a minimum of five specific details that would show a reader the same person. Melissa moves through the room, noting that students are enthusiastically discussing the portraits and building on each other's comments. The students do this for approximately thirty minutes and then, at the end of class, the groups share their descriptions of their portraits.

Melissa is pleased with the work they have done. As a follow-up writing assignment, Melissa asks the students to write a description of a friend from their idea sheets. They follow the same procedure, thinking of words to describe that person in the moment that they are remembering and then imagining details that make them describe the person that way.

Activity Five: Guided Imagery/Describing Setting

Moving along in her unit plan, Melissa begins later that week to work on describing setting with the students by having them do a guided imagery activity. She instructs her students to close their eyes and describe a scenario where they are being chased by a rabid dog. She pauses after each question, allowing students to think of and relate details. As she did with the shell game and the picture descriptions, she writes the details the students generate on the board. After they are done, she asks them to write a description of the imagined experience. They are allowed to use any of the details from the board, but they may also add new details that they have imagined. She says their goal is to have at least one specific detail or description of a detail in every sentence. Students use this simple rubric to self-evaluate their own writing and revise as necessary before turning in their descriptions.

Growing more and more confident with her students' progress, the following day Melissa asks students to think of a place from their idea sheets to describe. She has them think of a feeling that the place evokes and specific details of that place that help evoke these feelings. The students set to writing and Melissa nods to herself, thinking, "These kids can do the work we do with other students. You just have to believe."

And Melissa has witnessed firsthand how engaged the students are in class. As Hillocks (1995) draws out in his study of "flow," students experience this when they enjoy what they are doing, when the are able to gauge or discern that they are getting better or improving, and when they are interested in the task at hand. Melissa reflects on her colleagues and their devotion to the skill-and-drill worksheets they are using, and the constrained, prescriptive, "teacher-proof" pedagogy that they use in these classes labeled "at risk." How can this type of teaching elicit "flow" responses in students?

Crisis

That weekend, after her first two weeks of the unit, Melissa finally finds time to grade the work of the students. She wishes she could find time to grade during the week, but the demands placed on her from her other courses make it impossible for her to sleep much during the week, let alone grade student work on a daily basis. Besides, she has seen such excellent detail coming from students in her large-group discussions and small-group work that she feels confident it will be easy to write strings of superlatives on their papers. She sits down with a cup of coffee, takes out the stack of papers from her book bag, and eagerly begins to read, pen in hand. After reading the first few descriptions of friends, however, Melissa cringes and turns to the stack of settings. She is crestfallen. After reading through the sets, she decides that the writing the students did independently was more of the problematic, dull writing that she had seen in the pretests. What happened? She saw them having fun, experiencing "flow," and producing high-quality work in class.

On Monday she decides to share her frustration with some of her coworkers, looking for some advice on what to do next. Her feelings of deflation are exacerbated rather than diminished. One colleague, Martin, offers her a workbook of basic grammar skills. He invokes his mantra that students cannot handle writing longer compositions until they can master the sentence. Another colleague tells her that she has already spent more than enough time on narrative writing, and that she should just give them low scores and move on to the next bullet in the curriculum; two weeks is a long time to spend on anything, after all. When Melissa considers the amount of time and energy that setting up the narrative unit has taken her, she wonders whether all the work has been worth it. Indeed, this is only one component of the students' state assessments and the department chair has emphasized they must prepare all students for all components prior to the tests. Maybe it's time to move on to grammar work. Melissa has an hour before classes begin and she is not sure which direction she wants to take.

We argue that, to be sure, Melissa does need to make a change in pedagogy. But it does not have to be a change in favor of constraint. Rather, it demands putting into practice the suggestions of Hillocks—develop classroom environments that properly scaffold instruction, provide students with opportunities to practice what they are learning, and use curriculum and pedagogy steeped in the method of inquiry. And most of all, reflect on her practice. Hillocks (1995) writes, "The point is *that the assumptions we make and the theories we hold have a powerful effect on what and how we teach*" (28, emphasis Hillocks). Reflective practice demands that we question our assumptions, what seems natural to us, and that we inspect the theories that undergird our practice. To do this kind of reflection is to dismiss the idea that there exists some easy, foolproof prescription for teaching success. To do this kind of teaching is to recognize the craft of the profession; the need to observe, self-assess, and constantly tailor our teaching to the particular group of students a teacher is working with at a given time. Hillocks, drawing on Bloom, writes:

> [W]e need to forget about generalized notions of intelligence and aptitude and concern ourselves instead with working out where students are in relation to specific learning tasks in the curriculum... what students have to know to accomplish that, and how they can enjoy learning those things. (22)

Melissa needs to use reflective practice and the method of inquiry, endorsed by Hillocks for writing curriculum, on her own teaching. Hillocks writes, "In Dewey's (1938) terms, this process [of reflection] that originates in doubt and moves in a rational way to resolution constitutes inquiry" (1995, 30). So when Melissa doubts or questions an aspect of her teaching, forms a hypothesis, tests the hypothesis, and arrives at a judgment of effectiveness, she is incorporating inquiry into her practice. This is our recommendation for Melissa, the at-risk teacher: use reflective practice in the spirit of inquiry to provide an ongoing assessment of her teaching and students' progress so as to make the needed revisions of the process/methods of instruction. Inquiry, in this way, supports a tension or dialogue between practice and theory, and this *is* reflective practice. This is, in fact, what Melissa is about to engage in—a conversation between her theoretical understandings and beliefs about teaching and what happens in her classroom.

Activity Six: Revision

Melissa gets through that Monday, but has not made a decision regarding where next to go. Not only is she at risk of giving up on inquiry-based activities in her classroom, she feels like she is at risk of giving up on teaching all together.

Ironically, it is not another teacher, but a friend who offers Melissa hope. That evening Melissa calls a friend and tells her what's going on, how she's feeling. After listening to Melissa recount all the activities and read a few samples of the students' writing, she says, "I don't know, Melissa. It seems like the kids can do what you're asking them to do. They just aren't getting it when they are doing it by themselves. It's mystifying, but if I were this confused by one of my clients, I would just ask them what they were thinking. And if I were this disappointed, I wouldn't accept it. I would demand that they redo it." That's it! Melissa decides to bring the problem to her students through a lesson on revision. Maybe the students have enough of a demand on them when recalling specifics from their own life and are unable to add much meaningful detail when composing the narrative.

The next day, Melissa shows her students a very basic description of a picture of a young girl in a classroom:

Describing the Girl #1

The girl in the picture seems sad. She's holding something and looking real hard at it. She's a very cute kid. Her hair is in a barrette, and she has freckles.

She asks them, "What else could we ask this writer about so that she could write a better description?" She writes the questions on the board, and asks students to copy them onto their handout as they replay: "Why is she sad?" "How can you tell she's sad?" "What makes her cute?" "What do her freckles look like?" "What is she looking at?" "What is it like?" "What is she thinking about?" For each question that they ask, they put a number above the line in the writing where they would like to see the questions answered.

Next, she shows students the picture and asks them to answer the questions. The class spends some time working quietly, answering the questions. Melissa asks for a few volunteers to share some of the lines they have written. Together they add different sentences into the basic piece. Again, the students have produced a much more descriptive and sophisticated piece of writing.

Describing the Girl #2

The girl in the picture seems sad. She is holding her hand to her face and slouching in her seat so hard that it looks like she's trying to disappear. She isn't disappearing though. She is a cute kid. Her hair is in a barrette. Some of it has been curled, but the rest of it is sticking out like hay. She has so many freckles you couldn't even begin to count them. But, she isn't happy. Her eyes can't stop staring at the red D that's staring back at her. She can't stop thinking about what her mother will say to her when she brings it home.

After doing this activity, she tells her students about her dilemma with their writing. The papers that they wrote individually lacked a lot of detail. She passes back their stories and asks them to think of questions about their own writing and to add details using the numbered revision system that they practiced. She tells them that she expects to see a minimum of ten new details. Then, she gives them time to think and revise in class. When she receives the revised versions, she sees the payoff for taking the time to model the revisions. What follows are two sets of original compositions and revisions. What they reveal is how much improved the revisions are from the original compositions.

Stilianos One

A place that I like is in Southern Greece were I live. I picked the beach which is not even 5 min. away from my house in Greece. Hen you go to this beach you see people laying down on the sand sun tanning. The sand is hot with seashells scattered about and crabs running from rock to rock. Far off at sea, barley visible you might see some oil tankers crossing the Mediterranean Sea. In the ocean you will see kids playing or building sand castles on the shore. If you happen to go snorkeling or scuba diving you will see fish, turtles, and if you go deep enough you might get lucky and see a school of dolphins.

Stilianos Two (revision)

There is a place far off past the Atlantic Ocean that I like to think about. The place I like to think about when I am depressed is in Western Europe. It is Southern Greece where I live when I go on vacation in the summer. When you goto this beach you will see people lying down on their towels laid down on the hot sand like seals on a rock. The sand is hot like a frying pan. Sitting in the sand you can feel the sand burning on your shoulders like you are an ant and there is a boy on top of your ant hill focusing his magnifying glass on you. You can also fell the hot sand sticking in–between your toes like mud. Seashells are scattered all over as if they were confetti. Crabs running from rock to rock. Far off at sea, barely visible as if it were a flea, you might see an oil tanker crossing the Mediterranean Sea. The oil tankers are orange and black and it seems as if they were barely moving. In the ocean you will see children playing as if they were back home in a park; or building sandcastles on the shore as ancient empires would. If you happen to go snorkeling or scuba diving you will see fish as if you were in *Finding Nemo,* with fish all kinds of colors as if there was a rainbow in the ocean; and you might see some turtles too, gliding across the ocean like a bird in the sky. If you go deep enough you will see a school of dolphins jumping in and out of the water at the same time as if they were doing a routine; jumping in and out like fish in the rivers swimming up stream.

Justin One

My truck's cab is small and green. In the inside there is a long, brown leather bench seat. The carpet, door panels and ceiling are all blask. Its' steering wheel is also black with a shiny chrome horn in the center. The gear shifter that sticks out of the steering column is also green with a big, round, black knob. Its dashboard is small and green like the rest of the truck. In the dash there is a radio that is old fashioned looking but it is new and the speakers are under the seat and they sound awesome. On the dashboard there are any small round dials and instruments which show how much gas there is and the level of oil pressure and the temperature of the engine. There is also a knob on the left hand side under the dashboard to adjust the heater and defroster. The heater itself has a big motor which is enclosed in a gray metal case which peeks out from under the dashboard. The parking brake is a chrome handle which is close to the floor on the left hand side. The glove box is over on the passenger side of the dashboard and it is shiny chrome with a button in the middle to open it. On the back of the cab is a small rounded window that is old fashioned looking.

Justin (Revision)

My truck's cab is small and green like a box turtle. In the inside there is a long, brown leather bench seat. The carpet, door panels and ceiling are all black like the inside of the turtle's shell. Its steering wheel is also black with a shiny chrome horn that sits there like a clown's nose. The gear shifter that sticks out of the steering column is also green with a big, round black knob like a clown's arm waving. Its dashboard is small and turtle green like the rest of the truck. In the dash there is a radio that is old fashioned looking but it is new and the speakers are under the seat and they sound awesome just like being at a concert. On the dashboard there are many small, round dials and instruments which are like windows that peer into the engine, show how much gas there is and the level of oil pressure and the temperature of the engine. I there is also a knob of the left hand side under the dashboard to adjust the heater and defroster. The heater itself has a big motor which is enclosed in a gray metal case which peeks out from under the dashboard like a snail from under a shell. The parking brake is a chrome handle which is close to the floor on the left had side. The glove box is over on the passenger side of the dashboard is like a treasure box with its shiny chrome button in the middle just waiting for someone to push it to see what's inside it. On the back of the cab is a small rounded window that is old fashioned looking just like the glasses worn by a little old man.

Melissa is reaffirmed in her decision to use inquiry as a means of teaching narrative writing with her students—all her students. She has learned, however, that not all her students will make connections between activities in class and their own writing right away. Rather, she needs to reflect on these students, think about which step in the sequence is not working, and then think out a set of steps these students could take to get them to transfer what they do in class to what they do with their own stories. In these narrative writing activities, Melissa needed to reflect on a step that was implicit in her sequence and, through analysis of the task she was asking students to do, spell out explicitly what needed to be done to make the necessary leaps. The revision activity modeled the kind of internal dialogue she hoped her students would internalize after the initial activities. Rather than give up on them and assume they just couldn't do it, or give up on herself and assume she just couldn't teach them, Melissa remained optimistic and committed to constructivist pedagogy. This commitment, however, did not mean "staying the course" and teaching all kids the same way. It meant revising her curriculum to meet the needs of this particular group of students.

Later Activities

After experiencing success, Melissa is recommitted to completing the unit. She involves students in lessons where they observe and describe sounds, bodily sensations. They role-play dialogues, and look at exciting ways to begin narratives. Finally, she has students write stories about a learning experience they had. They write their narratives in class and are given the opportunity to revise by asking questions and adding details. This time she finds herself happy with the growth that she sees in the student writing.

First Day of High School, by Gustavo (Pretest)

Right now I'm going to start y first day of high school. As I walk toward the school I am seeing all different kinds of people, short, tall, light skin, dark skin, etc. Without a doubt I'm so nervous because many of my friends older brothers or sisters that go here said that older kids pick on younger kids, and sometimes send them to Wings that don't even exist. As I stop in front of the doors I' saying to myself, "Prepare to be beaten up." As I walk through the holeways I'm seeing some of my friends and weird people. Some are dressed with really baggy clothes some are dressed like rock stars. Suddenly I get lost, and don't know where I am. So I asked a Big Brother, that's what we call seniors, and sends me to B wing, but I didn't trust him so I went to the office just to find out he was right he did send e to the right direction. Later that day I meet with my friends at lunchtime, and talked about how our first day in High School was until this point including me. So far I was wrong about high school. It was pretty good. Later that day when the clock struck 2:55 it was the sigh that school was over so I whent outside, and got on my bus and got home without trouble.

Facing The Fear, by Gustavo (Posttest)

"Ok I'm Going I'm Going!" I kept yelling to my friends as I was standing on the diving board shaking like a piece of Jello with my life vest across my watery chest. We were swimming in gym class well not exactly because I didn't know how to swim so my teacher was teaching how. In order to complete the lesson everybody had to jump out of the diving board, but I just couldn't it was to high. I kept standing on the long green diving board and they were looking at me with huge eyes like if they were toads searching for a fly.

Then a couple of people said, "Come on you wuss don't just stand there jump!"

After hearing that I felt ashamed because they were right I was a wuss

"He would Jump when his ready don't pressure him," said my gym teacher in a deep scary voice.

Every time I try to jump the picture of me drowning as a little kid would come like a nightmare. I wanted to give up, but if I didn't jump now then when would I. I remained calm. I walked forward to end of the diving board. As I walked I could feel the diving board shake. My toes were holding on to the diving board like if they were glued on.

My teacher said, " Good, Good now jump when you are ready."

"Come on you can do it," my friend Alex said.

I leaped into the air like a frog. BAM! When I landed in the water it sounded like if somebody had drop a bomb in to the earth and cut it in half. Water splashing everywhere like a hurricane. I realized that I had done a belly flap that was the reason my stomach hurt when I landed into the clear water. When I checked my stomach it was red like a tomato. By jumping of the diving board this means I could jump again and again without being scared.

Conclusion: Continuous Reflection

Who is this "at-risk" and "struggling" teacher? It is Melissa. And it is us—Julianna and Jamie. It's the teacher who works hard, tries her best day after day, and takes risks. It's the teacher who, like Sisyphus, fails to make things work and yet persists. We believe it's important and ethically incumbent on us to not stop pushing the stone, even when we feel it slipping. But rather than pushing the rock the same way over and over again, the optimistic/constructivist teacher will improve her curricular design and instruction by using the methods of inquiry and reflection on her own teaching practice. And so, rather than fixating on "at-risk" students, fixate on the belief that it is possible to conduct student-centered, inquiry-based instruction with *all* students, just not in the same way every time.

References

CISNEROS, S. 1989. *The House on Mango Street*. New York: Vintage Books.

CSIKSZENTMIHALYI, M., AND R. LARSON. 1984. *Being Adolescent: Conflict and Growth in the Teenage Years*. New York: Basic Books.

HILLOCKS, G., JR. 1975. *Observing and Writing*. Urbana, IL: NCTE.

———. 1995. *Teaching Writing as Reflective Practice*. New York: Teachers College Press.

———. 1999. *Ways of Thinking, Ways of Teaching*. New York: Teachers College Press.

WRIGHT, R. 1945. *Black Boy: A Record of Childhood and Youth*. New York: Harper & Brothers.

2 Inquiry Versus Naïve Relativism
James, Dewey, and Teaching the Ethics of Pragmatism

Jeffrey Conant Markham
New Trier High School
Winnetka, Illinois

My MAT program under the guidance of George Hillocks was a year of gathering what might be called super-compressed information and experience. Like the other groups that came before and after us, we were given challenges that seemed unbearable in their difficulty and complexity. These challenges came in all forms—classroom discussions and activities, reading assignments, teaching projects, and writing assignments. After each, I was surprised that I managed to do what was asked and would find myself saying, "Alright, if it doesn't get any harder than this, I think I'll be OK." Of course, each assignment was more difficult than the last, but one aspect of Hillocks' genius in teaching was that he knew exactly where our zone of proximal development was at each step of the way. In truth, it took me years of teaching to unpack everything I learned from the program. That said, it is probably foolish for me to reduce Hillocks' teaching philosophy to one statement, but if I had to, it would be this—that the classroom ought to be a place of sustained, relevant discovery. What makes the discoveries relevant, and how a teacher sustains this sort of environment, varies from class to class, student to student, and teacher to teacher. The object of this chapter is to consider discussion and discovery in the classroom with specific attention to relevant matters of ethics.

Like most other MAT programs, ours included a philosophy of education class. On the first day, our professor, Philip Jackson, proposed what I would come to understand as a very Deweyan point of view: that education is essentially an ethical endeavor. Later in this chapter I hope it will become clear what he meant, but for now, I'll simply agree with him and add that my own career has become increasingly focused on ethics—almost everything we read and discuss has an ethical dimension, and allowing our students to avoid this dimension, for me, represents a real failure. The problem, of course, is how to make this dimension compelling; how to make it the subject of sustained, relevant discovery. As anyone who has taught high school students has found out, we meet a certain amount of resistance when matters of ethics are presented in the classroom. I've explored a great many sources in an effort to meet this resistance and have thereby greatly enriched my own education. Inasmuch as we're all in the teaching profession together, I would like to believe that it is a collaborative effort and that my own discoveries and experiences may be useful to others. The following is an account of one such discovery that has enabled me to develop sustained ethical inquiry in the classroom.

William James

For any English teacher who is interested in having discussion and inquiry at the center of the classroom dynamic, the work of William James is an invaluable source of inspiration and insight. James was fluent in five languages by the age of nineteen, studied painting as a young man, earned an MD degree from Harvard, and was kept on to teach physiology. The mechanical stuff of medicine bored him but he remained at Harvard to teach psychology and then, later in life, philosophy. It would be difficult to name anyone else who rivals James in knowledge of the human condition; and his ability to see the interrelationships between the arts, the mind, the body, and the psyche is apparent in all that he wrote. While psychologists thought him too philosophical, and philosophers thought him too psychological, the modern educator can use his philosophy as a key not only to the works of educational theorists (Dewey foremost), but also to unlock various sticky doors in the minds of his or her students. I am, in short, amazed that so few educators seem to be aware of James and what he did for modern education. This chapter is an attempt to bring more attention to what is so obviously an invaluable resource, and to demonstrate how immediately useful his work is to us as teachers of English— especially as we discuss ethics with our students.

The Problem of Naïve Relativism

If discussion is the lifeblood of the classroom dynamic, then we must do everything we can to make sure it flows freely. There are numerous impediments to spontaneous and inspired group interchange; indeed, much of what we read in professional journals is concerned, finally, with this problem. In a group discussion of ethics, however, one of the most numbing obstacles is an attitude of nonreflective relativism that many students feel entitled, if not obligated, to adopt. Certainly we've all heard students make various claims such as, "You can't prove that anything is absolutely true, so my truth is just as good as your truth." Or, "There's no such thing as truth, so you can't say someone is wrong." Or more contextually, "Osama bin Ladin thinks he's right, so that means, to him, he is."

Probably the most frustrating aspect of naïve relativism is that it does nothing to promote dialogue. Our minds function by using comparisons, and as soon as we accept the notion that comparisons are impossible, the conversation flounders and stops. It helps a bit to demonstrate that the purely relativistic point of view is logically untenable, for what sense does the following proposition really make: "It is absolutely true that there are no absolutes"? Nevertheless, this quip will likewise produce little conversation because it, too, quickly leads to the observation that we don't know anything for certain and that comparisons are arbitrary. In point of fact, even if absolute truths do exist, we are not privy to them, but we do use the concept of "truth" every day. In a discussion of *Hamlet*, for example, a class might find itself evaluating Hamlet's inclination toward violence as a solution to his family problems. One student will state that it is right to meet violence by violence; another will say that this approach is never virtuous; while a third will say that it is up to Hamlet because he has his own idea of what is true for him. Indeed, we often say that something is true, or that it's closer to the truth than something else. What exactly do we mean by these statements, and how are we able to make them in the first place?

The Truth of an Idea Depends on Its Usefulness

For James, the most important criterion of an idea's truth-value is its usefulness in the context of life as a person is actually living it. All our students are genuinely concerned with how they might get the most out of their lives, and they have a natural attraction to ideas that seem useful to them. In other words, pragmatism already plays a role in their lives even though they don't know it. James summarizes his basic position by observing that an idea "'is useful because it is true' or 'it is true because it is useful.' Both of these phrases mean exactly the same thing" (James 1978, 98). Unfortunately, to equate truth simply with what is useful or with what "works" for us seems to be just another way of asserting the relativist position just considered. After all, the idea of flying a couple of airplanes into the World Trade Center works just fine for al Qaida. It is at this point that many believe they've heard enough from James and simply write him off as a naïve or even crass relativist. The reason why he isn't either of these things is discussed in the following pages as the subtleties of his philosophy are considered. Admittedly, the subtlety of pragmatism presents a number of difficulties and easily misleads even the careful reader to think that she has finished before she has yet started. Nevertheless, it is truly worth struggling to understand what James means because his ideas smack of so much common sense and are immensely useful in spite of their apparent complexity.

Part of the difficulty of reading James is that he uses the tool of logic while he simultaneously points out its shortcomings. In his 1896 essay "The Will to Believe," James asserts that, "We want to have a truth; we want to believe that our experiments and studies and discussions must put us in a continually better position towards it…. But if a pyrrhonistic skeptic asks us how we know all this, can our logic find a reply? No! Certainly it cannot" (James 1992, 463). In other words, logic can help us understand why we feel sure of some things, but it will never allow us to prove anything with absolute certainty. While this point of view might seem to keep him trapped in a relativistic system, he is merely recognizing our limitations and considering how we must make the best of our situation. Logic is a limited tool after all, and even in James' day it had been a long time since anyone had seriously thought it could reveal absolute truth. James would have us lower our gaze and use logic to look at how we live—at what we actually do in certain situations in order to understand how the action of our lives both creates, and helps us understand, our truths.

Nevertheless, in the context of late nineteenth-century philosophy, James' view on the limitations of logic was more radical than most, and was subject to condescension and ridicule. In particular, Bertrand Russell and G. E. Moore made a number of scathing attacks that helped to exasperate as well as unite James and his peers. In spite of what seemed to be "woolly thinking," James was, in reality, quite clear-sighted and anticipated much of what would become the focus of twentieth-century philosophy. The essence of his shift in perspective is indicated by his idea that "[pragmatism is] the attitude of looking away from first things, principles, 'categories,' supposed necessities: and of looking towards last things, fruits, consequences, facts" (James 1978, 32). Logic and a priori concepts cannot be seen as givens that we must begin with and on which we must build our ethical positions. Rather, we ought to start with a consideration of what our thoughts and actions will produce; we ought to start with what we know at present and then anticipate how these ideas will play out in the real action of our lives. To the degree that they work well, ideas will be useful and, therefore, true. But what does "working well" really mean? How is it possible to assert that one idea is ethically superior to another?

Truth Is Both Made and Revealed in the Action of Our Lives

Since James accepted that we have no access to absolute, objective truth, he consequently realized that truth isn't something that will stand still and pose for us. Instead, he realized that it moves all around us and through us and that we actually contribute to making an idea true with the action of our lives. As he puts it, "it is in the game." But how do we help to make truth and to what degree are we then able to evaluate what we've "made"? James offers some pretty specific directions to aid us in the evaluation of our ideas. He suggests that "true ideas are those that we can *assimilate, validate, corroborate,* and *verify*. False ideas are those that we cannot" (italics are mine) (James 1978, 97). With the addition of these verbs, we notice that the original criterion, "an idea is useful because it is true or it is true because it is useful," has been made a degree less relativistic. It's also important to notice that these are all active verbs. If we are to recognize true ideas through a process of assimilation and verification, we must accept the notion that truth is not a static abstraction. Rather, truth is an ongoing action, a living thing that we experience in the moment and anticipate in the future. To us, truth never appears to stand still because we must always assimilate ideas as we verify them. And it is this dynamic of assimilation and verification that helps to produce the feeling or "sentiment" of truth. For this reason, James observes that "truth happens to an idea." Nevertheless, while it is always characterized by a certain "mobility," the living quality of truth does not mean that anything is true—far from it.

Great Minds Think Alike: The Tradition of Progressive Teaching in America

Since the preceding ideas have been presented in the abstract, I'd like to pause for a moment and recall an element of the thesis—that insofar as we put inquiry at the center of the classroom we are much indebted to James, who stands at the beginning of a long line of progressive educators in America. No doubt, this genealogy is carried on in a full-blooded sense by the work of George Hillocks, who likewise puts inquiry center stage. From the point of view of this chapter then, I'd like to assert that to the degree that we don't "download" fixed ideas into the minds of our students and to the degree that we demand that they see their education as a process of corroborating, verifying, and assimilating new ideas, is to the degree that they are young pragmatists who realize that learning must be dynamic and unceasing. Further, if we were to learn only one thing from Hillocks it would be this: It is up to us, the teachers, to create an environment of inquiry in the classroom. And I believe that this environment of sustained, relevant discovery finds its historical roots in pragmatism. Thus, we are all deeply indebted to James and can only benefit by using his theory of meaning.

Our debt to Dewey is at least as great as it is to James, and as modern educators we must continue to revisit the work of John Dewey—often a formidable task. Yet I believe that his writing is made much more lucid once we consider him in relation to James; in other words, understanding pragmatism is essential to understanding Dewey. While the latter was nearly twenty years younger than James, and while most of what Dewey wrote was published after James' death (in 1910), the two nevertheless had a profound effect on each other. Their correspondence stretched over eighteen years and has the tone of mutual admiration as they worked through the implications of pragmatism in terms of ontology, epistemology, and, especially, Dewey's focus—the relationships between thinking, teaching, society, and morals. The last statement in *Democracy and Education* serves well to sum up Dewey's position:

> All education which develops power to share effectively in social life is moral. It forms a character which not only does the particular deed socially necessary but one which is interested in that continuous readjustment which is essential to growth. Interest in learning from all the contacts of life is the essential moral interest. (Dewey 1944, 360)

The notion of "continuous readjustment" is intimately tied to the attitude toward truth that we've considered so far in James: that it's a process of assimilation and verification of ideas. That said, there remain a few elements of pragmatism that have yet to be considered. Bringing Dewey into the discussion will help us by both clarifying pragmatism and showing us how it is at the heart of inquiry.

True Ideas Lead to a Better Life

If, to James, true ideas are useful, and if we know them by an ongoing process of assimilation, corroboration, and verification—the question still remains how we might actually judge one idea better than another in a context that is not simply subjective. In other words, if pragmatism isn't relativism, then exactly what becomes our basis for assessing the moral superiority of one idea compared to the next? James suggests, essentially, that we have to look at the big picture.

> True ideas lead us to useful verbal and conceptual quarters as well as directly up to useful sensible termini. They lead to consistency, stability, and flowing human intercourse. They lead away from eccentricity and isolation, from foiled and barren thinking. The untrammeled flowing of the leading process, its general freedom from clash and contradiction, passes for its indirect verification. (James 1944, 103)

Again, the key idea here is not found in a static conceptual framework, but in the flowing movement of life itself. Truth is recognized in ideas that make life consistent, stable, and positive—ideas that leave us with the reality and the promise that life will be harmonious, fruitful, and good.

Dewey is on the same page in this respect. For him, too, ideas must be seen in context where their value is determined by how they affect flowing human interchange. In his essay, "Morality Is Social," Dewey states:

> The facts upon which [morality] depends are those which arise out of active connections of human beings with one another, the consequences of their mutually intertwined activities in the life of desire, belief, judgment, satisfaction and dissatisfaction. In this sense conduct and hence morals are social: they are not just things which ought to be social and which fail to come up to scratch. (McDermott 1981, 721–22)

Here "the facts" are seen to have moral value only in the context of real social interaction, not apart from it. Again, what is useful to us is not an abstraction, but something vital, mutable, and dynamic.

The Truths We Share Beget New Truths as We Live

In his essay "The Moral Philosopher and the Moral Life," James makes the observation that there would be no ethics or morality if there were only one person in the world (McDermott 1977, 610–29). As soon as other people are added to her world it becomes necessary to communicate and compromise and understand—in essence to formulate a system of ethics. Thus, for James, the reason why facts or ideas function in social contexts, and the reason why some function better than others, is that people are tied together, albeit somewhat loosely, in a web of shared ideas and values. It is this functional aspect of ideas that James has in mind when he uses the term "instrumental truth." Taken individually, each idea is instrumental in the effectiveness of the other ideas that are connected to it. Hence, we are able to judge the truth-value of ideas because they must be seen in the context of other "shared" truths—truths which in their own context are instrumental to the validity of other truths, and so on. James observes this point early on in *Pragmatism*. "For how much more [ideas] are true will depend entirely on their relations to the other truths that also have to be acknowledged" (James 1978, 41). These "other truths" are, of course, various ideas that "work" for us (i.e., that are true for us) to increase our ability to have consistent flowing exchanges with one another. Further, it becomes the job of the intellect and indeed education to apprehend these ideas and learn how and why they have become true so as to guide us ethically in the future. As educators, we recognize this "job of the intellect" as inquiry, and can look to Dewey to see the intimate connection between inquiry and ethics.

The process of learning about the dynamic system of shared truths is, in the end, the purpose of education. In the essay "The Construction of the Good," Dewey describes our lives with and without intelligent, ethical behavior trained by the educative process.

> When theories of values do not afford intellectual assistance in framing ideas and beliefs about values that are adequate to direct action, the gap must be filled by other means. If intelligent method is lacking, prejudice, the pressure of immediate circumstance, self-interest and class interest, traditional customs, institutions of accidental historic origin, are *not* lacking, and they tend to take the place of intelligence. (McDermott 1981, 583)

Thus, if we allow ourselves to rely on systems of values that are not in common to the greatest number of people; if, in other words, we base our actions on ideas that are "true" only in a self-interested sense through the insulating forces of tradition, custom, and isolated institutions, we then forfeit intelligent method and ultimately our ability to act ethically. The tragedy of 9/11 provides a perfect example of this warning. On that day prejudice, the pressure of immediate circumstance, and self-interest overpowered intelligent method. The good of a relative few was privileged over a number of values that are shared in a global context. And consequently, the effect of al Qaida's attack did not add to consistency, stability, and flowing human intercourse. To whatever degree that it did the opposite is the degree to which we could rightfully call the action unethical.

The preceding example demonstrates that James and Dewey are able to avoid relativism not because there are absolutes, but because ideas affect all of us absolutely. Each proposition we consider must be evaluated in the context of life now and in the future. If we are able to see the "truth" of ideas in the context of free-flowing human interaction; and if we are able to accept the idea that such interaction is possible only if a system of shared truth exists within a social context, we can understand how it is possible to judge one idea against another. We are able to confidently say that some ideas are more true, more ethically effective than others, by observing how they work through the process of inquiry.

Taking Pragmatism, Ethics, and Inquiry into the Classroom

Chances are, any classroom based on inquiry is already making use of a number of the concepts that underlie pragmatism; nevertheless, it is possible to make a systematic introduction of it through a series of classroom approaches. In the long run, these approaches would provide students with the tools necessary to examine various ethical claims in a meaningful and lively way. The fundamental concepts of pragmatism might be introduced by asking students to consider the following questions: (a) How do we use the word *truth* in everyday discourse? (b) In what ways is truth equivalent to usefulness? (c) How do we effectively "assimilate, validate, corroborate, and verify" our ideas? In other words, how do we learn new ideas and accept them as true? (d) How is "instrumental truth" made useful in the context of shared truths? (e) Do global human truths exist—instrumental truths on a grand scale?

At this point, I am reminded of a discussion I had in class a few years ago. We had been reflecting on our ability to judge the actions of other people, and for the most part, my class thought that we were obliged to leave other cultures alone. I began to toss out examples of various atrocities, and the worst thing I could think of that day was torturing two-year-olds, supposing that surely here we could take a stand. Much to my surprise, many of my students held fast to their position and claimed that while they might not like it personally, they weren't able to condemn what people in another culture found useful, even if it involved the torture of small children. After class, I realized that my students had merely clung to the idea of tolerance because they were either afraid to be "hegemonic" or because they realized that taking a stand anywhere would lead to much more difficult reflection and discussion.

By now, I hope I've helped to make it clear that inquiry and pragmatism go hand in hand; and one of the great virtues of a classroom characterized by inquiry is that simpleminded relativism is revealed to be a lazy and useless point of view. In his essay "Morality Is Social," Dewey observes that "intelligence becomes ours in the degree in which we use it and accept responsibility for consequences" (McDermott 1981, 713). Let us teach our students to bravely wrestle with truth. While they will never win absolutely, they will come to realize that the strength gained from such a contest will empower their intelligence and sense of responsibility.

The Meaning of "Truth"

While we are all quite comfortable using the word *truth* throughout the day, a closer look at how we use the word might bring us face to face with a number of assumptions and contradictions that ultimately cloud our thinking. The following reflections on what we mean by "truth" are meant as a theoretical backdrop for the creative teacher's own approach to dealing with this topic. I suspect that presenting these ideas in a lecture format would be quite deadly to class involvement; nonetheless, taking a closer look now will help us later. For example, when we say, "that's true," we might mean a number of things. On the simplest level, something is true when it agrees with observable reality. If my wife were to observe that it's raining, I might then look out the window, see the rain and say, "that's true." That some schools of philosophy find ways to doubt the veracity of such observable events is useful here only as a bridge to the next category of truth. Ultimately, logic cannot conclusively prove that it's raining or even that what is outside my window exists, but it can help to support the "law of inference." When I say, for example, that it's true the sun will rise tomorrow morning, I am merely stating an inferentially based hypothesis. Because the sun has come up every morning for as long as any of us can remember means only that there is an extremely good chance it will happen again, not that it definitely will. Nevertheless, such inferential truths are as good as real truths in our everyday lives. What other kinds of truths fit into this category? If dropped, a ball will fall to the ground; water seeks its own level; plants die if they don't get enough water—these truths are all related because they are so repeatable as to be virtually certain; and because they deal with the observable, physical universe.

What of inferential truths in the social sphere? There are a number of observations we generally consider to be true because they fit into the "common sense" category. Again, this category does not lay any special claim to truth, but common-sense observations do have a very high probability of truth through repeated application in our daily conduct. When we utter homilies and such, we're tapping into this sort of "truth." The character of Polonius is, of course, the very prophet of such truths—"Neither a borrower nor a lender be;/ For loan oft loses both itself and friend,/ and borrowing dulls the edge of husbandry." While it is impossible to prove that such statements are true absolutely, their sense is verified enough times throughout our lives to carry the feeling of truth. Finally, there are commonly held moral truths in virtually all societies that transcend the more context-specific homiletic ones. For example, a basic premise of the United Nations' Declaration of Human Rights is that all humans are entitled to dignity and freedom. These normative statements seem true to us because we can't imagine humans fighting for their dignity or freedom to be taken away. They seem absolutely fundamental to the nature of healthy and happy human beings.

Again the point of reviewing the various categories of truth is to inspire ideas in the creative mind of the teacher, who will then find the most appropriate way to help her students come to terms with the word *truth*. How do we use the word *truth* in everyday discourse? Do we ever imply the use of one connotation, but mean another? Do the people we talk with have a different estimation of truth's certainty? What is our objective when we use the word? Is it different in different circumstances? Reviewing the various uses of the word *truth* and the various complications its use creates will help sensitize students to the issues raised by applying pragmatism.

Classroom Activity: The "Use" of Truth

This activity is intended to demonstrate James' notion that "truth" is not found as a static object but in the action of our lives. If truth "happens" to an idea, then an idea remains true as long as it's happening, so to speak. The first element of this classroom sequence would be to work with the statement "an idea is useful because it's true and it's true because it's useful." James' proposition is fairly easy to work with because its opposite is so clearly false. For example, if I were to claim that a person always benefits by breaking promises it isn't hard to imagine the kind of life that person would have. In the end, he would find himself completely alone, reviled by all he's ever met. Therefore, "break all promises" is not useful—it carries no truth-value. And since we all have an intuitive understanding of James' idea, one could easily ask his students to review any commonly held truth in terms of usefulness. One could simply write "Murder is wrong" on the blackboard and ask the following questions: To what degree is this proposition useful? Is it always useful? Under what conditions? What could we mean by "useful" in this context? Useful to whom? For what purposes? And so forth.

After looking at the proposition "murder is wrong" in view of the preceding questions, the class could brainstorm more propositions commonly held to be true—"Treat others as you would like to be treated." "It's wrong to steal." "It's unfair to take advantage of those weaker than yourself." And so on. After a list is made, a teacher could break the class up into small groups and assign each group a "truth" to examine in light of its usefulness. After the group work, each group would report its findings and thus prepare the class for an extended discussion and evaluation of James' basic proposition. Having done so, they might decide if usefulness is a helpful criterion. More than likely, they will decide that it is, but will also agree that it isn't enough. Are there modifications that need to be made? What are they? Why are they necessary? The following exercise is intended to anticipate and deal with these questions.

Classroom Activity: "Truth" in Action

The usefulness of an idea is best demonstrated in the action of our daily lives. Since usefulness can be determined only in the context of action, and since truth is related to what's useful, we must look to ideas that we can actually validate, corroborate, and assimilate into our daily lives. Indeed, true ideas often bring with them the feeling that we *must* apply them to our lives or suffer self-deception and hypocrisy.

A teacher might make a "truth table" having to do with a certain class of morals; let's take those having to do with stealing, for example. On the extreme side, she could write, "stealing in any form is always wrong." Somewhere in the middle of the continuum she could write, "while sneaking into a movie is a form of stealing, it's not really unethical." On the other extreme, she might write something like "stealing is wrong only when you get caught." Such continuums are easy to make for any ethical topic: violence, infidelity, lying, and so forth. In any case, the point would be to see which "level" of ethical propriety each student is willing to "validate and assimilate" into his or her own life. Again, "assimilation" in this context means to genuinely adopt into one's daily decision-making process. We know that an idea's been assimilated if we feel guilty once we've violated it.

Classroom Activity: "Truth" in Context

This activity would represent an effort to clarify what James means by "instrumental truth." Again, his idea is that an idea is useful partly because it fits within a structure of other useful ideas that are also accepted by a majority in a group. There are a variety of approaches a teacher might take to look at this dynamic. He could have the students brainstorm a list of every rule or idea that appears to be a part of their school code of conduct and discuss whether each is accepted by all or not. The rules that would be most interesting here are the ones that they are expected to accept, but don't. If James is correct, their refusal to accept a rule is because it is tied to other notions that they also have difficulty accepting. For example, a few years ago in my own school the administration decided that it would prohibit camouflage clothing of any kind. While this was a justifiable rule since it followed in the wake of the Columbine tragedy, it was generally resented and often broken by the student population because it was tied to other notions that they had trouble accepting. Since there was no dress code to begin with, many students felt that the administration was exercising its whim or fiat without bothering to justify it to the students. They also felt that there was no direct correlation between wearing camouflage and teen violence, and therefore they rejected not only the "whim" of the administration but also the logical correlation presented as fact. Here James' notion of instrumental truth became visible in that the administration relented after only two years and lifted the ban on camouflage.

Alternately, a teacher might present one rule or law from our society, such as the drinking age set at twenty-one, and have the class examine all the other ideas that are related to this idea that seem to support it. For example, the drinking age is twenty-one because of issues having to do with health, conduct, driving, judgment, and so on. To take the last one, it is generally assumed that teenagers as a group display poor judgment more often than people who are well into adulthood. It's a truism that alcohol impairs one's ability to make good decisions, so it makes sense that we should prohibit drinking until an individual is a bit older and more capable of deciding well. The idea here would be to outline the constellation of ideas that surround a rule or law and observe what supports it. Having done this, a group could easily discuss whether this dynamic of interrelated ideas in fact creates a sense of truth.

Classroom Activity: "Truth" in a Global Context

Finally, a class could pursue the class of "truths" that appear to be accepted by all or most humans, regardless of place or context. Perhaps the best place to begin a lesson on this topic would be the "Universal Declaration of Human Rights" created by the UN in 1948. This document can easily be found at www.un.org/Overview/rights.html and is a unique attempt at defining instrumental truths for all humans because it is the result of many nations working together to determine a basic set of ethics that transcend gender, age, race, and location. While one could argue that not all nations are represented in this effort, it is, at any rate, the best we have and quite worthy of close scrutiny. In James' terms it is a document of ideas that are interdependent and useful, each of which we can validate, corroborate, and assimilate.

The Universal Declaration contains a preamble followed by thirty articles, all of which could produce hours of class discussion. For instance, Article 1 states: "All human beings are born free and equal in dignity and rights. They are endowed with reason and conscience and should act toward one another in a spirit of brotherhood." In terms of the approaches just outlined, we can ask quite a few questions about any aspect of this article. The UN asserts that we must act toward one another in a spirit of brotherhood; but is this useful to us in all cases? Is it an idea that we can validate and assimilate? What other ideas is it tied to that we already accept? The Declaration is a wonderful tool for examining the usefulness of pragmatism, but more important, it allows us to take a step that James himself couldn't have taken inasmuch as he died long before 1948. After a detailed examination of the Universal Declaration, students are able to discuss whether there really are ideas that are true for all people. Of course, if there are such ideas, then the claim that "my truth is just as valid as your truth" becomes either nonsensical or simply not very useful.

Ethics, Pragmatism, and an Environment of Inquiry

In his essay "The Will to Believe," James makes the distinction between two types of philosophers: the rationalist and the empiricist. Both believe that truth somehow exists but each has a very different attitude toward it. The rationalist will seize on a truth and be absolutely certain that it is true, while the empiricist will sense truth but never allow herself to be absolutely certain about it. Consequently, she must keep up her search through the practice of pragmatism, attempting to validate, corroborate, and assimilate new ideas.

The truth of James' approach seems best proven by the fact that our most current and meaningful research on pedagogical practices still finds pragmatism useful. In his book *Teaching Writing as Reflective Practice*, Hillocks proposes that

> If education is the process of coming to understand the world around us and how to act in it, and if the world around us is in a constant state of change, then education must endeavor to prepare students to deal with what no one else has dealt with before. (Hillocks, 1995, 211)

In other words, truth is produced by a collective effort that is always located in the present. As the present changes, so must our ability to evaluate what is useful and true for us now. This is not to say that some things in our lives won't always remain true; rather, our position toward truth must remain lively and open. Thus Hillocks, like James and Dewey before him, would have us create an atmosphere of empiricism in our classrooms. They would have us create young pragmatists who are devoted to an unceasing examination of what they know and why they know it. Perhaps the final word here should be from James, whose prose style often captures not only our personal struggle with truth, but also the struggle each of us faces in the classroom as we wrestle with meaning, ethics, and right action.

> If this life be not a real fight, in which something is eternally gained for the universe by success, it is no better than a game of private theatricals from which one may withdraw at will. But it *feels* like a real fight—as if there were something really wild in the universe which we, with all our idealities and faithfulnesses, are needed to redeem; and first of all to redeem our own hearts from atheisms and fears. (James 1992, 502)

References

DEWEY, J. 1944. *Democracy and Education.* New York: The Free Press.

HILLOCKS, G., JR. 1995. *Teaching Writing as Reflective Practice.* New York: Teachers College Press

JAMES, W. 1978. *Pragmatism* and *The Meaning of Truth.* Cambridge, MA: Harvard University Press.

———. 1992. *William James: Writings 1878–1899.* New York: Literary Classics of the United States.

McDERMOTT, J. J., ED. 1977. *The Writings of William James: A Comprehensive Edition.* Chicago: The University of Chicago Press.

———. 1981. *The Philosophy of John Dewey: Two Volumes in One.* Chicago: University of Chicago Press.

PART

2

WRITING INSTRUCTION

3

Dialogue Folders
Creating Space to Engage Students in Conversation About Their Writing

KEVIN PERKS
Noble High School
North Berwick, Maine

In the novel *A River Runs Through It*, Norman MacLean (1976) writes, "All good things, from trout to eternal salvation, come by grace, and grace comes by art, and art does not come easy" (5). While MacLean is referring to fly-fishing in this passage, his words also ring true for the craft of writing. Any writer or student of writing knows that learning how to write does not come easy. For years I have watched my students struggle to learn this craft. Like most of us, they grapple with many of its facets. For example, on a daily basis I see my students fret about choosing creative and meaningful topics. I observe them wrestling with the differences between revising and editing. I watch as they struggle to carve space in their own lives so they can write on a consistent basis. I witness their impatience as they labor and play with words. The many hurdles I see my students overcome and struggle with seem endless at times.

As a teacher of writing, I see myself as a coach whose goal it is to help students become effective and, I hope, graceful writers. Slowly, over the years, I have come to the realization that if my students are ever going to increase their command of the craft of writing in my classroom, I need to provide a great deal of space for them to write and communicate with them about what they do as writers. By the term *space*, I do not refer just to physical space, but also to consistent time and opportunity to engage them in dialogue about writing, particularly their own. However, fostering and sustaining such opportunities is a daunting task.

In this chapter, I offer a strategy for creating and sustaining opportunities for students to converse with their teachers about their writing. I begin by reviewing the work of Hillocks and Nystrand, who emphasize the importance of dialogic writing instruction. Next, I review literature on writing conferences where I point out the strengths and weaknesses of traditional approaches to conferring with students. The final section of this chapter is a description of one classroom strategy that has helped my students become better writers by creating space where they can talk about and reflect on their own work with others. The strategy that I share owes much to the work of George Hillocks, Jr. (1986, 1995, 1999), who has frequently emphasized the importance of reflective teacher practice.

Procedural Knowledge of Writing

In order for students to become better writers, it is essential for them to talk about what they are doing as they are writing. Hillocks (1995) argues that good writing instruction focuses on teaching the *procedural knowledge* of writing. Procedural knowledge emphasizes the "knowledge of how to do things; how to write an effective argument of policy, how to write an empathic narrative....[I]t also involves how to decide what to do in a new situation and how to think about what to do when the what is new" (216). Procedural knowledge differs from *declarative knowledge*, which is "the knowledge of what" (1999, 27). As Hillocks writes, such knowledge "has only a very weak effect or no effect on improving student writing" (121–22). Hillocks' argument rings true in my classroom. I have found that as students get better at talking about *how* their writing is going, they also become better writers. However, many students enter classrooms feeling uncomfortable talking about their own work. Often when I ask them to talk to me about a piece they have written, the most common reply is, "Take a look at it and tell me what to fix." When students say things like this, they are giving up ownership.

Dialogic Instruction

Helping students maintain ownership of their own writing has evolved into the backbone of my writing curriculum. If we wish our students to craft thoughtful pieces with strong voices, how can we ignore their voices *as* they write? Nevertheless, I have found that it is easy to forget to pay attention to students' voices. I am not alone in this. Nystrand and collegues (1997), in a extensive survey of more than one hundred eighth- and ninth-grade language arts classrooms, found very little evidence of dialogic instruction in the classrooms; instead, he observed that the most common form of instruction was monologic in nature—what he refers to as *recitation*. While dialogic instruction refers to instruction that values the voices and views of the students in shaping the content of instruction, monologic instruction is teacher dominated and provides little room for the students to influence instructional aims. When, however, his researchers did observe dialogic instruction in practice, they frequently found students achieving at higher levels. Thus, as students engage in the procedures of writing, it is important that we encourage them to discuss their writing with us so they have opportunities to articulate what it is they are doing as they write, what they are struggling with, and *how* they are proceeding. The question then becomes *how* to engage our students in such discussions. For many language arts instructors the writing conference provides a solution, albeit an imperfect one.

The Writing Conference

In many language arts classrooms writing conferences are opportunities for students to talk with their teachers about their own writing. In recent years many texts have described benefits and various approaches to writing conferences (Anderson 2000; Atwell 1998; Calkins 1994; Graves 1983, 1994; Murray 1985). In addition, many colleges and high schools have developed walk-in writing centers where students can engage in conferences with writing consultants, instructors, or peer tutors. The widespread use of writing conferences as a tool for teaching writing is not a surprise.

Writing conferences are ideal contexts to engage students in dialogic instruction and procedural knowledge so that we can understand how they are going about their work, and can gain insights into how to further support them in their efforts. Some argue (Anderson 2000; Atwell 1998; Calkins 1994; Graves 1983, 1994) that conferences provide a space for students to talk about their own work. Graves (1983) insists, "As long as children talk, not only does the teacher gain more information about the subject, but the teacher acquires perspective on what will help the children" (138). Conferences also provide opportunities for negotiation and collaboration between student and teacher (Sperling 1990, 1992). According to Sperling (1992), they can be "seen as a context embodying the social construction of written language acquisition, a context in which the student comes to 'inherit' the conventions of written language through a bilateral pursuit of those conventions with a more able adult" (318).

Even though writing conferences have the potential to be effective for helping students improve their writing, many concerns still arise. One primary frustration is that conferences are often too short and too infrequent. Most teachers have so many students that it is not feasible for them to have thoughtful conversations with all of them on a regular basis. The writing workshop approach (Atwell 1998, Calkins 1994) offers strategies to confer with all students on a regular basis; however, such an approach is still limited. In his thoughtful discussion of writing conferences, Anderson (2000) mentions that most of his writing conferences are about five minutes long. He claims that this "is enough time to have a quality conversation with each student, and (in a class of thirty students) see each of them every six to eight days" (169). He continues to mention that some conferences may be only three or four minutes long.

While I agree with many of Anderson's assertions, I disagree that quality conversations can regularly take place in five-minute conferences. Anderson states that when looked at on the whole, one five-minute conference every week or so will yield "twenty to thirty conferences per student in a school year" (170). Add this up and you get about two hours of discussion with each student on average. I commend Anderson's attempt to meet with all students, and I believe his strategies, which mirror those of others who espouse the writing workshop approach (Atwell 1998; Calkins 1994; Graves 1994; Murray 1985), are valuable in the writing classroom; but we must recognize such conferences for what they are. Five minutes is only enough time to check in with students to gain an understanding of what they are doing and to give them a little support and guidance. That is all.

An additional concern with writing conferences is that, because one-on-one time with students is so precious, teachers have a tendency to dominate the discourse. Thus, one of the primary purposes of a writing conference, which is to hear from the student, is often undermined. Some studies (Flurio-Ruane 1986; Newkirk 1995) show how teachers dominate the conversation that occurs during writing conferences. As a result, students feel the need to retreat from the teacher's agenda (Nickel 2001). One reason for this may be that students are unfamiliar with the discourse used by the teacher and miscommunication arises (Evans 1994); another may be that students view the conference as a performance (Newkirk 1995) and thus feel inhibited. Nor are there multiple opportunities to reflect or build on previous conversations or clarify miscommunications, since writing conferences are such infrequent events.

My own experiences with writing conferences mirror the preceding concerns. I believe that writing conferences are valuable tools in the writing classroom, but I also experience many of the same frustrations. I never feel as if I can meet with students face-to-face frequently enough. I often feel that I try to get too much accomplished in a single conference because I know it might be weeks at best before I conference with a particular student again. I also know I dominate the agenda during conferences even when I wish the student would play a greater role. Almost as if in response, most students are more than willing to let me maintain control of the conference. For example, when I ask a student "How's it going with your writing?" many respond with questions like, "What do *you* think needs to be fixed?" They need help taking the reins.

Dialogue Folders

In response to my needs and the shortcomings of writing conferences, I designed a strategy that blends the use of dialogue journals (Baskin 1994; Cziko 1995; Holmes and Moulton 1995; Peyton 1997; Peyton and Staton 2000; Turewicz 1983) with the format of the writing conference. I created what I call dialogue folders. I started using these folders in my creative writing classroom and now use them in all of my classes. To start off with, each student is given a folder that remains in the classroom. Each student puts his or her name on it. In the folder attached to a clip is a set of blank pages. On the inside of the folder cover I have the students write a version of the following three questions:

1. How is my writing going?

2. What is the next step in my writing?

3. What specific questions do I have that will help me receive feedback about my writing?

These questions are intended to provide some structure for the students as they begin to write to me. I also provide students with examples of what good entries look like. For example, I often start by showing my students the following entry:

Mr. Perks,

My writing is going good. My next step is to write some more. Can you read the draft I put in my folder and tell me if I need to fix anything?

After reading this, I ask the students how much thought would have been required to write it. We also talk about how helpful this entry would be in guiding a reader to provide useful feedback.

I contrast the previous entry with the following from an actual student.

Mr. Perks,

I think that my writing has been going good so I'm going to start typing up my poems. I want to start typing up but I'm nut shure what I should do after that. In my typed poem can you look for any messtakes and if I need to fix anything or put anything into my poem, can you look at my poem and see if I focus on any other kind of motive besides friends. It doesn't seem like my poem has any other motive but I wanted to base it on if I could add another motive into my poem. Like can you give me some ideas about how I could if I want to redue my poem what could I base it on besides friends but keep the poem the same.

When I go over this entry with the students, they often point out how much more helpful such an entry is in guiding a reader into giving helpful feedback. When I first read this entry, I knew that the student wanted help in branching out from the topic of friendship. I was able to read her poem and focus on looking for other themes within her work.

After a few more examples, the students begin to get an idea of the kind of entries they are being encouraged to write. At the end of each class I ask the students to write to me in their folders. I also request that they include samples or selections of their writing work for me to look at. By the beginning of the next class I will have read their entries and their work and will have written back. This continues throughout the entire semester. It is also important to note that it is impossible to write to all of my students every night. In some classes, I put students into groups of three. Each day we use the folders, I have the students write to each other. At the end of the class, one student in each group must also write to me and give me samples of his or her work. Thus, I need to respond only to a handful of students in each class every night. This is very manageable yet still allows me to have consistent dialogue with my students about their work. I also find that I can provide my students with guidance on how they are giving feedback for each other, thus supporting the development of peer revision skills.

Results

The folders have yielded many of the benefits I have hoped for and more. Each time I implement the dialogue folders, I discover many positive outcomes as the semester progresses. These results only improve as I continue to explore the range of ways the folders can be used. Since I began using the folders as a tool in my classroom, I continue to find the following:

1. Many students get better at talking about their own writing.
2. My ability to engage in reflective practice increases.
3. Opportunities to differentiate instruction increase.
4. Students' motivation to write appears to increase.
5. Student writing improves.

STUDENTS LEARN HOW TO TALK ABOUT THEIR OWN WRITING   As the students begin writing to me in their dialogue folders, it becomes clear that many of them do not know how to talk about their own writing. At first, they just answer the three questions I posed at the start. But they soon begin to transcend these question such as a dialogue between us forms. For example, Elissa's first entry in her dialogue folder contained only brief answers to my questions.[1] She wrote:

1. How's it going?—Okay
2. Where do you want to go? Improve my writing skill as a poet.
3. How can we (teachers) help? ?

Her response to the third question was only a question mark, which made it clear to me that she was not sure how we could help. During the next class Elissa wrote a poem but shared no insights about it and asked for no feedback. The following is my response to her:

> Elissa,
>
> This poem is interesting. I like the sense of all the different emotions. I'd like you to work on this a little more. If we can get all of these emotions rooted to something the reader can *see* (i.e., an event/object), this poem will be great. If you have questions, ask me! GREAT JOB!!

Elissa replied by making some changes to the poem and asking the following in her next entry: "Do the changes I made take away from the poem?" That was all she wrote.

   These initial attempts by Elissa to talk about her work contrast greatly with the way she communicated by the end of the semester. In the following entry she struggles with a poetry review:

---

1   When I transcribe student writing in this chapter, I record it as it is written in the folder. I also make it a point not to correct grammar and spelling in the folder. I believe that doing so will inhibit the students from writing fluently. Think about a conversation you have with an individual who always corrects the grammar of others. It only sets up a barrier within the dialogue and impedes communication.

When I actually started to sit down + write this last night I realized that I didn't really know what I was doing. I could do the brief biography + the listing of some of his poems. But the analysis part was a disaster. I could understand what he (Yeats) was talking about in the poem, and it is easy to write about. I really couldn't figure out how to write about alliteration, etc. I don't know how I could show that. Do I define alliteration + give examples that he uses? Or do I write about how using alliteration made his poetry better? Was I supposed to analyze more than 1 of his poems? How many? How should I analyze his poems? I have a hard time telling what some things are? What do I do if I don't understand the poem? Or my view of what he is saying is totally off? What did I do wrong? Where should I go w/ this? Was the brief biography what you were looking for?— Truly LOST Elissa

This entry is representative of many of Elissa's end-of-semester entries. By this time she was no longer using the questions as a guide; it appeared she did not need them any longer. It was clear that she had become comfortable describing how her writing was going and discussing questions that were puzzling her. She also got much better at describing her own confusions and developing specific questions that helped support her writing. Elissa's growth in talking about her own work is representative of the growth I see in many of my students.

REFLECTIVE PRACTICE INCREASES   Another outcome of using the dialogue folders is the opportunity for me to engage in reflective teaching (Hillocks 1995). Hillocks describes six important dimensions to what he calls "frame experiments," a term he gets from Schön (1987). For Hillocks, frame experiments are critical to reflective practice in that they promote thoughtful inquiry about instruction. The six dimensions Hillocks identifies are:

1. analyzing current student progress in relation to general course goals;

2. positing some change or range of possible changes sought in the writing of students;

3. selecting or devising a teaching strategy or set of strategies to implement the desired change;

4. devising a plan for implementing the teaching strategies;

5. assessing the impact of the teaching strategy in order to "discover consequences and implications of [the] chosen frames"; and

6. confirmation or change of the strategies used. (1995, 33)

By using dialogue folders as a tool to foster conversation with students about their writing, I am able to meet all six dimensions that Hillocks describes; during face-to-face conferences, I am unable to do this. For example, when students put samples of their writing in their folders, I have the time to read their writing and think about the kind of feedback that will be helpful. I can consider how well they are progressing toward the goals we have set in the class as well as ascertain the kind of feedback they are requesting from me.

Consistent with the second and third dimensions Hillocks describes, the folders provide a space where I can explain and describe changes I would like to see in the students' writing. I also have the time to devise a strategy. Oftentimes I will include published work with my feedback as a model for what I am attempting to teach. To illustrate: consider a student who is working on a fantasy story. Her story has a similar motif to that of W. W. Jacobs' "Monkey's Paw." I am able to give her a copy of the story and ask her to compare her plot to that of the short story. I can also articulate the changes I want to see in her writing, which has a more refined plot.

In regard to the fourth dimension of reflective practice, devising a plan for implementing a strategy, dialogue folders allow me to implement almost any plan. In the preceding example, I felt the student would benefit from reading a piece of published writing that modeled what she was trying to accomplish. On other occasions, I may find that I need to have a face-to-face conference with the student; if this is the case, the folder is where I schedule this conference.

Finally, dialogue folders are excellent vehicles to assess student work and thinking. Feedback on my strategies is reflected in subsequent entries as well as in their writing. Since the folders stay in the classroom or with me, there is a permanent record to which I can always refer. This record provides a foundation from which to target common challenges my students are facing and helps me design lessons to target their needs. Not only do the folders help in designing effective lessons, but they are also excellent supports for differentiating instruction.

OPPORTUNITIES TO DIFFERENTIATE INSTRUCTION INCREASE　　While dialogue folders allow me to find common challenges the students are facing as writers, they also allow me to differentiate instruction to a much greater extent than I would if conducting face-to-face conferences. Through the folders I am able to determine and address students' individual needs as writers. For example, on any given night I may give one student feedback and advice on how to write flashbacks, and with another have a conversation on how to write effective imagery.

While the opportunity for differentiation exists in most writing conferences, the dialogue folders allow me to target specific needs on a regular basis. As the semester progresses, the students become better and better at targeting their own challenges. One way to look at this is that the dialogue folders help students explore their own zone of proximal development (Dixon-Krauss 1996; Vygotsky 1978, 1986; Wertsch 1985, 1991). According to Vygotsky, the Zone of Proximal Development (ZPD) describes the point at which a learner can accomplish a task with guidance and support, with the goal of eventually performing the task without support. Often, teachers are left with the task of determining exactly how much support is necessary to help students achieve independent mastery. But, when students can articulate the challenges they are facing in their own learning, the teacher can better scaffold (Palincsar 1986) instruction based on the students' own observations.

When students learn how to articulate their own frustrations, we gain greater insight into where they are developmentally in their writing. Such information is invaluable to a teacher. Here is a sample of the questions students ask.

- *Is my writing descriptive enough?*
- *I am not sure how to go about building a chorus and writing one. What do I need to make a good chorus?*
- *I think that if I shortened [my short story] there would be too many loose ends. What do you think?*
- *When I go to revise my work I find myself wanting to throw a lot of stuff away. I know this is good for revising but should I keep any of it for later? Also, when I take out a lot I find that I'm writing an entirely new song. Is this revising?*

Questions like these become more and more common in the dialogue folders as the semester progresses and are essential when deciding what support and guidance students may need. Prior to implementing dialogue folders in my class, I often felt as if I were shooting in the dark; that is, not sure if suggestions I was giving students were providing the support they needed.

The best evidence I have to demonstrate the success of dialogue folders is the work the students end up producing as well as their own feedback regarding the dialogue folders. I have found that two of the best ways to evaluate a teaching practice are by assessing the final product or performance and by asking the students themselves.

MOTIVATION TO WRITE INCREASES Every semester that I implement writing folders, the students' motivation to write appears to increase. I infer this from the improvement I see in their work. The feedback I receive from the students also reveals their motivation. For example, at the end of each semester I have students fill out a self-assessment questionnaire. A couple of items on this sheet ask students how useful they have found the dialogue folders, and to what extent the folders have supported them in their writing. Almost all the students report that they value the use of the folders. The only negative feedback I have received occurred when I was not prompt in responding to the students' entries. When I have difficulty replying, the students are always quick to admonish me—usually good-naturedly— demonstrating the extent to which they value the dialogue we have fostered.

I stress that it is not the folders themselves that are motivating but rather the dialogue that is fostered through the folders. It is my contention that after the early grades in primary school, students learn how *not* to participate in their own learning. For example, the dominant discourse pattern in many classrooms is the Initiation/Response/Evaluation pattern or IRE (Cazden 2001; Mehan 1979; Nystrand 1997). During this style of discourse, the teacher initiates a question to which a student responds briefly. The teacher concludes the interchange with succinct feedback or evaluative comments. Frequently there is little room for students to act as full participants. It is difficult to envision a less motivating way to learn. Dialogue folders, on the other hand, offer an opportunity for students to take the reins of their own learning. Current research in motivation also supports my claim that fostering dialogue about writing enhances motivation to write.

One current theory of motivation is the Self-Determination Theory (Deci et al.1991; Ryan and Deci 2000a, 2000b, 2000c; Vallerand 1993, 2000). This theory posits that individuals are motivated when they feel as if their actions are self-determined. Ryan and Deci identify three primary supports people need in order to feel motivated. The first is the need to feel a sense of autonomy (i.e., self-determination). In other words, they need to feel as if they have control over decision making—in this case, with their writing. Second, they need to feel competent. The students who always appear the least motivated are the students who think they are terrible writers. Conversely, the students who are the most motivated oftentimes think they are excellent writers. It can be tricky dealing with such students because many of them find critical feedback demotivating. Third, individuals need to have a strong sense of relation. This emphasizes the importance of the social context in many situations in which motivation is a concern. While I may feel competent and autonomous in doing what I am requested to do, if I am working with others whom I dislike, find intimidating, or disrespectful, my motivation may decrease.

Dialogue folders provide all three supports. For example, one of my main goals is to help students learn how to guide me in providing the kind of feedback they desire. As a result, they become more and more self-determined in their own writing as the semester progresses. I also make it a point to provide positive feedback. The more students learn to set the agenda, the more successfully I can provide positive feedback that they will find useful. This in turn increases their sense of competence as writers. Finally, by fostering a sustained dialogue with students over extended periods of time, we begin to develop a strong rapport around writing. Many of the students with whom I have worked continue to come back to conference even when they are no longer in any of my classes.

STUDENT WRITING   When we consider the benefits of fostering sustained dialogue with students, it is not surprising that students' writing improves as a result. To illustrate this, consider the work of Elissa again. Elissa's growth during the semester mirrors that of many students who have used dialogue folders. Below are two poems Elissa wrote. The first was written at the beginning of the semester; the second is a poem that was developed to a significant extent through our written conversations. These poems speak for themselves.

Poem 1

I saw in the flash of a light
An eternity
In which there was no end
A beautiful place of hope and endless light
I knew no pain
And felt no fear
It is where happiness reins

And where sadness disappears
My heart is saddened, how can I speak
Words of comfort can not appease
The pain that is
It pierces the heart with great agony
The joy that the morning has brung
Is shattered with sadness and tears that have sprung
With the day not yet begun
I don't know how I will live
This day is a tragic one

Poem 2

Flirting

> You stole my pen
> When I sat beside you.

I whined.

> You laughed.

I made a false attempt to get it back
   Trying to pry it from your hand.
     In vain I sat and ignored you.
Surrendered.

> You smiled.
> And poked me in the side with
> the pen.

I stole yours.

> Grabbing at my hand you pulled it
> Towards your body.
> Forcing it open to take
> Back what belongs to you.

I elbowed you in the arm.

> You shrugged your shoulders
> And mocked me
> With your smile

I kicked you in the leg.

> You'll only hurt yourself,
> Was all you chuckled.
> And you mocked me
> Once more.

I jabbed you with the pen.
   The bell rang, and we went our different ways.
    Later, I saw you in the library

> You smirked at me
> From the other side.

I blushed at your grin,
   and turned my eyes away
     because I had nothing
left to steal.

One may argue, and rightly so, that many factors play a role in bringing about student achievement. Dialogue folders are only one tool among many others that I utilize to teach my students. While I could provide many pre- and postwriting samples to demonstrate the growth of my students, I cannot separate the many variables that are involved in helping students learn how to write. For me the most convincing evidence occurs on a daily basis, as I see students opening up and becoming more comfortable talking about their writing. Regularly I see what they are writing, what they are struggling with, what they are playing with. Because of this I can see them growing as writers. As a teacher, this is proof enough.

Fostering Sustained Conversations

In this chapter I do not intend to sell a particular teaching method; rather I provide dialogue folders as an example of how we can foster sustained conversations with students about their writing. As educators, we are hard-pressed to teach students as much as we can in very little time. Crowded classrooms and short periods make the teaching of writing a laborious task. Yet despite all the impediments we cannot forget how important it is to get to know our students well, in this case as writers. Writing is often a personal and intimate endeavor. Many students feel uncomfortable sharing their work because classrooms can be intimidating places. We need to do whatever we can to foster classroom environments where students feel safe to write, explore, and share their work. We can only do this successfully if we take the time to get to know them as writers. We cannot expect this to happen if students do most of their writing at home. Nor can we expect great changes if we conference with them once or twice a semester. We need to develop spaces where we can foster sustained dialogues with them as writers. This is a must if a teacher wishes to establish a true writing community.

References

ANDERSON, C. 2000. *How's It Going? A Practical Guide to Conferring with Student Writers*. Portsmouth, NH: Heinemann.

ATWELL, N. 1998. *In the Middle: New Understandings About Writing, Reading, and Learning*. 2nd ed. Portsmouth, NH: Heinemann.

AULLS, M. W. 1998. "Contributions of Classroom Discourse to What Content Students Learn During Curriculum Enactment." *Journal of Educational Psychology* 90 (1): 56–69.

BASKIN, R. S. 1994. *Student Feedback on Dialogue Journals*. Unpublished Report. Educational Resources Information Center (ERIC) Documentation Service No. ED 375 627.

CALKINS, L. M. 1994. *The Art of Teaching Writing*. Portsmouth, NH: Heinemann.

CAZDEN, C. B. 2001. *Classroom Discourse: The Language of Teaching and Learning*. Portsmouth, NH: Heinemann.

CZIKO, C. 1995. "Dialogue Journals: Passing Notes the Academic Way." *The Quarterly of the National Writing Project and the Center for the Study of Writing Literacy* 17 (4): 1–11.

DECI, E. L., R. J. VALLERAND, L. G. PELLETIER, AND R. M. RYAN. 1991. "Motivation and Education: The Self-Determination Perspective." *Educational Psychologist* 26 (3, 4): 325–46.

DIXON-KRAUSS, L. 1996. *Vygotsky in the Classroom: Mediated Literacy Instruction and Assessment.* White Plains, NY: Longman.

EVANS, K. 1994. "That's Not What I Meant": Failures of Interpretation in the Writing Conference. Paper presented at the annual meeting of the conference on college composition and communication, Nashville, Tennessee, March 16–19.

FLURIO-RUANE, S. 1986. Taking a Closer Look at Writing Conferences. Paper presented at the Annual Meeting of the American Educational Research Association, San Francisco, April 16–20.

GRAVES, D. H. 1983. *Writing: Teachers and Children at Work.* Portsmouth, NH: Heinemann.

———. 1994. *A Fresh Look at Writing.* Portsmouth, NH: Heinemann.

HILLOCKS, G., JR. 1986. *Research on Written Composition: New Directions for Teaching.* Urbana, IL: ERIC/NCRE.

———. 1995. *Teaching Writing as Reflective Practice.* New York: Teachers College Press.

———. 1999. *Ways of Thinking, Ways of Teaching.* New York: Teachers College Press.

HOLMES, V. L., AND M. R. MOULTON. 1995. "A Contrarian View of Dialogue Journals: The Case of a Reluctant Participant." *Journal of Second Language Writing* 4 (3): 223–51.

KUTZ, E. 1997. *Language and Literacy: Studying Discourse in Communities and Classrooms.* Portsmouth, NH: Heinemann.

MACLEAN, N. 1976. *A River Runs Through It and Other Stories.* Chicago: University of Chicago Press.

MEHAN, H. 1979. *Learning Lessons.* Cambridge, MA: Harvard University Press.

MURRAY, D. M. 1985. *A Writer Teaches Writing.* Boston: Houghton Mifflin.

NEWKIRK, T. 1995. "The Writing Conference as Performance." *Research in the Teaching of English* 29 (May): 193–215.

NICKEL, J. 2001. "When Writing Conferences Don't Work: Students' Retreat From Teacher Agenda." *Language Arts* 79 (2): 136–47.

NYSTRAND, M., WITH A. GAMORAN, R. KACHUR, AND C. PRENDERGAST. 1997. *Opening Dialogue: Understanding the Dynamics of Language and Learning in the English Classroom.* New York: Teachers College Press.

PALINCSAR, A. S. 1986. "The Role of Dialogue in Providing Scaffolded Instruction." *Educational Psychologist* 21 (1, 2): 73–98.

PEYTON, J. K. 1997. "Dialogue Journals: Interactive Writing to Develop Language Literacy." *Emergency Librarian* 24 (5): 46–48.

PEYTON, J. K., AND J. STATON. 2000. *Dialogue Journal Bibliography: Published Works About Dialogue Journal Research and Use.* Washington, DC: National Clearinghouse for ESL Literacy Education.

RYAN, R. M., AND E. L. DECI. 2000a. "The Darker and Brighter Sides of Human Existence: Basic Psychological Needs as a Unifying Concept." *Psychological Inquiry* 11 (4): 319–39.

———. 2000b. "Intrinsic and Extrinsic Motivations: Classic Definitions and New Directions." *Contemporary Educational Psychology* 25: 54–67.

———. 2000c. "Self-Determination Theory and the Facilitation of Intrinsic Motivation, Social Development, and Well-Being." *American Psychologist* 55 (1): 68–78.

SCHÖN, D. A. 1987. *Educating the Reflective Practitioner: Toward a New Design for Teaching and Learning in the Professions.* San Francisco: Jossey-Bass.

SPERLING, M. 1990. "I Want to Talk to Each of You: Collaboration and the Teacher-Student Writing Conference." *Research in the Teaching of English* 24 (3): 279–321.

———. 1992. "In-Class Writing Conferences: Fine-Tuned Duets in the Classroom Ensemble." *English Journal* 81 (4): 65–71.

TUREWICZ, E. 1983. "Dialogue Journal Writing in the Secondary School." Unpublished dissertation. Sydney, Australia: Riverina College of Advanced Education.

VALLERAND, R. J. 1993. "On the Assessment of Intrinsic, Extrinsic, and Amotivation in Education: Evidence on the Concurrent and Construct Validity of the Academic Motivation Scale." *Educational and Psychological Measurement* 53 (1): 159–73.

———. 2000. "Deci and Ryan's Self-Determination Theory: A View from the Hierarchical Model of Intrinsic and Extrinsic Motivation." *Psychological Inquiry* 11 (4). 312–19.

VYGOTSKY, L. S. 1978. *Mind in Society: The Development of Higher Psychological Processes.* Cambridge: Harvard University Press.

———. 1986. *Thought and Language.* Translated by A. Kozulin. Cambridge, MA: MIT Press.

WERTSCH, J. V. 1985. *Vygotsky and the Social Formation of Mind.* Cambridge, MA: Harvard University Press.

———. 1991. *Voices of the Mind: A Sociocultural Approach of Mediated Action.* Cambridge, MA: Harvard University Press.

4 Inquiry, Dialogue, and the Teaching of Writing

JOSEPH M. FLANAGAN
York Community High School
Elmhurst, Illinois

I've been teaching for ten years and, although trained to encourage the authentic exchange of ideas in the classroom, I can recall my own high school experiences in the early 1980s where we rarely, if ever, attempted to discuss anything in a structured or meaningful way. My recollections of classroom discussion include the daily banter with which students would greet each other every day, and our successful attempts to draw our teachers off topic and get them talking about their personal lives or something that might have popped up in the news that week. Students still attempt to draw their teachers off topic as often as they can, and as a seasoned practitioner of the tactic who honed his skills sharply and met with great success, I have come to appreciate the efforts of these students. However, the grown-up adult teacher side of me resists the urge to engage kids in conversation merely for the sake of doing so. The notion of reducing teacher talk and maximizing student talk is a concept to which George Hillocks introduced me early on in my teacher training. It is a concept that revisits me whenever I attempt to engage students in discussion.

I recall the first time I cotaught a class that was a part of Hillocks' MAT program at the University of Chicago. I had never taught a day in my life—except for, of course, the days we managed to wrangle control of the classroom from our English teachers back in high school—and I know that my classmates and I attempted to prepare for our emerging roles as teachers exactly as Hillocks had trained us. One of my classmates engaged our experimental seventh-grade class in a scenario activity that encouraged the students to generate several criteria about heroic behavior. I then helped the students to test the criteria. The idea was to have the students write a preliminary narrative about a person in their lives whom they regarded as heroic. In Hillocksian fashion, I modeled the assignment and, in doing so, rendered what I thought was a touching portrait of the woman I had just married, Nancy. I recall reading my narrative to the class. It was only a paragraph long but while I read it I noticed something that the two coteachers before me had not yet experienced: absolute quiet and complete fixation on the teacher (me). The students were entranced by my tale and I felt, for the first time in my not-yet-established career, that I had the class in the "palm of my hand" (the nonsensical nature of this teacher myth had not yet been made clear to me). I finished out the lesson by giving students the rest of the class to begin fleshing out their own paragraph-long responses. They did so while I and my co-teacher colleagues circulated around the room (just as we had been taught) to help students and monitor progress.

I was feeling pretty good about what I had done. As we sat in an empty room at a circle of desks and my fellow neophyte teachers finished congratulating me for the lesson—or for actually surviving the experience—Hillocks chimed in with the constructive criticism that redirected our enthusiastic review of my lesson and brought us back to the serious task of educating the youth of America.

"That was a little bit chatty today," he said. "We need to get the *students* talking more."

Hillocks' sentiment has been at the forefront of my efforts as a teacher since that day. I have been pleased to learn, as I have made my way through the teaching ranks, that his call for the need for more student talk is supported by studies that have focused on what actually goes on in English classrooms in America. Nystrand (1997) found that students don't get the chance to talk very often in class and when they do, the speaking they do tends to be more recitation than the commentary more typically associated with solving or addressing a unique problem. We know also that students learn well when given the chance to exchange ideas and that the most effective exchanges are often among themselves and not with their teacher. Teachers are then challenged to construct an environment where students have the chance to talk to each other in ways that are significant, relevant, and meaningful to them.

The cornerstone of the Hillocksian view of English education—engaging students in relevant inquiry that calls on them to develop their reading, writing, listening, and speaking skills—turns out to create fertile ground in which to accomplish this difficult work. I began my teaching career practicing ways to engage kids in inquiry in order to prepare them to read a specific text. But over time I have come to value more highly the discussions that we have in class that result from the inquiry frames. In other words, the discussions that we have in class to *prepare* for our reading or writing often become actual classroom texts that provide further opportunity for students to enhance their ability to communicate effectively.

As Hillocks (1995) asserts, effective classroom inquiry cannot take place without worthwhile inquiry frames that provide the scaffolding necessary to help students attain reasonable goals. Inspired by the work of philosopher Stephen Toulmin (Toulmin, Rieke, and Janik 1984), Hillocks most often refers to this process as argument. A great deal of work has been done recently to express the importance of implementing a coherent framework for discourse in order to help students engage in higher-level thinking. One of the most valuable contributions Hillocks has made is asserting that when students are exposed to argument, regardless of their perceived ability level, they can then engage in high-level inquiry:

... constructing arguments is closely tied to conducting inquiry and to epistemological assumptions. The strategies of inquiry are inextricably engaged in the development of argument. As we set out to conduct an inquiry, we necessarily conduct an argument, an argument whose claim is continually reshaped by our changing perceptions of the problem, its data, and its context. The more we work with a problem, the more likely we are to deconstruct and reconstruct our thinking about it. (1995, 129)

I've come to appreciate that making students more aware of their own arguments, particularly through the analysis of the discussions they have in class and the resulting dialogues that may then be used as actual texts in the classroom, their ability to argue well and understand the logical underpinnings of what is said in class are both increased tremendously. Students develop a clearer understanding of how to solve problems, develop rules of engagement that lead them to problem solving, and actively practice the measures they've created. They become more familiar with fundamental elements of argumentation, become more willing to challenge each other and develop argument skills, and see a greater value to classroom discussion, thus rendering classroom discussion more meaningful.

The Claim Game

The first task of a teacher who wishes to embark on this meaningful path of student learning is to teach argument. Many resources exist for teachers to engage in this process but none, perhaps, more valuable than Joe Williams and Greg Colomb's "The Craft of Argument" (2004). One valuable tool to introduce argumentation is a procedure they call The Claim Game. In the game, students are briefly introduced to fundamental elements of argumentation such as claim, reason, evidence, warrant, and acknowledgment and response to opposing viewpoints. Teams of students are armed with colored cards, each corresponding to one of the elements of argumentation. Students engage in a conversation on virtually any topic, and as they speak they discard the card that represents the element of argumentation that coincides with the type of statement they make. If a student makes a claim, he or she throws down a claim card. If they offer evidence to support a claim, they throw down an evidence card. The process continues until one team has successfully discarded all of their cards.

Argument and Emotion

The Claim Game provides students with a basic knowledge of argument. Students then move on to activities that reinforce their understanding of argumentation and acclimate them to the idea that argumentative exchanges are fluid and organic. "Argument Is War," another activity Williams and Colomb created, stresses the need to distance students from the commonly held perception that argument is more a *negative* than a *logical* undertaking. In order to introduce this misperception and open up a discussion regarding its roots in our culture, I give students a series of open-ended prompts and ask them to characterize a situation of conflict:

1. The boxer resisted, but his opponent (describe a specific thing that the opponent does that helps him win) and eventually won the bout.

2. It was a grueling contest that saw Sally (describe a specific thing that Sally does in her attempt to win), but I finally won the race.

3. Last night at the dinner table, while discussing Elmhurst's curfew policy, my mom made some good points, but I convinced her to let me stay out late by (describe something you could do that would successfully convince your mom that you're right).

4. During the debate, Shuba resisted the points that Mark made but the way he (describe something Mark could do to win the debate) was too much for her.

5. Whenever I want to influence someone to believe something that I want them to believe, all I have to do is (describe your most reliable way of convincing people of something).

Students are not surprised to see that most of their colleagues suggest that the boxer "knocked out" his opponent in the first sentence, but do become more aware of the baggage associated with argument when they find that many of their colleagues have used similar pugilistic references to resolve the conflicts depicted in the later conflicts. Students are likely to suggest that "Mark crushed her ideas" when referring to the debate he had with Shuba, and are also likely to suggest that whenever they want someone to believe something all they have to do is "bribe them," "threaten them," or "bend them to my will." Through this activity students learn to recognize the latent tendency to view any conflict, even the most civil kind, as potentially disturbing or unpleasant.

Following this experience, and using a procedure designed by Williams and Colomb, students go on to brainstorm any thoughts, statements, or ideas that come to mind when they think of argument. Particularly, students brainstorm ideas related to winning an argument, building up evidence for an argument, or resisting an argument. A typical range of student responses to these prompts includes the following:

Winning an argument
- laying the smack down
- taking it to him or her
- killing the opponent
- stomping them into the ground

Building up evidence for an argument
- loading my pistol
- cocking my gun
- I'm armed and dangerous!
- I'm a donkey on the edge...

Resisting an argument
- running away
- turning the tables
- resisting the enemy
- surviving the onslaught

A brief review of the sentiments just expressed indicates the high drama and emotion that students associate with argument. This emotion and drama need to be corralled and built on by teachers who wish to engage their students in authentic discussion. Williams and Colomb suggest one way to assist students in making the transfer: ask students to view five to ten minutes of a popular talk show or news program and look for evidence of the items that appear in their brainstormed lists.

Television talk shows provide fertile ground for students wishing to examine the way they hear people talk about things that influence the way they see the world. Students who viewed the conservative columnist Anne Coulter on a political pundit program found that she "was acting very rude and interrupted the man in gray's sentences . . . and told the man in gray to 'stop your whining,' which also suggests that she was angry with him." Students who witnessed British Prime Minister Tony Blair defend himself against accusations brought forth by the opposing party during "Prime Minister Questions and Answers" on C-Span found that Blair "recognized the faults of the opponents in his argument" and accused them of "playing politics and not even thinking about the good of the people or the nature of the situation." Regardless of students' analysis, they come away with a greater understanding of how people assess the things they are told by people who are trying to convince them of something. This is the kind of critical analysis teachers should try to replicate in the classroom as often as possible.

Developing an Argument

These activities prepare students to engage in a number of discourse opportunities that will encourage them to develop a point and defend it in the face of reasonable opposition. The extent to which a teacher can foster these abilities is limited only to his or her own imagination. Modern-day headlines provide many opportunities to garner information that can be manipulated and altered to assist students in making connections between the literature they read and their own perceptions and beliefs about the world around them. Illinois English teacher Thomas McCann has developed a reputation of creating contextualized inquiry frames that assist students in engaging in argument. One such activity, "The Foster Child," which McCann wrote, places students in a variety of positions and asks them to determine which action would be the most fair (see Figure 4–1).

Students are encouraged to study the views of several persons involved, including Greg and Marjorie Goldsmith, the foster parents; Mr. and Mrs. Benedict, the maternal grandparents; Bill Ball, Carmen's father; and Melissa Crawford, the representative of the Department of Family Life and Welfare (DFLW) agency. The

FIGURE 4–1   *The Foster Child*

The Foster Child

The Situation

A few years ago in Chicago a woman who was addicted to crack cocaine gave birth to a baby girl. The mother's name is Hope Ball, and she named her daughter Carmen. Bill Ball, the father, abandoned Hope long before the child was born. The mother neglected and abused Carmen when the little girl was just an infant. Neighbors reported the mother to the police. When she was arrested for abuse, the police discovered a stock of stolen merchandise in her apartment. With the mother in jail, the baby became a ward of of the state; however, the baby was soon placed with foster parents.

Greg and Marjorie Goldsmith took Carmen in to their five-hundred-thousand-dollar house in an affluent and fashionable subdivision called Utopia Hollow in the suburb of Masonville. Greg and Marjorie are both college graduates. Greg works as a stockbroker for a prestigious investment firm in Chicago. He earns at least two-hundred-fifty-thousand dollars per year. His job is stressful, but he does not work extraordinarily long hours. Marjorie Goldsmith does not work outside their home. Most of her time is spent caring for her children—Patrick, Ginny, Beth, and Carmen, their foster child. At the time Carmen came to live with the Goldsmiths, Patrick was seven, Ginny five, and Beth three. Twice a week Marjorie works as a volunteer: two hours on Thursday nights at Mason Memorial Hospital and two hours on Monday nights answering calls and counseling for the Battered Women Hotline. Both Greg and Marjorie are active members of St. Blaise Episcopal Church in Masonville. Greg and Marjorie Goldsmith would like to adopt Carmen as one of their own children. They believe that they would be able to supply Carmen with all the material comforts she could desire. They could afford to send her to the best schools and provide her with enriching travel experiences. They are likely to be able to afford to provide Carmen with music lessons or ballet lessons or other kinds of valuable cultural experiences. They live in a very safe neighborhood in a community that has a reputation for having fine schools. Greg and Marjorie assert that although Carmen might be different in appearance from the other children, her classmates would be accepting and sympathetic toward her. They note that Carmen has already been accepted as a member of the family and believe that it would be traumatic for her to leave the only parents she has ever known. They believe that the rest of the Goldsmith family would also suffer emotionally from the loss of Carmen.

After Carmen lived with the Goldsmith family for two years, her maternal grandparents, Mr. and Mrs. Benedict, arrived in Chicago. They traveled from

Continues

Reflective Teaching, Reflective Learning edited by McCann, Johannessen, Kahn, Smagorinsky, and Smith (Heinemann: Portsmouth, NH); © 2005.

FIGURE 4–1   *The Foster Child* (continued)

Mission, Texas, for the burial of their daughter, the natural mother of Carmen. The grandparents had held out hope that their daughter Hope would leave jail, conquer her drug addiction, and regain custody of her own daughter, Carmen. The grandparents understood that the foster-home situation was temporary, so they never attempted to take Carmen into their own home. After Hope passed away in jail, however, Mr. and Mrs. Benedict attempted to gain custody of Carmen. Mr. and Mrs. Benedict believe that Carmen would have many advantages if she were allowed to live with them. They acknowledge that they are not rich—they farm for a living—but they are committed to providing for all of Carmen's basic needs. They believe that there is an advantage to having the child living with her blood relatives. They believe they are naturally inclined to show her love and affection. They also note that in Mission, which is in a rural area near the Mexican border, Carmen would grow up in a wholesome environment away from the crime, pollution, and other hazards of the city.

In the midst of the dilemma, Bill Ball, Carmen's father, returned to Chicago. Upon learning of his wife's fate and the situation surrounding Carmen, he immediately sought to claim custody of his daughter.

The Policy

The Department of Family Life and Welfare (DFLW) usually governs the placement of children in foster homes when they become wards of the state. It is the policy of the DFLW that children in foster care cannot be adopted by the foster parents. The policy exists so that children who are placed temporarily in foster homes will not be taken away from the natural parents. In addition, the DFLW wishes to maintain a network of families who are willing to take in foster children. If the families adopted children permanently, they would be less willing to accept additional foster children.

Reflective Teaching, Reflective Learning edited by McCann, Johannessen, Kahn, Smagorinsky, and Smith (Heinemann: Portsmouth, NH); © 2005.

purpose of their study is to develop a clearly stated and well-defended position about who should be awarded custody of Carmen Ball.

Students write a brief first-person narrative from the point of view of an assigned character and then take part in a large-group discussion in which they advocate the position of the character they represent. A typical conversation emerging from this activity takes on any number of twists and turns. The dialogue that follows was transcribed by a student in the class who was assigned to record the main ideas of the conversation as specifically as possible knowing that after the conversation, the class would be analyzing the dialogue.

Crawford: I think we should give the child to the father. That's the policy.

Bill: I agree. The mom was on crack. When I left I didn't know about the child. I would have stayed if I had known.

Marjorie: Yeah, but you just left. You should have called or something.

Bill: I've also got a new job. I'm a construction worker now. Why send the kid to some fake family? I'm better.

Marjorie: Look at all that she'll have with us...

Greg (to Bill): You're only one person. You can't handle the responsibility.

Bill: The grandparents can't be good parents. Look how the daughter turned out.

Mrs. Benedict: What happened to her isn't our fault. She fell into bad company.

Bill: You're too old, anyway. Besides, your daughter probably got her habit from you.

Mrs. Benedict: Our daughter had a full ride to college and was doing well. Then she met Bill. He can't take the child. What is he going to do with the child while he's working?

Bill: I have plans to send her to day care.

Mr. Benedict: If you put her in day care there will be no bonding.

Greg: We have lots of money! The child will have more opportunity with us. Money is everything! Besides, we've had the child for two years. She knows us. You should bypass the policy and let us keep her.

Bill: Everybody... just read the policy. How can a farmer raise a child? What are you going to do, carry the baby on your back when you're out in the fields?

Mr. Benedict: When we work on the farm we work in shifts.

Bill: You're old and you don't have that many years left. That wouldn't be good for the child either.

Crawford: You left the child once before, who's to say you won't leave the child again?

With the background of this type of discussion in place, students are in a better position to discuss and write about issues of fairness that they see in the texts they read in class. In addition to helping students develop knowledge prior to engaging with a text, the discussion affords the opportunity to evaluate what is said and why it is said. Armed with copies of the transcript, students collaboratively describe what each speaker was trying to accomplish with his or her words. Parts of the transcript are repeated below but are now shown with the students' attributions.

Crawford: I think we should give the child to the father. That's the policy.

The agent is making a claim.

Bill: I agree. The mom was on crack. When I left I didn't know about the child. I would have stayed if I had known.

The dad is trying to discredit the child's mother.

Marjorie: Yeah, but you just left. You should have called or something.

The Goldsmiths are trying to discredit the dad so he doesn't get the child back.

Bill: I've also got a new job. I'm a construction worker now. Why send the kid to some fake family? I'm better.

The dad is trying to make himself look better and more deserving.

Marjorie: Look at all that she'll have with us...

Mrs. Goldsmith is referring to evidence of her wealth.

Greg (to Bill): You're only one person. You can't handle the responsibility.

Mr. Goldsmith is presenting another opposing viewpoint.

Bill: The grandparents can't be good parents. Look how the daughter turned out.

The dad is using evidence to attack the other parties.

Mrs. Benedict: What happened to her isn't our fault. She fell into bad company.

The grandmother made up evidence to defend herself.

Bill: You're too old, anyway. Besides, your daughter probably got her habit from you.

The dad made up evidence to discredit the grandparents.

Mrs. Benedict: Our daughter had a full ride to college and was doing well. Then she met Bill. He can't take the child. What is he going to do with the child while he's working?

The grandmother has made up more evidence to call the dad into question and attack his position.

Encouraging students to think about and classify what they say provides them with a deeper understanding of the fundamental elements of argumentation and how those elements work together to create a persuasive effect.

This type of reflective analysis can be reapplied in future discussions. In another contextualized inquiry frame, students in my class participate in an activity I call The Truth Is Out There. Students play various characters in a scenario that involves a star high school quarterback who may or may not have colluded with coaches to alter the outcome of a football game.

First, we read the scenario (Figure 4–2). Then, students are assigned roles to play in a scene where the quarterback is questioned. Each character, or role, comes with relevant background information about that character, including their personal motivation, what they remember about the game in question, and what they think of the people involved (Figure 4–3). Students are given this information and time to familiarize themselves with their characters before the role-play activity begins.

The following is a brief excerpt from a transcript of a role-play that one of my classes did based on The Truth Is Out There:

Ian [playing Kai, the quarterback]: You guys are making a big to-do about it . . .

Jim [Dr. Jones]: You're a star quarterback but don't care about the record. I think you did something. This is really weird. You wouldn't want scouts to see you break the record, knowing that they're there . . . you didn't want a scholarship to get you there.

Ian [Kai]: With a big record like that, people will always suspect something. I don't want to have to put up with that.

Jim [Dr. Jones]: You don't want an astounding accomplishment?

James [Board Member 3]: Did you have a chance to make the playoffs?

Ian [Kai]: I don't know. (*James notes the two contrary facts*). Maybe the story looks worse but the newspaper is getting their facts wrong. I didn't throw the game. I threw a long pass to help us come back.

Ken [Reporter 1]: You want to play football in college . . . wouldn't the record help that?

FIGURE 4–2   *The Truth Is Out There*

The Truth Is Out There

The Situation

The game between the Cuyahoga Comanches (6–4, 4–1) and the Mount Leo High Warlocks (4–5, 3–4) marked the season's end. Playoff eligibility had already been decided for each team. Cuyahoga would be moving on to the playoffs while Mount Leo would be moving on home. Although the record for each squad had little significance, the record for Mount Leo senior Kai Bobkowski was very important.

Cuyahoga won their final home game in a 42–20 romp. The Comanche's coach, Antwyne Golliday, relied on a strong running game and stingy defense to take the lead by half-time and hold a comfortable margin for the second half. Cuyahoga went on to meet Deer Park (7–3) in the first round of the IHSA playoffs.

The loss to Cuyahoga and the losing record were disappointments to Mount Leo and their coach, Neal Taylor, but they could celebrate the milestone of senior quarterback, Kai Bobkowski. With Saturday's performance, Bobkowski broke the Central State Eight Conference career passing record, formerly held by Griff Jurgens of Chatham Glenwood. A 30-yard completion to teammate Jacque Robinson with time expiring left Bobkowski with 5,006 yards for his career.

The previous record, held by Jurgens, who now quarterbacks the University of Northern Iowa, was 4,998 yards. In breaking the record, Bobkowski became only the twelfth player in Illinois prep football history to exceed 5,000 career passing yards. Reflecting on the accomplishment after the game, Bobkowski noted that it "meant a lot to me...a lot."

This sentiment was supported by many of the collegiate scouts who were in attendance at the game. Burt Campis, a scout from Division I Indiana University, said, "Bobkowski obviously is a skilled player. A record like this one boosts his stature greatly."

At the time of the game, Bobkowski hoped to continue his football career at an Ivy League school. He had yet to sign a letter of intent with any school.

The Dilemma

Within a week of his final, record-breaking football game, Kai Bobkowski found himself at home at his bedroom desk writing a letter to the president of the Central State Eight athletic conference requesting that his passing record be erased. During the seven days after the record-setting game, Kai Bobkowski found himself questioning whether he would ever be given the chance to fulfill his

Continues

FIGURE 4–2 *The Truth Is Out There (continued)*

childhood dream of playing collegiate football and whether Mount Leo High School coach, Neal Taylor, the best coach Kai ever had, would ever coach another football game.

The Outcome

The record-breaking game drew not only local, but national, attention. Much of the controversy derived from coverage the game drew from local and national sports radio shows and newspapers. A number of prominent officials in the community served by Mount Leo High School have called for specific action. In an emergency meeting, the Mount Leo High school board is meeting to sort through the events, weigh all the evidence they uncover, and decide what should be done.

Reflective Teaching, Reflective Learning edited by McCann, Johannessen, Kahn, Smagorinsky, and Smith (Heinemann: Portsmouth, NH); © 2005.

Ian [Kai]: I want other considerations to take precedence...

Ken [Reporter 1]: But doesn't the record do that? Only twelve in Illinois have done that.

Jim [Dr. Jones]: Do you have any reason to suspect Coach Taylor? Was he ever away from your bench?

Ian [Kai]: I focused on the game, not the coach. I don't think so...he would focus on the game.

Jim [Dr. Jones]: Could you answer my question?

Ian [Kai]: No.

Jim [Dr. Jones]: You might be biased because you have a close relationship with this Coach Taylor. What kind of history have you had with this man? Don't you want to talk about it?

(Laughter)

Ian [Kai]: That's just wrong...

Jim [Dr. Jones]: Answer the question.

Ian [Kai]: He's been my coach for a long time.

Mike [Board Member 1]: Perspective is the key to viewpoints...most people here feel you're hiding something...You keep saying "somewhat," "maybe,"... direct answers might help you define your point. You are hiding something from us? steroids? Maybe something personal—you told the Central Eight that you wanted to "preserve the integrity of this great conference." What hurt the integrity? Did you take steroids?

Ian [Kai]: There were no steroids...forget about that...I wanted to keep the losing out of the spotlight.

Mike [Board Member 1]: Is that your answer to everything? You lost. Why does that matter?

FIGURE 4–3   *The Truth Is Out There*

The Truth Is Out There

The Characters

KAI

Here's what Kai knows...

Kai asked officials to erase his record-setting pass after learning that his coach made a deal with the opposing team to let him complete it.

Kai's Springfield Mount Leo High School team let Cuyahoga High School score a touchdown with a minute left in Saturday's game, which Cuyahoga won 42–20. In exchange, Cuyahoga made no effort to keep Bobkowski from completing a 37-yard pass that gave him a record.

Kai had an inkling of what was happening when Cuyahoga, which won 42–20, and ended Mount Leo's playoff hopes, scored so easily. Coaches were yelling for him to go back out on offense, "so I just went out there and did what I was told to do." Kai knew he was close to Jurgens' record, but he didn't know how close until the pass play he was told to run unfolded.

Kai recalls seeing Coach Taylor on the sidelines, yelling at teammate Jacque Robinson that this is how far he needed to go (on the field), so Kai knew that's what was going on.

Kai was too upset by the loss to think about the record until about six days later. Radio talk shows and phone lines had been lit up all week and newspaper editorial pages were weighing in on the incident daily. Kai heard the rumors and gossip all week and it got to him. Kids were saying things about him, like, he threw the game in order to get the record and improve his chances at a scholarship.

After the game, Kai's coach told him that both coaches acknowledged arranging the deal during a time out. The pass to teammate Jacque Robinson was set up between Mount Leo coach Neal Taylor and his rival, Antwyne Golliday of Cuyahoga. With less than thirty seconds to play, Taylor and Golliday agreed Cuyahoga would score again, kick the ball back to Mount Leo, and not contest Bobkowski's career-capping pass, which ended with Robinson running out of bounds.

The completion gave Kai 5,006 yards for his career, setting a record for the Central State Eight Conference and making him one of twelve Illinois high school quarterbacks to pass for more than 5,000 yards. But in a letter to the president of the conference, Kai asked that the pass be stricken from the record books.

In his letter, Kai said, "While I admittedly would like to have passed for the record, as I think most high school quarterbacks would, I am requesting that the Central State Eight does not include this pass in the record books."

Continues

Reflective Teaching, Reflective Learning edited by McCann, Johannessen, Kahn, Smagorinsky, and Smith (Heinemann: Portsmouth, NH); © 2005.

FIGURE 4–3 *The Truth Is Out There* (continued)

Bobkowski said the yardage he passed for in his career "required a lot of cooperation and hard work from my teammates. I do not wish to diminish the accomplishments that were made in the last three years."

Kai knows that if he does get a college scholarship, he owes it all to Coach Taylor. Kai's coach, Neal Taylor, has trained and supported Kai since Kai first started playing football. Kai credits Taylor, a former Division I college star quarterback, for teaching him everything he knows. Coach Taylor has been a second father to Kai, who is often found at Coach Taylor's house around dinner time, playing with Coach Taylor's three children, who are all under the age of eight.

Kai knows that if his coach is implicated in a scandal suggesting that he did something wrong, the coach will lose his job, his reputation, and his ability to provide for his family, something that could push Coach Taylor and his family into poverty.

Kai knows that he cannot allow this to happen. He will do whatever it takes to avoid the truth coming to light in a way that negatively impacts Coach Taylor, even if this means giving up the opportunity to play collegiate football. During the questioning, he will protect Coach Taylor, while also trying to protect his own interests as long as he can.

DR. JONES (HEAD OF THE SCHOOL BOARD)

Here's what Dr. Jones knows...

Dr. Jones knows that Kai Bobkowski asked officials to erase his record-setting pass. Dr. Jones believes that Kai did this after hearing that his coach made a deal with the opposing team to let him complete the record-setting pass, but Dr. Jones is not sure.

Dr. Jones, who was not at the game, has heard that the Mount Leo High School team let Cuyahoga High School score a touchdown with a minute left in Saturday's game, which Cuyahoga won 42–20. Dr. Jones believes that in exchange for that touchdown, Cuyahoga made no effort to keep Bobkowski from completing a thirty-seven-yard pass that gave him a record.

Dr. Jones does not know why Mount Leo let Cuyahoga score so easily. He would like to know more details about what happened during the game, and is relying on Kai Bobkowski to provide some details.

Dr. Jones would also like to know if Kai observed Coach Taylor acting suspicious in any way during the game.

Dr. Jones thinks that it's also possible that Kai knew he was close to Jurgens' record and, thinking that the game was lost, did something to secure the record for himself. This belief has been mentioned by a number of people on sports radio

Continues

Reflective Teaching, Reflective Learning edited by McCann, Johannessen, Kahn, Smagorinsky, and Smith (Heinemann: Portsmouth, NH); © 2005.

FIGURE 4–3 *The Truth Is Out There* (continued)

shows and in the local papers. Dr. Jones knows that several scouts from college football programs were at the game and thinks that it is plausible that Kai might have thrown the game to secure the passing record and improve his chances of getting a college scholarship.

Dr. Jones has heard a rumor that, after the game, Kai's coach acknowledged that both coaches arranged a deal during a time out. Dr. Jones believes that the pass to teammate Jacque Robinson was set up between Mount Leo coach Neal Taylor and his rival, Antwyne Golliday of Cuyahoga. Dr. Jones believes that Taylor and Golliday agreed Cuyahoga would score again, kick the ball back to Mount Leo, and not contest Bobkowski's career-capping pass, which ended with Robinson running out of bounds. Dr. Jones does not think it a coincidence that this strange completion, coming off of a conceded touchdown, gave Kai 5,006 yards for his career, setting a record for the Central State Eight Conference and making him one of twelve Illinois high school quarterbacks to pass for more than 5,000 yards.

Dr. Jones knows that Kai Bobkowski has written a letter to the president of the Central State Eight athletic conference. The president will not release the letter, but Dr. Jones has heard that in the letter to the president of the conference, Kai has asked that the pass be stricken from the record books. Dr. Jones wonders why Kai Bobkowski would do this.

In an email response from the president of the conference, Dr. Jones was told that he cannot have a copy of the letter, but the president provided this quote from Kai's letter: "While I admittedly would like to have passed for the record, as I think most high school quarterbacks would, I am requesting that the Central State Eight does not include this pass in the record books." The president of the conference also shared this quote from the letter: "The yardage I passed for in my career required a lot of cooperation and hard work from my teammates. I do not wish to diminish the accomplishments that were made in the last three years."

Dr. Jones is aware that Kai Bobkowski and Coach Taylor have a unique history. He knows that Kai owes a lot to Coach Taylor. Dr. Jones will ask Kai about this history and try to ascertain just how close Kai Bobkowski is with Coach Neal Taylor.

Dr. Jones believes that something wrong happened during the football game and that either Kai Bobkowski, or Coach Taylor, engaged in some questionable activity that cost the school a football game and a chance at the playoffs, and damaged the reputation of the high school he has worked so hard to support. Dr. Jones is a skilled corporate attorney by trade and is not known to let people off the hook very easily.

Continues

Reflective Teaching, Reflective Learning edited by McCann, Johannessen, Kahn, Smagorinsky, and Smith (Heinemann: Portsmouth, NH); © 2005.

FIGURE 4–3 *The Truth Is Out There* (continued)

BOARD MEMBER 1

You are a long-standing member of the board who supports Dr. Jones and thinks he is on to something. You find fault with everything Kai Bobkowski says and point out how his answers are continually evasive and vague. You were at the game and can specifically recall details about the play that incriminate Coach Taylor. You are suspicious about what Kai Bobkowski did at the game, as well.

BOARD MEMBER 2

You are a long-standing member of the board who believes that Kai Bobkowski, a young man with a lot on his mind, is doing the best he can given the circumstances. You find the continual badgering that he receives from Dr. Jones and other board members excessive and you stand up for Kai Bobkowski at every opportunity. You believe that Dr. Jones has a personal grudge against Coach Taylor and will do anything to remove him from his position.

PARENT OF A FOOTBALL PLAYER 1

Your son has had an outstanding year on the football team despite Coach Taylor's efforts to botch the season at every turn. You have specific details of questionable events that have occurred throughout the season to suggest that Coach Taylor is up to something. You support Dr. Jones' inquiry and think he is on to something. You find fault with everything Kai Bobkowski says and point out how his answers are continually evasive and vague. You were at the game and can specifically recall details about the play that incriminate Coach Taylor. You are suspicious about what Kai Bobkowski did at the game, as well.

PARENT OF A FOOTBALL PLAYER 2

Your son has had an outstanding year on the football team. Coach Taylor has been an inspiration to your son and the team and, although they did not make the playoffs, you believe they had a great season. You are at the meeting to support Kai Bobkowski, a young man with a lot on his mind, and you believe he is doing the best he can given the circumstances. You find the continual badgering that he receives from Dr. Jones, and other board members and parents, is excessive and you stand up for Kai Bobkowski at every opportunity. You believe that Dr. Jones has a personal grudge against Coach Taylor and will do anything to remove him from his position.

Continues

Reflective Teaching, Reflective Learning edited by McCann, Johannessen, Kahn, Smagorinsky, and Smith (Heinemann: Portsmouth, NH); © 2005.

FIGURE 4–3   *The Truth Is Out There* (continued)

REPORTER 1

You have worked for the *Springfield Clarion* for a long time and have covered Mount Leo football games for too many seasons to count. You can recall specific details of questionable events that have occurred throughout the season to suggest that Coach Taylor is up to something. You support Dr. Jones' inquiry and think he is on to something. You find fault with everything Kai Bobkowski says and point out how his answers are continually evasive and vague. You were at the game and can specifically recall details about the play that incriminate Coach Taylor. You are suspicious about what Kai Bobkowski did at the game, as well.

REPORTER 2

You have worked for the *Springfield Herald* for a long time and have covered Mount Leo football games for too many seasons to count. You have been continually amazed at the outstanding quality of football that arrived at Mount Leo when Coach Taylor took over and can recall specific details that support your belief. You believe that Coach Taylor has been an inspiration to the team and the community, and although they did not make the playoffs, you believe they had a great season. You are at the meeting to support Kai Bobkowski, a young man with a lot on his mind, and you believe he is doing the best he can given the circumstances. You find the continual badgering that he receives from Dr. Jones, and other board members and parents excessive, and you stand up for Kai Bobkowski at every opportunity. You believe that Dr. Jones has a personal grudge against Coach Taylor and will do anything to remove him from his position.

Reflective Teaching, Reflective Learning edited by McCann, Johannessen, Kahn, Smagorinsky, and Smith (Heinemann: Portsmouth, NH); © 2005.

Mitch [Board Member 2]: (*to Mike*) Do you have a bias?

Jim [Dr. Jones]: Could you explain why you told the Associated Press "I felt disrespectful the way I got it . . ." Wouldn't that mean you did something wrong?

Ian [Kai]: No. There's no way we were going to make points that way—the other team not playing.

Jim [Dr. Jones]: So how is that disrespectful? But what about "past and present football players"?

This excerpt from the conversation demonstrates the exchange and uptake that take place when students are authorized to inquire into a well-structured problem with a defined context. In addition to discussing what they thought should happen to the high school quarterback in question, students were asked at the conclusion of this conversation to reflect on what they noticed about the way people in the conversation sought to *discover* the truth and what they noticed about the way people in the conversation sought to *cloud* the truth. They reviewed the transcript line by line and speaker by speaker and classified specific parts of it according to their observations of what people said and how they behaved. This analysis allowed students to generate the following lists of characteristics:

People Who Attempted to Discern the Truth

questioned motives

established facts

established significance

attempted to establish a theory

diverted attention to get to real issues

established a state of mind

showed bias in their questions

clarified answers

questioned physical states of being

questioned morals

questioned legitimacy

questioned importance

repeated certain questions

demonstrated persistence

attempted to rattle people

asked leading questions

pointed out contradictions

reduced questions to obvious facts

People Who Attempted to Cloud the Truth

downplayed significance

avoided answering questions

attacked people, not ideas

made excuses

asked off-the-topic questions

gave indirect and vague answers

got defensive

> failed to answer either yes or no
>
> were evasive
>
> questioned the question
>
> questioned accusers' morals
>
> relied on stereotypes

Students were able to associate any one of these criteria with specific phrases from the transcript from which the statements were generated.

With these student-generated lists in place, students were in a better position to evaluate the behaviors and motivations of characters in the texts they later read in class. For example, later in the year, when evaluating the extent to which it is acceptable for the characters in Miller's play *The Crucible* to ascertain the truth from the citizens of Salem, students found the task easier because they were armed with the criteria they had developed. These criteria helped them write an analysis of the words and actions of Danforth, who does the bulk of the questioning, and John Proctor, who is on the receiving end of the inquiries. With background knowledge like this, students were prepared to create and defend their own opinions. One student reviewed the text and suggested that Danforth believes that Hale is "questioning his own authority and making Hale feel like he can't say anything else to Danforth. He is being very controlling which makes him seem to have authority and Hale feels defeated."

Many people associate writing instruction with the examination of model compositions, peer review of drafts, and conferences between teacher and writer. But writing instruction also entails the mindful development of procedural knowledge about argument and about decision making, much of which requires learners to engage in the processes that they will transfer to their writing. Simply put, if we want students to write reasonable arguments, they need practice in arguing reasonably. Discussion supports this effort. Students' examination and reflection about what they actually do and what they should do as they argue, awakens them to procedures that they can employ to their advantage in many situations, and teaches them to be more critical viewers, listeners, and readers as well.

References

HILLOCKS, G., JR. 1995. *Teaching Writing as Reflective Practice*. New York: Teachers College Press.

NYSTRAND, M., WITH A. GAMORAN, R. KACHUR, AND C. PRENDERGAST. 1997. *Opening Dialogue: Understanding the Dynamics of Language and Learning in the English Classroom*. New York: Teachers College Press.

TOULMIN, S., R. RIEKE, AND A. JANIK. 1984. *An Introduction to Reasoning*. New York: Macmillan.

WILLIAMS, J., AND G. COLOMB. 2004. The Craft of Argument. Unpublished manuscript, University of Chicago.

5

The Other Writing Process
Using Inquiry to Teach Writing

TIM PAPPAGEORGE
Maine South High School
Park Ridge, Illinois

Not long ago, as another year of classes began, I asked my tenth graders, "Do you ever look for the easiest and simplest way of finishing a writing assignment?" It was a seemingly innocent question: Who could help but agree? But then I rephrased it: "How many of you look for the quickest, easiest way of writing a paper because you don't want to spend a second more on it than you have to?" Lots of grins and laughter. As we talked, my students admitted that they viewed writing as a chore to complete rather than a journey of discovery. We may have taught our students to be too efficient in the writing process, to move through it without much real thought. They can brainstorm, draft, and publish with a stark kind of deftness. But to what point?

Influenced by Hillocks (1995) and Nystrand (1997), I have since attempted to prompt my students to talk and think in ways that support meaningful writing. Johannessen, Kahn, and Walter (1982) have shown how to construct specific prewriting activities that challenge students to create short, meaningful pieces of writing. The activities I find most useful (1) genuinely challenge students' ways of seeing important issues, (2) give them the opportunity to discuss what they are thinking, and (3) focus their attention on smoothness and continuity (the *flow* of writing). It is also absolutely essential that I respond to the resulting writing by making comments and asking questions in the margins.

These prewriting activities are not always linear—don't always follow a neat pattern. I see them as "jam sessions" rather than the studied practicing of scales; there will be time for precision and exactness later. Three activities of which I'm particularly fond are scenarios, replays, and dialogue games.

Scenarios

Hillocks (1995) models the art of crafting subtle scenarios (whether anecdotes or more extended case studies) as a way to visualize potential topics and tease out the key questions surrounding them. I gear my scenarios toward gray areas my students will find interesting; the resulting discussion helps them clarify their thoughts on the key questions.

For example, I developed a set of five "morality scenarios" (Figure 5–1 shows two of them) in conjunction with our reading of *Our America* (Jones and Newman 1997), a nonfiction memoir about urban issues. The book follows the lives of two boys who grow up in the Ida B. Wells housing projects on Chicago's South Side. Students also read additional interviews and journal articles about why violent crime happens in these environments. The attendant questions of nature versus nurture, choice versus environment, along with the consequences of moral decisions, inform their investigation of possible topics.

The rules for using scenarios are simple. I pass out the handout and ask students to follow along while I read the first one aloud. I then ask students to rate the morality of the character from 1 to 5, with 1 being most moral and 5 being least moral. They quickly do so, and we discuss their reasons. I have them read the remaining scenarios individually and rate the morality of the character featured in each. After five or ten minutes, I ask students to discuss their ratings in groups of three, explaining their reasons and identifying one scenario on which they all agree and another on which they differ. We then discuss each scenario as a class, drawing out the controversies.

The Joe Dittering and Roger Johnson scenarios in Figure 5–1 always trigger a difference of opinion. "Roger Johnson isn't a bad guy!!" one student will say.

FIGURE 5–1 *Everyman, Everywoman: Morality in Context*

Everyman, Everywoman: Morality in Context

Joe Dittering, a Chicago public accountant, recently finished a very busy time of year in his office—tax season. As usual, he bragged to his colleagues about how he was again able to squeeze a few more bucks away from Uncle Sam for his clients. When Marcus, a colleague, said, "Joe, you're not *really* breaking tax codes, are you?" Joe smirked, laughing under his breath slightly, saying, "Let's just say I used my creativity! Ya know what I mean?"

Roger Johnson lives in the Robert Taylor Homes, at 53rd and State Streets, on Chicago's South Side. His sixteenth birthday just around the corner, he has maintained a gang-free philosophy throughout his life. Until now. Repeated pressures and threats to his younger brother, Ishmael (age eight), have forced him to join the local gang, the Hornets. Later that year, Roger finds himself a part of some activities he never would have imagined. One evening, in the heat of an encounter with another gang, the Overlords, Roger fatally wounds another young man his age. Weeks later, Roger feels bad for what he did, but can do nothing to repay the family of the deceased, since he never knew his name.

"Look, he regrets what he has done, while Dittering doesn't!" Another retorts, "But Johnson killed someone!" Someone else says, "But isn't breaking the law, as Dittering seems to have done, just as bad?! I mean, wasn't Johnson forced into it?"

And so the debate rolls on, engaged and vivacious, as the students explore the issues. I encourage as much *uptake*—student-to-student dialogue—as possible, since student interaction and discussion is the goal of the exercise (Nystrand 1997). I record the salient ideas on the board, but the students offer up the reasoning. They then apply one or more of these ideas in a written paper on *Our America*.

I have used the same activity to help students see how to construct common rhetorical structures such as process analysis or cause and effect. For example, in connection with process analysis, I have students combine textual examples, original anecdotes, and research to explain how or why a certain phenomenon, such as racism or street gangs, exists.

In my experience, it has been key to give the actual assignment a day or two after first piquing their interest with the prewriting activity and getting them thinking in the mode of discourse the assignment demands. If I give them the assignment right away, students ironically stop thinking and start applying a sort of bogus writing process, a set of rote mental actions to get the assignment done as quickly as possible without thought.

I also avoid model writing until the third or fourth day of working with a given inquiry activity. I need to give the students time to understand and explore the activity before I ask them to apply this kind of thinking to a larger writing task. Only after students have struggled with the activity themselves are they ready to examine someone else's work. I also make sure to display a sample of my own writing; or, using an LCD projector, I write one on the spot, thinking aloud as I go, so, they can see how I'm solving the problem of the assignment. The initial goal is to get the students talking and writing shorter responses that mimic the larger papers they will soon be working on independently.

There is also a difference between inquiry-based, inductive activities such as scenario work and typical "brainstorming" sessions in which students identify topics based on their interests or experiences. Questions, such as *how do people become racist? why does poverty exist? how do we come to trust people? what happens when people lose their innocence too young?* flow naturally when brainstorming follows an inquiry-based prewriting activity. But in the absence of genuine inquiry, brainstorming sessions bear little fruit.

Replays

Replays are another way to encourage students to inquire into and think through their topics and thus improve the quality of their writing. Here's how they work. Without looking at any notes, a student retells, or *replays*, his topic from beginning to end in a timed, two-minute exchange with a partner (the partner can be another student or you; I always first quickly remind students that in active listening, the partner nods and otherwise nonverbally affirms the speaker). The listener writes down two questions for the speaker, and the speaker has a chance to respond. Then the roles are switched. A replay can be used at any stage of the writing process. If done early on, it helps the writer form and define her topic; later in the writing process, it helps her remain organized. As is obvious, the activity is also a lot of fun.

I used replays in connection with the process analysis assignment I introduced using the scenario technique. The prewriting scenarios produced high-quality, authentic topics: The questions really seemed to matter to the students and were posed with integrity. For example, one student, in connection with Elie Wiesel's *Night* (1960), wrote "Why Savagery Exists," connecting the events in the book to an incident receiving a lot of media coverage that year, in which a high school football game degenerated into hazing and brutality. The student described the event in living color ("Girls were brutally and savagely beaten, punched, slapped, kicked, and pushed around"), then made authentic connections to his life: "This reminds me of a time I was playing football with friends in eighth grade. About twelve friends of mine and I were playing football after school at Brickton park. Everybody was having fun until after getting tackled, two people got into a fight. These were my friends, just as some of the juniors and seniors from Glenbrook North probably were, but [we] got angry because we were playing a rough game of football." In making this connection, the student carefully illustrated his point about savagery— that violent spectacle often leads to violent action. To round out his analysis, the student created a literary connection to Wiesel's novel: "In Germany, German people gradually thought it was acceptable to mistreat Jews and blame them for economic problems, just as the high school seniors thought it was acceptable to mistreat the younger, smaller juniors."

Dialogue Games

Prior to an assignment to explain how to do something (clearly delineate or analyze a process), I gave each group of three students a note card bearing a "how-to" topic (*how to break up with someone, how to have the best summer ever, how to be happy, how to help a friend who's depressed*) and asked them to generate a list of five tips to help a peer facing that particular challenge. (Interestingly, this prewriting activity, and the assignment as a whole, challenged students to imagine an audience for their paper, thus making the piece more lively and specific.)

Each small group leaned in and discussed their options before recording their ideas on large sheets of white paper with bright-colored markers. After a few minutes, they shared their ideas with the class, prioritizing the most essential steps and identifying common mistakes to avoid.

Last year, when the process-analysis assignment landed near Valentine's Day, I created same-gender groups and posed questions about dating: *what is the ideal date? what mistakes should your date be sure to avoid?* After small groups of boys identified the ideal movie to see on a date, the girls offered their critique, and vice versa. After some witty and humorous back-and-forth, I asked students to compose a short process-analysis journal entry: *give someone advice on creating the perfect date or the perfect homecoming dance, and warn him or her about at least one pitfall as well.*

Providing Models: Student Essays, Professional Writing, and Teacher Think-Alouds

After these initial prewriting strategies have led students to begin to define their own topics, I model some of my own writing. Students can then ask why I've included a particular idea or example. This kind of dialogue enhances (and allows me to trouble-shoot) the writing process.

For example, for a process-analysis paper about racism, I presented the idea of identifying the qualities of a "diverse mind"—or how to maintain an open mind—ostensibly one that is freer from narrow-minded or racist thinking: (1) widely read and travelled; (2) open minded; (3) able to identify one's own stereotypes; (4) flexible when wrong; (5) courageous. In the essay I shared with them on the overhead projector, I cited both literary and personal experiences, as this is what I expect the students to do. One of the quotations I included came from *Our America*: "Don't think of us ghetto kids as different. You might not want to invite us to your parties, you might think we'll rob you blind when you got your back turned. But don't look at us like that" (Jones and Newman 1997, 83).

We also examine student work. Sometimes the examples are from previous years, and sometimes I take home a stack of paragraphs from my current students, examine them, respond with questions on content, and pull out a good example or two to discuss (with the student's permission) on the overhead. Over the years, I have found that there is no better way to increase the creativity of students than to celebrate it. As I read a given student paragraph to the class, pumping it up, struggling students get an idea from listening to the model, and the author of the paragraph benefits by hearing his or her work read aloud. Ideally, I orally publish something from every student's prewriting or a final draft at some point in the semester.

Examples from professional writers serve two excellent purposes but have one terrible drawback. Let's look at the good points first. Students generally like reading examples of published writing because they see the range of topics one can write about. Also, they often discover that writing can be fun and that approaching a familiar topic from a new vantage point makes for a good essay. For example, in class this year, I played an audio recording of a Tom Bodett essay (1996) while teaching my students the cause-and-effect rhetorical strategy. In this piece, the author notes the differences between men and women and makes the argument that men should be able to cry too. He furthers his argument by saying that men should view it as "just another bodily function" like "writing your name in the snow." While I worried that this gender humor might be too subtle, the students caught right on and had a great laugh. Another benefit of using a professional model is the innovative way that the professional essayist will use a rhetorical strategy. In this case, Bodett uses a cause-and-effect strategy informally; another example, the Stephen King essay "Why We Crave Horror Movies" (1983), uses the same strategy in a different way, with colorful examples that only a renowned horror writer could produce.

But there is one fly in the ointment: professionals create their own riffs on the melody. By taking the original strategy in question, whether it be classification, comparison/contrast, process analysis, analogy, or any other, and reconfiguring it, changing its scope, or taking whatever other liberty, the professional writer stays loose and swings with the interest of the reader while still benefiting from the rhetorical strategy in question. When students try to model themselves after the *organization* of these essays, however, they often get confused. Thus, I recommend using professional writing examples either at the beginning of the activity or at the very end; if used at the beginning, the goal is for students to see the range of possible ideas; at the end, students are able to see a creative instance of the strategy in use. In between, I usually have my students read primarily student examples, typically at a level they stand a good chance of being able to replicate with some help. The goal is to challenge the students' thinking, to push them to the top of their zone of proximal development (Vygotsky 1962).

Using Visual Organizers

Nearly every teacher of whom I have been a colleague has introduced his or her students to visual organizers. Visual organizers help students organize their thoughts, and many computer programs, such as Inspiration,[1] provide them. The question then becomes, how do we encourage our visually stimulated students to use graphic organizers to fuel and shape their method of inquiry rather than end it?

Too often, when we make a writing assignment, we display the pat, five-paragraph, three-point organizer (Johnson et al. 2003) on the board and encourage students to fill in each box, mentally and physically, with examples or observations that fit. The graphic organizer becomes *prescriptive* rather than *descriptive*—that is, the organizer tells students what to write rather than helps them describe and outline their own thoughts about the topic. We encourage this constrained rhetoric because many students are still primarily concrete in their thinking; they need to be able to write like this for standardized tests, and they have been taught this way throughout grade school (Hillocks 2002).

The Hump

This may seem like a digression, but it may be the most important point I make. In any inquiry-driven approach to writing, good writing takes effort—and not only on the part of the students. We teachers must exercise the kind of perseverance a good coach demonstrates after a losing streak. If we are truly challenging students to think, they are likely to bump up against the frustration created by the new demand. Students need to feel the challenge of something totally new, but we must see to it that they are not overwhelmed by it.

---

1 Snapse. 2004. *Inspiration.* Computer Program from Snapse, Inc. San Rafael, CA.

The writing process, as we often practice it, is so prescribed that students proceed on automatic pilot. In contrast, this same process can be used in connection with inquiry strategies and a genuine challenge to write something worth saying, something that matters to a defined/imagined audience, something that inherently requires students to hold up the familiar to the light of their own observations and synthesis of thought.

But the hump is real, and facing it requires courage and tact. I tell my students that the assignment requires some front-loading on their part, and they usually respond to the challenge. They plead for a model (*what do you want my paper to look like? how many paragraphs? how many pages?*), and I promise them they'll get one—but only after they have had a chance to engage in the topic in an authentic way in the process of exploring the rhetorical strategy that is the centerpiece of the assignment. I usually handle it like this: "Are you in a hurry? Do you have someplace you have to be right now?" That elicits wry grins and a level of trust: They realize that we'll all get there together and on time. For the classes that need it, I sketch out the calendar of writing events so that they can see how this new, somewhat chaotic process will help them land safely and complete the assignment successfully.

Back to Visual Organizers

So how can visual organizers help students over the hump, help them fuel their own inquiry approach to the topic? I have my students think of the topic first, then do a replay or a scenario or conversation, and only later fill in the visual organizer.

Here's an example. My tenth graders were working on a comparison/contrast paper in conjunction with Salinger's *Catcher in the Rye* (1945). The assignment was to intuit the connection among dissimilar items or issues or discern the subtle differences among similar items or issues.

I designed a worksheet (Figure 5–2) to help the students think about and discuss the comparison/contrast strategies before we moved on to using the visual organizer. The topics on this worksheet were culled from interest inventories (Hillocks, McCabe, and Campbell 1971)—informal surveys of students' interests in music, hobbies, school activities, and so forth—that the students had filled out earlier in the year. Fly-fishing versus line fishing is on the list because there were five students who very much enjoyed fishing and loved to talk about it; in a different year, this prompt would probably fall flat. However, a discussion of a good burrito is probably appropriate every year. As students decided which strategy, comparison or contrast, would work better with their larger point or thesis, they discussed the topics as well.

Their discussion of Taco Burrito King (a local small chain) versus Taco Bell provided some engaging traction. At first, some thought it worthwhile to compare the two. "In what ways are they similar?" I asked. The students mentioned that both were Mexican restaurants, both sold burritos, and both served the food quickly.

Then another group brought out the contrasts. "At TBK, they have the King," which I took to be an enormous burrito. "Yeah," another student said, "and all the staff are actually Mexican and speak Spanish among themselves and to some

FIGURE 5–2 *Comparison/Contrast Discussion*

Comparison/Contrast Discussion

This exercise will give you a dry run at thinking through a topic to see if it is better to work with similarities or with differences and also to check whether there is a thesis lurking anywhere.

Directions: Pick three of the topics listed below and state whether it would be better to find similarities or differences. Then, think about your audience and purpose for writing (who needs this information?) and come up with a thesis or insight based on this analysis. Use the questions to help move you toward forming an interesting thesis.

Taco Burrito King Versus Taco Bell

- The similarities are obvious, but what are the differences?
- When should you go to one or the other?
- Where's the "so what"?—what kind of thesis could you generate from this?

Fly-Fishing Versus Line Fishing

- Why would you do one or the other?
- Is one of them preferred?

Adam Sandler Versus Jim Carrey

- Should you go with differences, since the similarities are easier to point out?
- What thesis can you draw from this?

Listening to Versus Playing Music

- What does a person gain from playing music over simply listening to it?

Smack the Penguin Versus Pong (Video Games)

- Are the similarities the way to go here? Why?
- Why do dumb, basic video games remain popular?

Reflective Teaching, Reflective Learning edited by McCann, Johannessen, Kahn, Smagorinsky, and Smith Heinemann: Portsmouth, NH); © 2005.

customers. And it's always great for people-watching! You never know *who* is going to come in there!" Then this, from someone else: "But don't go in there too late at night, there's *always* thugs in there." Laughter. The discussion continued down seemingly unimportant paths: how the burritos tasted at each, how the places were decorated, and so on.

When they'd finished, at least a dozen good points were on the chalkboard, each supplied by a different student. "Okay, now," I baited them, "what is a good point you could make about these two restaurants? They're not that different, right? Both are just burrito joints, right?"

One student had the answer: "TBK is more of a mom-and-pop place. It's more authentic, while Taco Bell is a national chain and it's more uniform."

I summarized, "So, you think TBK is a more authentic Mexican American food experience?"

What could we all do but say yes?

Interestingly, the discussion was also completely authentic, as I had no idea we would end up with this thesis, although I had the general suspicion that a contrast strategy would fit the topic better.

The next step was to work visually with other possible topics, not yet zeroing in on *The Catcher in the Rye*. (My students were beginning to wonder whether—hope?—I'd forgotten that part.) We moved, as a class, into the writing lab so that we could use Inspiration, a computer program that provides templates of graphic organizers but also allows students to create their own from scratch. The assignment for the day was to use the Inspiration comparison/contrast template to create a graphic organizer related to a new topic of interest. The same thing can be done by hand; it's just that the computer program adds novelty and interest. Also, Inspiration allows the user to create extra bubbles, so the number of subpoints implied by the graphic organizer is flexible—a key factor in making it *descriptive* rather than *prescriptive*. Possible subpoints unfold one by one.

That night, as I examined the graphic organizers my students had created (in this instance, maps of a variety of possible topics), I could see their original thoughts very clearly. I was impressed with the kind of inquiry already in evidence, so I made overhead transparencies of some of their maps to discuss in class the following day. One contrasted *Saturday Night Live* with another comedy show, *MAD TV*, and included some interesting observations about what's funny, what's not, and the specific characteristics of the two shows. With the visual organizer as a basis for our thinking, we discussed several specific examples and ended up with a great thesis: *MAD TV* is geared toward a younger, often junior high school-age audience, while *Saturday Night Live* is geared toward an older audience (the news segment being one manifestation).

The final papers on *The Catcher in the Rye* were also outstanding—interesting and clearly products of independent thought. One student, for example, likened Holden Caufield to Dr. Phil, both being prone to overindulging their advice-giving personalities. Another wrote about how his view of religion differed from Holden's.

Observing and Writing—The Remix

Much has already been written about the benefits of combining observing and writing—of playing observational writing games (Hillocks 1975, 1986, 1995) that help students write more engaging and realistic narratives. In my experience, students generally enjoy the novelty of these activities and find them stimulating, and the results are powerful.

Not as much has been said about using observing and writing activities to develop nonfiction essays, particularly in connection with the common strategies of extended definition, analogy, comparison/contrast, process analysis, cause-and-effect, and so forth. The long view must be taken, here, to see the full benefit.

Typically, we teachers bring out these fun activities—describing shells, *National Geographic* photos, audiotaped sounds—as a discrete miniunit during a larger unit on narrative writing. Then, later in the year, we flip to the left side of the brain and teach literary analysis or some other more academic, highly structured essay. It's easy to fall into the prescriptive trap (it's a siren's call), and the writing is often barely worth reading. I'll go so far as to say that we often don't read these types of essays as much as check them off against the rubric: good, bad, and ugly.

However, it's possible to teach structured writing so that the process is fun, if taxing (remember the hump), and the final product is authentic and filled with original observations. We can guide students to be so observant of the world around them that they *must* create new meaning when they combine these observations with what they are learning in their courses. At the very least, the new thought is a synthesis; at most, it ventures into new areas of inquiry, discovery, and definition.

Here's an example.

Each year I challenge my students to write an extended-definition paper that includes examples from the texts we have studied as well as personal anecdotes of things they have seen or experienced firsthand. Midway and again late in the writing process, I introduce observing and writing activities. One is something I call "fists of fire," an exercise in which students clench their fists tightly for about a minute, slowly release them, and write a descriptive paragraph about the sensations they experienced. The mechanical nature of our body's tendons makes the fingers open like a rusty hinge, and students find the exercise engaging. And they are quick to point out that the same effect is achieved by applying pressure to the door jamb, squatting on the floor, "cherry picking" in midair, and other similarly masochistic activities. I typically have them follow through on at least one of these suggestions but require a descriptive paragraph afterward, reminding them that sensory description is the key to good writing—even analytical, expository writing.

As students complete rough drafts and individual paragraphs of the paper, I remind them to include this type of description.

Our exploration of various elements of inquiry-based writing yields strong final papers about interesting topics and typically include strong descriptive anecdotes. One year a student, in defining the nature of responsibility, described a scene from the film *Home Alone*: "When his family is gone, he manages to get groceries from the store, put up the Christmas tree, clean up the house, and have some fun, too." This student also made some nice connections to two short stories we had read earlier in the year.

Another student defined *home*, drawing examples from *Tuesdays with Morrie* and *Our America*. He connected these texts to the story of a family member who had badly injured his leg, nicely capturing the emotional nature of home: "He was stranded. All of a sudden, he felt this energy fill his body; he got up and started to walk. He didn't know where he was walking, but there was something leading him in that certain direction. When he reached the end of the woods, he found his father and mother waiting for him on the path he was walking toward." The line "he felt this energy fill his body" seems to have been the direct result of the "bodily response" observation games we had played.

Again, I need to point out that this type of writing is not developed in average tenth graders overnight, in one gimmicky activity. We need to commit ourselves to training our students in the art of deliberate and careful observation as part of a year-long writing curriculum, even if it is a "hidden" one. Each writing assignment, if at all possible, should create space for these engaging and productive activities. My students and I come back to descriptive writing on most major papers throughout the year, reinforcing the skill and sharpening our descriptive eyesight on each assignment.

Publication: The Final Appreciation

Research tells us that students write better when they have a clearer sense of audience. This can be achieved in many ways. A simple but compelling method I find helpful is something I call "dialogue boxes," a strategy I introduce at the close of several writing assignments throughout the year. As with scenarios and graphic organizers, the goal here is to move away from traits-oriented, positivistic peer response toward one of shared inquiry.

Very simply, I create a handout with text boxes like those in Figure 5–3. To frame the assignment, I arrange students in groups of four, each bringing with them a finished, polished final draft of the assignment. Conversations about what to include, how to edit grammar, which quotations to use, how and where to use description and topic sentences, and so on, take place over at least a day or two. The goal is to provide each writer with constructive feedback.

Each person gets a set of three dialogue-box handouts. As students read each essay other than their own, they respond thoughtfully to the content—not the form!—of the paper, and finally, write a question for the author *about the content of the paper*. I explain that the papers and dialogue boxes will be bundled together and handed in as a unit. If their responses are done well and thoughtfully, they'll get a next-higher-grade bonus on their papers; if done poorly, they'll get a next-lower-grade deduction; if their responses are average, their grade won't change. In other words, if they execute a thoughtful and considerate response to the readers in their group—students with whom they have been working with throughout the assignment—their B+ paper will end up an A–. If they do the minimum or don't try at all, the grade will remain a B or drop to a B–.

FIGURE 5–3 *Comparison/Contrast Discussion*

Comparison/Contrast Discussion

Comments from group member _____:

What did I learn?

What question do I still have?

Reflective Teaching, Reflective Learning edited by McCann, Johannessen, Kahn, Smagorinsky, and Smith Heinemann: Portsmouth, NH); © 2005.

Most students do an excellent job of appreciating the writer's viewpoint and then challenging him or her to consider it even further. Relative to the extended-definition-paper assignment I discussed earlier, one student wrote, "I learned evil is relative to those who perceive it to be so. [The student] illustrates that well, that evil in people is unrelenting, like the Nazis persecuting the Jews in *Night*. But who decides what actions are evil and what are pure evil, really?" The student who wrote about responsibility received some thoughtful feedback, as well: "From reading this paper, I learned a lot about responsibility and how important it is. You made some nice connections from outside reading and movies you saw. But what I'd like to know is if you had any experience where responsibility was important to you?" Another student finished her reflection on this same paper this way: "Do you feel that you handle your responsibilities maturely?"

Getting students to question one another is another hump to get over. They aren't used to it and need some encouragement. To help them, I circulate from group to group and ask a proficient student to read his or her sample question so that group members have an impromptu model from which to draw.

Conclusion

Briefly put, each writing assignment is an opportunity to challenge students to see their lives differently, to hold a magnifying glass—or at least a sporty monocle—up to an issue they find challenging or interesting. We can better facilitate authentic inquiry if we let students explore and talk about each stage of the writing process.

References

ALBOM, MITCH. 1997. *Tuesdays with Morrie*. New York: Doubleday.

BODETT, TOM. 1999. "Why We Cry." In audiotape *First Words* by Spaulding Gray, et al. San Bruno, CA: Audio Literature. Excerpted from *First words* by gang of seven. ISBN 1-882543-01-7.

HILLOCKS, G., JR. 1971. *Observing and Writing*. Urbana, IL: ERIC Clearinghouse of Reading and Communication Skills/NCTE.

———. 1986. *Research on Written Composition: New Directions for Teaching*. Urbana, IL: National Conference on Research in English/ERIC Clearinghouse on Reading and Communication Skills.

———. 1995. *Teaching Writing as Reflective Practice*. New York: Teachers College Press.

———. 2002. *The Testing Trap: How State Writing Assessment Control Learning*. New York: Teachers College Press.

HILLOCKS, GEORGE, B. J. MCCABE, AND J. F. MCCAMPBELL. 1971. *The Dynamics of English Instruction, Grades 7–12*. New York: Random House.

JOHANNESSEN, L. R., E. A. KAHN, AND C. C. WALTER. 1982. *Designing and Sequencing Prewriting Activities*. Urbana, IL: ERIC Clearinghouse on Reading and Communication Skills/NCTE.

JOHNSON, T. S., P. SMAGORINSKY, L. THOMPSON, AND P. G. FRY. 2003. "Learning to Teach the Five-Paragraph Theme." *Research in the Teaching of English* 38 (2): 136–76.

JONES, L., AND L. NEWMAN. 1997. *Our America: Life and Death on the South Side of Chicago*. New York: Washington Square Press.

KING, S. 1983. "Why We Crave Horror Movies." In *Models for Writers,* edited by A. Rosa and P. Eschholz (2003). New York: St. Martin's Press.

NYSTRAND, M., WITH A. GAMORAN, R. KACHUR, AND C. PRENDERGAST. 1997. *Opening Dialogue: Understanding the Dynamics of Language and Learning in the English Classroom*. New York: Teachers College Press.

SALINGER, J. D. 1945. *The Catcher in the Rye*. Boston: Little, Brown.

VYGOTSKY, L. S. 1962. *Thought and Language*. Cambridge, MA: MIT Press.

WIESEL, ELIE. 1960. *Night*. New York: Bantam.

PART

3

DISCUSSION AND ACTIVITY

6

The Role of Play and Small-Group Work in Activity-Based Instruction

DAVID A. RAGSDALE
Clarke Central High School
Athens, Georgia

PETER SMAGORINSKY
University of Georgia
Athens, Georgia

George Hillocks, Jr. has outlined a theory of instruction that stresses the active role of learners in developing their reading, writing, and language abilities. Hillocks (e.g., 1995; Hillocks, McCabe, and McCampbell 1971) emphasizes the *task* as the center of students' literacy instruction. This task might be writing extended definitions, writing arguments, reading ironic literature, reading a particular author's works, or engaging in some other performance that involves a distinct set of social practices, procedures, and forms.

To help students become more adept at these tasks, Hillocks' approach engages learners in a sequence of activities through which they gradually move from guided practice to individual performance. This approach has been described by some as "instructional scaffolding" (e.g., Bruner 1983). The teacher releases control of the process by having students work with increasing independence. Central to this process is a stage during which students collaborate in small groups on task-related work. Here they either develop or practice strategies that enable them to perform the given task on their own. This small-group stage provides students the opportunity to perform the task and its requirements in a setting that encourages experimentation and provides feedback from peers who are learning the same procedures and strategies. In most cases students ultimately go on to demonstrate their individual learning in a final assessment. Teachers who use instructional scaffolds of this sort assume that through the teacher's guidance and students' practice in small groups, students will learn the procedures they have practiced and experimented with during the small-group sessions and can now apply them in new situations.

This small-group phase is the subject of our inquiry in this chapter. Hillocks and his students have described the small-group phase in many publications (e.g., Hillocks 1975, 1995; Johannessen 1992; Johannessen, Kahn, and Walter 1982; Kahn, Walter, and Johannessen 1984; Lee 1993; Smagorinsky 1991, 2002; Smagorinsky and Gevinson 1989; Smagorinsky, McCann, and Kern 1987; Smith 1984, 1991). The beneficial effects of small-group work described in these publications have been expressed primarily in cognitive terms: that is, the task-based procedures that students learn during this phase of an instructional sequence and their ability to apply them in new learning tasks. In this chapter we focus on the benefits of the playful or experimental thinking and discussion that potentially take place in this sort of task-focused, small-group work. We describe how a set of activities designed for the high school classes of English teacher David Ragsdale included opportunities for playful exploration of a task's demands that contributed to students' development in two areas. One area is students' affective engagement with school learning, for which we rely on the work of Mihalyi Csikszentmihalyi and Reed Larson (1984) that investigates what they call *optimal experience*. The other area is the critical role of play or experimentation in learning, for which we draw on Lev Vygotsky's (1987) work in human development. We next outline each of these perspectives as they relate to a Hillocksian approach to the teaching of English, then describe events from David Ragsdale's class to illustrate how these factors contribute to multiple learning opportunities—for students and teachers—related to David's instruction.

Theoretical Framework

Affective Engagement with School Learning

In Being Adolescent: Conflict and Growth in the Teenage Years, Csikszentmihalyi and Larson (1984) map the affective terrain of the adolescent. Educators will surely find the results of their study discouraging: School is among the least emotionally satisfying settings in which teenagers spend their lives. Schools, the authors find, "are essentially machines for providing negative feedback" (198). More specifically, "The classroom provides largely negative feedback. It is opposite from the situation with friends where a wide range of novel, random, and crazy actions may be reinforced. . . . [T]he average student pays little attention to the goals of the classroom, and does so without enthusiasm or pleasure" (207). The typical student in the typical classroom, they find, is attentive to the teacher's instruction only about 40 percent of the time. Many a fine lecture, well-researched and thoughtfully prepared, has thus made little impression on the minds it is intended to enlighten.

Csikszentmihalyi and Larson are concerned that schools are so oblivious to teenagers' affective states that teachers teach in ways that students find neither useful nor stimulating. Students therefore rarely get into the *flow* of academic experiences. A flow experience is one in which people become so involved in what they're doing that they lose all track of time. A flow experience is potentially available through school learning, though was rarely found among the youngsters in Csikszentmihalyi and Larson's study. Rather, students found flow experiences during sports, arts, and other activities that they undertook voluntarily. On these occasions their levels of skill and the challenges provided by the activity produced a fine tension that resulted in complete engrossment.

The typical structure of the school day contributes to the low affect experienced by students. "[F]eeling happy and feeling active go together for teenagers," argue Csikszentmihalyi and Larson (1984, 97). Yet activity is by far the exception in school, especially in core academic classes such as English, where teachers are prone to monopolize discussions (Marshall, Smagorinsky, and Smith 1995). Csikszentmihalyi and Larson (1984) report that

> Classic academic subjects such as...English showed the lowest levels of intrinsic motivation, coupled with low affect and activation.... [C]lasses that provide more concrete goals and require more than intellectual skills, such as industrial arts, physical education, and particularly music, were associated with more favorable motivation and with positive affect. These classes involve students in some form of physical and sensory participatory activity, whereas math, English, and languages are entirely cognitive. (206)

The idea that English classes are "entirely cognitive" describes the instructional norm. One of Hillocks' contributions, and a staple of much teaching in the progressive tradition, is his emphasis on student activity, particularly in collaborative settings. This focus violates the norm identified by Csikszentmihalyi and Larson (1984) in at least two ways. First, they argue that "It is when they are working toward a goal in a structured activity that [teenagers] feel best." (99). The type of small-group work advocated by Hillocks, with its clear structure and concrete goals, meets this criterion well. Second, "intrinsic motivation is relatively high in informal activities like group work and discussions. This is also when students are most happy and active. Passive activities like listening to the teacher or to other students are much less pleasant" (206–207). The sort of group work advocated by Hillocks provides just this sort of informal, goal-directed, structured activity.

Csikszentmihalyi and Larson take pains to demonstrate that such activity is distinct from social situations in which teenagers simply hang out together. They find that *"it is in productive rather than leisure activities that concentration is highest"* (104; emphasis in original). Key to the activity, then, is that it is oriented toward the goal of producing something: an interpretation, a text, and so on. Potentially, a Hillocksian small-group activity has

- an overall structure that provides clear goals, a framework that contributes to high levels of affect among students;
- opportunities for informal work that contributes to students' levels of activity, motivation, and happiness;
- a need to produce something, a *goal* that elevates students' levels of concentration.

The final dimension we wish to extract from Csikszentmihalyi and Larson is strongly related to the discussion we take up next, Vygotsky's notion of the importance of play in learning. Csikszentmihalyi and Larson find that students described enjoyable occasions with friends "in terms of 'being rowdy,' being loud, crazy, and wild" (1984, 167). They continue:

> In some circumstances, yielding control may have a positive long-term effect. Dipboye... for instance, has argued that the deindivuation of collective excitement can renew one's sense of commitment to the social whole. In fact, numerous cultures provide structured occasions of group liminality—like the carnival, which was originally a religious orgy—precisely to serve this purpose.... The difference is that American adolescents enter this state without the assistance of cultural structures. Ritualized rowdiness has clear limits and specified outcomes. (171)

This "ritualized rowdiness" can be harnessed in the classroom in ways that do more than make students feel good. The deliberate creation of liminal structures—such as carnivalesque small groups whose tasks have clear goals and products—can also contribute to students' construction of socially acceptable boundaries. And, as we described, it can serve students' cognitive growth through the provision of opportunities for playful experimentation with ideas that extend students' potential for learning.

The Role of Play in Learning

Vygotsky (1987) argues that through focused play or experimentation, learners can extend their learning potential. In this view a person does not have a fixed intelligence but instead has a potential for learning that can be extended under the right conditions. A person has a *zone of proximal development*—that is, an individual learner's bounded "zone of...intellectual potential" (209) that is always being adjusted upward as one gains new knowledge and skills. The goal of a teacher, adult, or more capable peer should be to help learners do more—although not infinitely more—and solve more difficult tasks than they can independently.

In this sense a teacher's influence can be dramatic. Rather than simply presiding over students' biological development, teachers can accelerate development by providing appropriate guidance and support. Among the key factors in a learner's negotiation of this ZPD is the opportunity to play or experiment with ideas, an activity that can help push learning thresholds and create new juxtapositions of ideas. Play, then, can not only contribute to the affective dimensions of learning described by Csikszentmihalyi and Larson, but it also can promote cognitive growth by allowing students to push and extend their cognitive boundaries.

The zone of proximal development can also be viewed more broadly as the social context in which such learning takes place. We believe that a playful ethos should permeate a learning environment so as to enable learners (including teachers) to experiment, make mistakes, try new ideas, and push the boundaries of their previous understanding. Doing so stretches learners' (and teachers-as-learners') thresholds for learning to generate the possibility for something fundamentally new. Creating such an instructional context also opens the whole class to the possibilities afforded by new ways of thinking. These new ideas can include a teacher's experimentation with instructional ideas that in turn create playful opportunities for students to become more accomplished learners.

The Role of Play in Activity-Based Teaching and Learning

We would like to revisit a key facet of Hillocks' approach, using Csikszentmihalyi and Larson and Vygotsky to illuminate how goal-directed, task-oriented small groups contribute to students' learning. For Hillocks, the small group often serves as an initial or intermediate stage in students' learning. In small groups students work inductively toward the development of strategies, or practice strategies first introduced by teachers, all as part of a learning process in which they ultimately perform on related tasks independently.

Hillocks has primarily described small-group work in terms of its cognitive benefits, particularly in terms of the strategies students learn for thinking about how to solve task-related problems. We would like to expand on that discussion. First, we see Csikszentmihalyi and Larson's views on affective engagement as relevant: Such small-group projects are among the most emotionally satisfying settings for students in school and, when oriented toward a clear product, contribute greatly to students' concentration on academic tasks. Given that these two factors are generally absent in students' experiences in school, small-group activities may potentially play a unique role in instructional planning. Second, we see both Csikszentmihalyi and Larson and Vygotsky emphasizing the importance of play—the rowdy, experimental transactions through which learners extend the boundaries of their own learning. Such opportunities are available in the liminal settings provided by small groups.

We next provide illustrations from the high school English class of David Ragsdale to show how the creation of a playful environment promotes the learning of students and teacher. David's account is a first-person narrative of a teaching experiment he conducted in his junior English class. David had taken several master's-level courses with Peter Smagorinsky at the University of Georgia and had been particularly impressed with activities designed by Hillocks and his students for teaching students task-related strategies for writing. David, who had experienced frustration in teaching writing in his first years in the profession, felt that these activities offered hope for engaging his students in schoolwork and improving their writing.

In terms of his classroom ethos, then, he took an experimental approach to his teaching. The activities themselves involved small-group, task-oriented procedures that had the potential to engage students in the sort of ritualized rowdiness prized by Csikszentmihalyi and Larson. Finally, David's account illustrates a reflective practitioner at work, making changes in his teaching and reflecting on them through the production of a written text. This act of formal reflection represents an additional experiment on David's part, one that cast him as a learner who, like his students, both developed and represented his thinking about what he'd learned through his instruction.

David's Teaching Narrative

Nestled in the heart of a university community, Clarke Central High School is the home of my research. Initially established in 1951 as a replacement for the original Athens High School, the present campus was home to the segregated White area secondary school. Although a few African Americans were allowed to enroll, the school stayed "Whites only" until 1971, at which point it was renamed Clarke Central High School. Presently, the school's ethnic demographics reflect the broad diversity not only of the community but also of the state of Georgia as well. Current demographics show enrollments of 60 percent African American, 25 percent European American, 15 percent Latino. The school's minority populations have been growing steadily, while the school's European American student body has dwindled considerably during the last ten years.

Class Context

This unit has been tailored for one section of eleventh-grade Advanced College Preparatory American Literature/Composition (ACP). While the course nomenclature indicates that this class is advanced in nature, it is actually the median-level course offered in the English department, with American Literature/Composition Advanced College Preparatory/Gifted (ACP/GF) being the honors equivalent and American Literature/Composition College Preparatory (CP) as the lowest of the offered levels. Despite the "advanced" nature of the class, several of the students read below grade level, have limited access to books, and demonstrate low achievement on the traditional writing assessments imposed on them.

Unlike the upper-level gifted classes (which have proclivities toward being almost exclusively White and upper-middle-class) and the lower-level CP class (which typically enrolls lower-income Black students), the ACP track has an interesting split. In my four years in the county, at each of the two high schools (one as a student teacher), ACP classes are nearly always 50 percent White and 50 percent Black. These students often come from extreme ends of the socioeconomic spectrum. Students who drive brand new BMWs and SUVs are enrolled with students who rely on public transportation as their sole means of travel. An outsider might think that this distinction in affluence and outlook would cause problems in class, but the ACP-level students typically engage in the most frank discussions of race and politics of any students in the building, regardless of academic track.

I originally piloted my study during the fall semester with twenty-six students, then refined my research during the spring term with a new class of twenty-three students. Thirteen of these students are male and ten are female. Across racial lines, the class is predominantly White, with eight Black students, two Latino students, one Asian student, and eleven White students. The students are generally very genial with each other and in most cases have known each other since middle school or earlier.

Instructional Challenge

My goals are not just to cover set material in the curriculum but to engage students in learning that they will find challenging yet enjoyable. I've often found that veteran teachers in the school tend to overcompensate for the loss of yearlong instruction due to block scheduling by loading up students with numerous projects, reports, and exams without considering student interest or motivation. I'm not saying that the curriculum should be explicitly tailored for student enjoyment, but rather it should be attentive to their learning styles with activities that foster discussion, learning, reading, and writing while studying and appreciating American literature.

Instruction

The school district produces a yearly high school program of study. In this year's curriculum American Literature/Composition is described as covering "a variety of literary genres and multicultural writers in a chronological or thematic pattern." With this framework in mind, I set out to design a pair of units that would fall under the theme, "How do we define the American Dream?" The first text we used was the Arthur Miller play *The Crucible*. The second unit centered around Reginald Rose's *Twelve Angry Men*. During the initial pilot in the fall, I taught both units. However, for this research I've focused my study on my students' response to *Twelve Angry Men*.

While I wanted the students to appreciate the literary merit of each work and how they related to our overarching question about the American Dream, I also wanted them to be able to engage in activities surrounding the plays that would provide them with goal-oriented collaborative work. The unit on *The Crucible* culminated in a comparison/contrast essay in which students explored the differences and similarities between the 1995 film version and the play we read as a class. The *Twelve Angry Men* unit's summative assessment was a group parody of the drama.

To introduce *Twelve Angry Men*, I had students form groups of three and gave them a survey to engage their interest in the subject matter at hand, particularly the failures of the judicial system to guarantee an unbiased trial of one's own peers (Figure 6–1). Discussion was heated as students rebelled against the notion of a bunch of strangers judging them for a wrongdoing. Soon after, we began reading the play and students assumed the roles of the twelve angry jurors, with me playing one as well. I provided students with a graphic organizer to help them access and record the knowledge they gained during the reading (Figure 6–2). Students listed the characters and described their backgrounds and appearance. They also recorded both their first and final impressions of each of the twelve jurors. This organizer of character traits would prove invaluable when the students moved on to the final assessment of the unit. Additionally, given that the play is so short, we watched both the 1960 and 1997 film versions to reinforce our ideas about the jurors. Once again, students used their graphic organizers to note their impressions of the twelve jurors and how their ideas about the jurors from the play compared to those in the film.

FIGURE 6–1 *Survey*

Part I. Survey

Directions: Please check the answer that best suits you in response to the following questions.

Do you believe in the American Dream?   Yes____   No____

How do you define the American Dream? _____

_____

_____

Have you ever watched an arrest made on TV, in the movies, or in real life?

             Yes____   No____

Have you ever been arrested?

             Yes____   No____

Is it possible that the police can arrest the wrong suspect?

             Yes____   No____

What rights do you have upon arrest? Check all that apply.

   Court-appointed attorney___   Right to remain silent___Right to a trial___

   Right to be judged by a jury of your peers___Right to question authority___

Which of these rights do you value most and why? _____

_____

_____

Is it possible that a jury may be biased?

             Yes____   No____

If so, what factors could bias a jury against or for a defendant? Check all that apply.

   Ethnicity of defendant___ Economic background___   Juror's own background___

   Ethnicity of juror___   Prior criminal background___   Personal beliefs___

Which of these factors could most affect a juror and why? _____

_____

_____

_____

Are jurors ever wrong in their verdict? Yes____ No____

What happens when all the jurors can't come to a consensus? _____

_____

_____

_____

FIGURE 6–2 *Twelve Angry Men Study*

Twelve Angry Men Study

CHARACTER CHART

CHARACTER NAME	APPEARANCE/ AGE	CHARACTER'S HISTORY	YOUR FIRST IMPRESSION	WHAT DO YOU THINK NOW?

Reflective Teaching, Reflective Learning edited by McCann, Johannessen, Kahn, Smagorinsky, and Smith (Heinemann: Portsmouth, NH); © 2005.

As we worked on the play, I wanted to introduce the students to a different form of writing than they had previously done for me during the semester. By this time, students had done freewrites, journal entries on assigned topics, expository writing, and so on. Now I introduced parody writing to the class. I passed out a handout detailing the tenets of a parody, based on Smagorinsky (1991) (Figure 6–3). We discussed our interpretations of this genre of writing in small groups. Because I have my students at tables, as opposed to traditional desks in rows, students worked with their self-selected peers at their respective tables. Students reviewed the handout and began work on their assignment. Their volume was louder than usual, but they seemed to move into discussion of the parody very quickly.

Their first assignment was to analyze commercials for everyday products. For example, why is it that all pickup-truck commercials show a burly guy riding over rough terrain or hauling a prodigious load of freight when most trucks seldom go off-road? Conversely, students looked at why all beer commercials have gorgeous female models in them when many beer drinkers are perceived as being corpulent, pot-bellied men. As a group, they decided on a product they wanted to make fun of and began work on a skit.

Students were given class time during three days to produce their three-to-five-minute skit, and I visited with each of the groups to touch base. One idea that stood out was doing a parody of the hair growth product Rogaine. As opposed to promoting hair growth, the group decided to create "Nogaine," a hair removal system for hippies. Their premise was that with one dose of Nogaine a "tree-hugging hippy is instantly transformed into a Wall Street businessman." Another group decided on a parody of Gatorade. Rather than replenishing an athlete's energy, their product, "Pimpade" replenished a "player's game" thus enabling him to talk to and pick up ladies. Yet another idea was a play on the Mastercard advertising campaign, "Shirt, $25. Jeans, $70. Movie tickets, $15. First date, Priceless. For everything else, there's Mastercard." My students' take on the idea was a man catching his fiancée cheating on him and his sweet revenge as "Priceless."

My closest involvement came with one group of students who wanted to parody a serious newscast. This particular group was among the least diverse, with four members, three of whom were male and one female. Because the group all had differing schedules, (it included two baseball players and a student with a full-time job), accommodating group time outside class had become extremely difficult. The students had agreed to meet before school the day before the production was to be screened in front of the class, but two of the four students couldn't make it. During class group time, the kids opted to meet after school that day to film and to finalize their script. I offered my classroom and agreed to videotape their performance.

After school, the males were all present, but due to job obligations, the young woman was unable to attend. As I watched the guys rehearse and hash out their ideas, they asked me to help with the script. I watched as the students, all of whom were C+/B– performers at that point in the semester, engaged in rich discussions of what would be funny and how to film the scene. Without my prompting, they again analyzed the set routines of news anchors and brainstormed ways of twisting that dialogue into a funny and compelling scene. They also discussed the sequence

FIGURE 6–3 *Parody*

Parody

A parody is a literary form in which a writer makes fun of a particular author or type of writing by exaggerating its features. You may be familiar with other types of artists who use parody for humorous effects. In the film, *This Is Spinal Tap!*, a group of comedians performs an extended parody of a rock-and-roll band, while the film's director does a parody of documentary films.

The musician Weird Al Yankovic has grown successful by doing parodies of popular songs. The television show *Mad TV* usually includes parodies of commercials or famous people for a humorous effect. The following procedures will help you produce effective parodies.

Part I: Presenting a Parody
Prewriting: Small Group

1. Advertisements for particular types of products tend to follow a formula. For instance, pickup-truck ads tend to feature tough-looking men driving along rough terrain as their vehicles absorb every bump and bounce while zooming onward. The music tends to be loud and aggressive, and often the vehicle is described as being far better than a particular competitor's.

   In a group of three to five students, do one of the following:

   (A) Think of a product that many different companies advertise according to the same general formula (such as the formula for pickup-truck ads). What do the ads for all of these companies have in common? Or
   (B) Think of a particular product for which all the ads tend to follow the product's own formula, such as the promotions for certain beverages. Identify the characteristics that the ads in the series have in common. Some areas to look for include the following:

   - A particular sequence of events
   - Types of characters (including animals)
   - Type of music
   - Setting
   - Type of image conveyed (sensitive, humorous, tough, etc.)
   - Benefits or advantages of product

2. After you have characterized the ad, work with your small group to prepare a parody of the type of ad you have studied. In order to prepare an effective parody, you should take a characteristic and exaggerate it so that it is funny. For instance, the tough-looking man in the pickup-truck ad might rip off a car fender and scratch his back with it before getting in his pickup, the truck might fall to the bottom of the Grand Canyon and keep going, and so on. Take several characteristics of the ad you have chosen and brainstorm ways in which to exaggerate them for a humorous effect.

3. Produce a parody for the class based on your work in steps 1 and 2. You may either perform the parody live before the class or videotape it.

Reflective Teaching, Reflective Learning edited by McCann, Johannessen, Kahn, Smagorinsky, and Smith (Heinemann: Portsmouth, NH); © 2005.

in which all newscasts are broadcast. Additionally, they assessed the way in which newscasters looked and talked. In doing so they were conducting the sort of genre analysis outlined in the parody assignment. I offered some suggestions on how to do on-the-scene reporting and was tapped to play a correspondent for Clarke Central News Network (CCNN).

At the end of the discussion, they decided to start the skit with the two anchormen, thinking they were off camera, swapping jokes and then proceed to a live broadcast of the news. After a short broadcast, the anchors would exchange heated words and one anchorman would leave the studio in anger. At this point, a belligerent cameraman would attack him. In embarrassment, the remaining anchor would cut directly to the on-the-scene reporter, who would broadcast the capture of Bigfoot and then interview a bystander.

The boys rearranged the room to resemble a studio as best they could, and I offered my blazer and tie to the anchors. We rehearsed the scene and went over our tentative scripts, which were written on the spot with each group member offering feedback and ideas until we were ready to film. All the while, the mood was light and humorous and at times rowdy. Yet, the boys were goal oriented and directed toward producing a quality product. I watched, with great interest, as the guys reviewed their idea against their assignment handout, which outlined their task, and were satisfied they were producing a parody.

The filming went very well after some rough starts, including the angry anchorman being pelted in the head with a rubber ball by the belligerent cameraman and falling into a storage locker, unrehearsed and downright scary because the student was dizzy for about five minutes. During my bit as CCNN correspondent Rick Sanders, we incorporated a school resource officer to help apprehend the runaway Bigfoot. I then interviewed the officer and still-dazed anchorman, now a typical high school student, on his thoughts about the capture. After filming, we reviewed the tape and were amazed at how well the product lived up to expectations and just how funny it really was.

Since they had three class days to produce their three-to-five-minute skit, some groups opted to tape-record their parodies at home or on campus, which seemed to be vastly more successful, and some groups performed their parodies live. After viewing the skits, many of which the class found incredibly funny, we began to analyze what we'd seen. Because the groups were self-selected, some of the groups of friends ended up doing more socializing than skit producing, and it reflected in their performance. Group members ranked each other on the following categories: accomplishment of task, individual enthusiasm, commitment to product, contributions, attendance, and intangibles. Despite being in a group of friends, the students evaluated each other fairly and recorded their shortcomings frankly and honestly. Groups also assessed the performance of their peers, evaluating the humor of the skit, how well it related to the product it was a parody of, and overall production values.

As we concluded our study of the play and film versions of *Twelve Angry Men*, groups went over their list of characters, impressions, and the differences between the film and play. At this point I had students stay in their parody groups, as they had almost universally gelled. Our task now was for each student to produce a parody of the very serious and dark play. I provided the students with a handout (based on Smagorinsky 1991) that built on the prior work they'd completed as a group (Figure 6–4).

Because the second task mirrored the first, the groups set to work relatively quickly, evaluating what could be made funny about the play. I circulated among the groups, spending about ten minutes with each, to help brainstorm and to facilitate discussion. While in groups, the students often read and reread the play to each other, finding key dramatic scenes in which they felt they could inject humor. Ideas that came up were twelve irate dogs, with each character represented by a distinct breed of dog portraying the individual's personality; that is, angry juror number 3 was a rottweiler and the stable and thoughtful number 8 was a sheepdog. Other ideas were twelve angry cheerleaders, as well as twelve "sassy" kindergartners.

It was enjoyable to see the banter among the students in deciding what was funny and what wasn't. At various points, students got a bit wild but were able to censor each other and to keep their ideas focused. Again, I gave students class time during the course of a week to work on their drafts and to offer peer counseling. Likewise, I continued to monitor and facilitate discussion and peer interaction. The students shared their rough draft of the parody during a peer read-around and editing session.

The peer read-around was very interesting to witness. While not every student had a rough draft to hand in, all the students seemed universally interested in the work of their peers. The reading session and subsequent conference elicited a great deal of laughter; however, not all the students were comfortable with the feedback they'd received from their peers and sought my advice. I conferred with a number of them and attempted to allay their misgivings. Because I wanted them to feel ownership of the parodies, I tried to keep my ideas to a minimum and tease out what problems and insecurities the students had about their own work.

Two days after the editing session, the students completed their final drafts and handed them in to me for assessment. Likewise, they brought a copy for their peers to reread. At this time I combined groups, with the six small groups merged into three larger groups to represent the "twelve angry people" that the students would portray in the next step of our assignment. Each student in the new larger groups read the work of his or her groupmates, and they then voted on which was the funniest parody to produce for the class, either live or via video.

Although the new groupings produced interesting dynamics—students with seemingly nothing in common in groups of seven or eight, with a tangible goal in front of them and a test grade awaiting their scripts and performances—they got to work. Additionally, since some groups had little prior knowledge of each other, my role as a facilitator was more important, because I had to spend time trying to tease out students' ideas and keep them talking with each other.

Since we ran long during the performances of the skits, many of the students weren't able to perform during class time. Rather than leaving at the sound of the bell, almost to a single student, they all asked to be allowed to see the final performances and to carry out their own. While it wasn't fun signing twenty late passes, I was overwhelmed by the group's enthusiasm and by the humorous skits based on a terribly grave play.

FIGURE 6–4 *Part II: Writing a Parody*

Part II: Writing a Parody

Prewriting: Small Group

1. Next you will produce a written parody. In a small group of three to five students, review the play we've just covered, *Twelve Angry Men*. Look in particular for common features, including the following:

   - Point of view
   - Sentence structure
   - Diction
   - Types of details
   - Phrasing and figures of speech/dialect
   - Attitudes
   - Style

2. Work with your small group to identify aspects of the writer's characteristics that you can exaggerate for a parody, and brainstorm for ways in which to exaggerate them.

3. With your group, think of humorous topics for your parody. As you know, Rose's play is steeped in conflict and tension. You might rewrite the play in the style of children on a playground. Or you could retell one of the conflicts in the style of *The National Enquirer*. The possibilities for incongruous matchups such as these are endless.

Producing a Draft

Write a parody based on the ideas you generated with the help of your small group.

Revision: Small Group

After you have written a draft of your parody, get back in your small group to share your writing. Respond to the parodies of your group members, pointing out passages that you feel are strong and suggesting ways to improve the writing, particularly with regard to the writer's exaggeration of the author's or narrator's particular characteristics. Make comments in the margins of the draft wherever you feel they would be helpful, and write a summary evaluation at the end of each draft you read. Feel free to discuss the parody with the writer and other members of the group.

Revision: Individual

Using the comments of your group members, produce a new draft of your parody. This will be handed in to me for assessment.

Presentation: Group

You will also provide a copy of your final draft for your group members to read. As with our last parody, you and your group will act out a rendition of your parody for the class.

Reflective Teaching, Reflective Learning edited by McCann, Johannessen, Kahn, Smagorinsky, and Smith (Heinemann: Portsmouth, NH); © 2005.

Reflection

In reflecting on the two units, I noted that the students had engaged with a pair of traditional texts, written more than forty years ago, in unorthodox units. Rather than just taking a multiple-choice Scantron test as many had been accustomed to doing, they actually had to create their own meaning for the texts. Through discussion in both large and small groups, students identified themes, conflicts, character motivation, and other traditional academic considerations in ways that had been unfamiliar to them—that is, in collaborative small groups. Rather than trying to stifle their group talk, I encouraged them to find meaning in the playful banter and jokes they made during discussion.

I also learned that I don't always have to be teacher-centered to make sure kids achieve my goals for the unit. While I observed their conversations and discussions, they raised points that I hadn't anticipated and that shed light on obscure aspects of the texts. It is incredibly hard for kids to stay focused on any task for ninety minutes. Likewise, lecture-driven instruction is effective at best for about fifteen minutes. But when given the leeway to find meaning through playful experimentation with serious texts, the students pushed the boundaries of what they thought they knew and how they thought they could learn the information. As one student told me during the parodies, "We do some crazy stuff in this class." Crazy? I don't know about that, but we certainly got some rich dialogue and products as a result of the ritualized rowdiness of their small-group activities.

References

BRUNER, J. 1983. *Child's Talk: Learning to Use Language.* New York: Norton.

CSIKSZENTMIHALYI, M., AND R. LARSON. 1984. *Being Adolescent: Conflict and Growth in the Teenage Years.* New York: Basic Books.

HILLOCKS, G., JR. 1975. *Observing and Writing.* Urbana, IL: National Council of Teachers of English.

———. 1995. *Teaching Writing as Reflective Practice.* New York: Teachers College Press.

HILLOCKS, G., B. J. MCCABE, AND J. F. MCCAMPBELL. 1971. *The Dynamics of English Instruction, Grades 7–12.* New York: Random House.

JOHANNESSEN, L. R. 1992. *Illumination Rounds: Teaching the Literature of the Vietnam War.* Urbana, IL: National Council of Teachers of English.

JOHANNESSEN, L. R., E. KAHN, AND C. C. WALTER. 1982. *Designing and Sequencing Prewriting Activities.* Urbana, IL: National Council of Teachers of English.

KAHN, E., L. R. JOHANNESSEN, AND C. C. WALTER. 1984. *Writing About Literature.* Urbana, IL: National Council of Teachers of English.

LEE, C. D. 1993. *Signifying as a Scaffold for Literary Interpretation: The Pedagogical Implications of an African American Discourse Genre.* NCTE Research Report No. 26. Urbana, IL: National Council of Teachers of English.

MARSHALL, J. D., P. SMAGORINSKY, AND M. W. SMITH. 1995. *The Language of Interpretation: Patterns of Discourse in Discussions of Literature.* NCTE Research Report No. 27. Urbana, IL: National Council of Teachers of English.

SMAGORINSKY, P. 1991. *Expressions: Multiple Intelligences in the English Class.* Urbana, IL: National Council of Teachers of English.

———. 2002. *Teaching English Through Principled Practice.* Upper Saddle River, NJ: Merrill/Prentice Hall.

SMAGORINSKY, P., AND S. GEVINSON. 1989. *Fostering the Reader's Response: Rethinking the Literature Curriculum, Grades 7–12.* Palo Alto, CA: Dale Seymour.

SMAGORINSKY, P., T. MCCANN, AND S. KERN. 1987. *Explorations: Introductory Activities for Literature and Composition, Grades 7–12.* Urbana, IL: National Council of Teachers of English.

SMITH, M. W. 1984. *Reducing Writing Apprehension.* Urbana, IL: National Council of Teachers of English.

———. 1991. *Understanding Unreliable Narrators.* Urbana, IL: National Council of Teachers of English.

VYGOTSKY, L. S. 1987. "Thinking and Speech." In *Collected Works*, volume 1, edited by R. Rieber and A. Carton, translated by N. Minick, 39–285. New York: Plenum.

7 Engaging Students in Authentic Discussions of Literature

LARRY R. JOHANNESSEN
Northern Illinois University
De Kalb, Illinois

ELIZABETH KAHN
James B. Conant High School
Hoffman Estates, Illinois

In the mid-1970s, as students in George Hillocks' MAT program in English, we learned the meaning of *authentic discussion*. At that time, Hillocks didn't use the term *authentic discussion*; he simply called it discussion. He saw discussion as a key component of an effective English language arts classroom—not as an end in itself but as essential to having students learn to engage in inquiry, to interpret literature, to develop effective arguments, to become empowered as learners, and to gain a better understanding of themselves and others. Hillocks not only taught the English methods courses, but also supervised our clinical and student teaching experiences. He was very clear about the characteristics of a good discussion. First, if the discussion lasts for more than ten minutes or so, then most of the students (say, 80 percent or more) should respond at least once. For an extended discussion (half an hour or more), virtually all the students should respond at least once. Second, the direction of the discussion should not be repeatedly teacher to student, teacher to student, and so on. Rather, sometimes—or better still, often—it should involve student-to-student conversations in which students respond to each other's comments without the prompting or intrusion of the teacher. Third, the proportion of *teacher talk* in relation to *student talk* should be below about a third (33 percent) of the total talk.

When Hillocks observed our classroom discussions, he employed a variety of methods to gather information for us to use in analyzing the interaction. He made seating charts showing the number of responses given by each student in the class; he drew interaction diagrams with lines showing the flow and the direction of the conversations. But his favorite method was the Flanders Interaction Analysis (Flanders 1965, 1970).

Flanders developed a system of ten categories to describe the verbal behavior of both teacher and students in a classroom (Figure 7–1). The first seven have to do with teacher talk (e.g., praise or encouragement, questions, lecture, giving directions, criticism). Categories 8 and 9 refer to student response, and 10 indicates silence. Every three seconds, the classroom observer indicates, by recording the number of one of the categories, what type of verbal behavior took place during the preceding three seconds. Consequently, after gathering such information for a class period or a portion of a class period, the observer would have several pages with columns of number sequences.

FIGURE 7–1 *Summary of Categories for the Flanders' Interaction Analysis System*

Summary of Categories for the Flanders' Interaction Analysis System

INDIRECT TEACHER TALK	1. *Accepts feelings.* Acknowledgement of student-expressed emotions (feelings) in a nonthreatening manner.
	2. *Praises or encourages.* Positive reinforcement of student contributions.
	3. *Accepts or uses ideas of student.* Clarification of, development of, or reference to student contributions. Often non-evaluative.
	4. *Asks questions.* Solicitation of information or opinion (not rhetorical).
DIRECT TEACHER TALK	5. *Lectures.* Presentation of information, opinion, or orientation; can include rhetorical questions.
	6. *Gives directions.* Direction or suggestion with which a student is expected to comply.
	7. *Criticizes or justifies authority.* Negative evaluation of student contributions or emphasis on teacher's authoritative position.
STUDENT TALK	8. *Student talk—response.* Response to teacher's question. Usually results in a predictable answer.
	9. *Student talk—initiation.* Talk initiated by students; includes introduction of new topics and unmediated responses to classmates.
	10. *Silence or confusion.* Periods of silence or inaudible verbalization lasting more than three seconds.

Source: Adapted from N. A. Flanders. 1970. *Analyzing Teaching Behavior.* Berkeley, CA: Addison-Wesley, p. 33.

Reflective Teaching, Reflective Learning edited by McCann, Johannessen, Kahn, Smagorinsky, and Smith (Heinemann: Portsmouth, NH); © 2005.

When Hillocks observed our teaching, he frequently used "the Flanders." In addition, he taught us the method and had us use it as well when we observed each other teaching. (As a result of the design of the MAT program, we were able to observe each other during our student teaching.) Hillocks frequently cautioned us that during a class period teachers often talk far more than they are aware. This was made dramatically and brutally clear to us when we examined Flanders analyses of our own discussions as we began teaching our secondary classes. Usually there were too many 4's (teacher-initiated questions) and 5's (teacher lecturing) and too few 9's (responses initiated by students). Too often there were long strings of one 5 after another, with only an occasional peppering of 8's (talk by students in response to teacher) and a few 9's (talk initiated by students). We found that when we were running a "discussion" in our classes, we almost always talked more than we thought that we had. We felt a great sense of accomplishment when we or our fellow MAT students were able to conduct a whole-class discussion that exhibited a large proportion of 9's (talk initiated by students) with few 5's (teacher lecturing). In these cases, we spent a great deal of time analyzing the various elements of the instruction in order to identify factors that we could replicate the next time we planned to have a class discussion.

Our repeated use of the Flanders taught us some important lessons. We learned to be more objective observers and evaluators of our own classroom discussions when no one else was present observing us. We learned how difficult it is to avoid the dreaded "5" when conducting a discussion, and how difficult it is to achieve a preponderance of long strings of 9's in a discussion. And, as a result, we strove over many years—and still to this day—to discover and to develop strategies that would enable us to have good discussions on a consistent basis with all levels of students we teach.

Recent research has demonstrated a strong connection between discussion-based approaches—those in which students frequently engage in authentic discussion—and student achievement in English language arts (Applebee, Langer, Nystrand, and Gamoran 2003; Langer 2001; Nystrand 1997). When these researchers talk about authentic discussion, they are talking about the same kind of discussion that Hillocks defined. They distinguish authentic discussion from recitation, the IRE pattern (teacher *initiates* a question which has a predetermined answer, student provides a *response*, and teacher *evaluates* the adequacy of the response).

Unfortunately, studies of classrooms reveal that students are seldom engaged in authentic discussion. Christoph and Nystrand (2001) and Nystrand (1997) report that, in the classrooms they observed, authentic discussion occurred on average for only fifty seconds per class in eighth grade and fifteen seconds per class in ninth-grade classes. In one sense these discoveries attest to the difficulty involved in generating and sustaining authentic discussion about important academic topics. But they are especially distressing when one considers the significant impact that meaningful discussion has on learning.

One question we have pondered is, why is authentic discussion hard to generate and sustain in the classroom? If these patterns are as pervasive as research suggests, secondary students may have come to expect the teacher to do most of the significant talking in the classroom. They may have experienced the IRE pattern so frequently that it is firmly engrained. Marshall, Smagorinsky, and Smith (1995) see the traditional pattern of classroom conversation as what Bakhtin (1986) refers to as a "speech genre" that becomes "'privileged,' or widely and perhaps dogmatically accepted as the 'right' way of communicating in particular settings" (7). Therefore, students may believe that classroom conversation is supposed to follow this pattern, with the teacher asking questions to test them on their knowledge, students giving brief answers, and then the teacher commenting—often at length—on the accuracy and sufficiency of their answers. When a teacher throws out an open-ended question with the hope of creating authentic discussion, students may not understand the expectations—they may see it instead as a question to test their knowledge.

Add to this the problem of students who can't think of a response on the spot, who can't remember what they read (or didn't read) the night before, or who don't have enough information available to generate a response. Add to this students' concerns about what kind of impression they may make on their peers or the teacher if they speak up in class. Finally, participating in a discussion—especially within a large group of twenty-five to thirty people—takes a certain amount of effort and energy on the part of the students as well as the teacher. At times there just doesn't seem to be any momentum.

On the other hand, authentic discussion sometimes occurs somewhat serendipitously. For example, Christoph and Nystrand (2001) describe one class in which IRE recitation tended to dominate. Then, in a discussion of *A Midsummer Night's Dream*, the teacher asked students who they thought was the most important person in the play. Immediately, four students offered markedly different responses, leading to a debate in which more than half of the class contributed vocally and in which those who did not participate vocally were unusually attentive and engaged. As the teacher encouraged students to present and defend their different viewpoints, the exchange between students turned into an instance of authentic discussion. Although this discussion was only 2:41 minutes long, Christoph and Nystrand (2001) report that it had a disproportionately large effect on students for the rest of the semester. For weeks after the discussion, several students continued to mention it to each other in passing between classes. Clearly, engaging in authentic discussion had a strong and lasting impact on the students and their understanding of the play.

But what can we as teachers do if we are not content to wait for the serendipitous? We have found and developed some strategies for generating authentic discussion that can overcome the impediments just suggested so that we aren't simply waiting and hoping that by chance a discussion may take place sometime. We began working with these strategies in Hillocks' MAT program and have continued to refine, update, and add to them over the years. Of course, they aren't foolproof. We both have encountered situations in which one of our tried-and-true activities just seemed to fizzle with a particular group of students or in a certain setting. But this has generally been the exception rather than the rule.

Next, we will discuss six strategies for encouraging and sustaining authentic discussion: (1) approaching the classroom as a forum for collaborative inquiry; (2) showing students the differences among types of questions; (3) using the uptake technique; (4) asking broader, more open-ended questions that focus on a key issue or interpretive problem; (5) providing data and time for students to think about responses; and (6) connecting questions/problems to students' lives and prior knowledge.

Collaborative Inquiry

We recently overheard two teachers discussing Mark Twain's *The Adventures of Huckleberry Finn* (1884/1965). One teacher indicated that she really had problems dealing with the ending in her class: "The way they treat Jim is demeaning and downright cruel. I don't know what to do with that." The second teacher responded, "The way I teach the ending is to explain to the kids that it's showing Tom's character, not Twain's viewpoint. Twain is in no way endorsing Tom's actions."

The comment by the second teacher suggests that he doesn't approach the classroom as a forum for collaborative inquiry. Instead he feels the need to lead students to a certain interpretation of the text—to provide an explanation of it to remove any confusion for them. He doesn't appear to seize on the ending as an opportunity to involve students in an exploration of different interpretations and to engage them as participants in an ongoing critical conversation about the novel.

Unless the teacher's goal is to have students grapple with a text so that they engage in the process of inquiry, the environment is not going to be conducive to authentic discussion. But what about questions that have a definite answer? Are we suggesting that there are never misreadings of a text? We have found that it is possible to take an inquiry approach even with a question that has a definite answer in a text. For example, our ninth-grade students often have difficulty understanding what happens at the end of Harper Lee's *To Kill a Mockingbird* (1960). Knowing that this is a difficulty for our students, we take an inquiry approach to the question of what happens to Bob Ewell. We begin discussion of the last chapters by asking students individually to write on a slip of paper how they think Bob Ewell dies and what they believe happens to him. We collect the slips of paper and quickly compile the results without identifying any names. Students typically write the following different ideas: Jem killed him, Ewell fell on his own knife, Boo Radley stabbed him, Mr. Tate stabbed him. We list the different possibilities that students come up with on the board and ask, "So which of these happened or does the text never reveal which happened?" We invite a discussion, letting students explain what they think happened, what didn't happen, and what evidence supports their views. We work hard to avoid giving answers and instead leave it to the students to address a comment such as, "Tate says in the book that Ewell fell on his knife." Over many years of working with the novel, we have always had students finally arrive at a consensus after they have listened to all the evidence that emerges in the discussion.

Types of Questions

Sometimes it is difficult to engage secondary students in authentic discussion about texts because, depending on the type of instruction that they are used to, they may think that there really isn't anything to discuss. Their reasoning is something like the following: "There are right answers versus wrong answers, and it is the teacher's job to see who knows the right answers and make sure that those who don't are corrected." Or "there are questions with no right or wrong answers. Anything can be right, so, therefore, what's the point of giving or listening to answers when all of them are right?"

We have found it helpful in these cases to show students that there are different types of questions one could ask based on relationships between reader, author, and text. Although there are several different question hierarchies or taxonomies that work effectively with secondary students, we have found that Raphael's (1982) Question-Answer Relationships (QAR) works well, particularly with younger students (Figure 7–2). One purpose of showing students the QARs

FIGURE 7–2   *Question-Answer Relationships (QAR)*

Question-Answer Relationships (QAR)

IN THE BOOK QARs	IN MY HEAD QARs
Right There The answer is in the text, usually easy to find. The words used in the question and the words used to answer the question are *Right There*, close together in the text.	*Author and You* The answer is *not* in the text. You need to think about what you already know, what the author tells you in the text, and how it fits together.
Think and Search (Putting It Together) The answer is in the story, but you need to put together different story parts to find it. Words for the question and words for the answer come from different parts of the text.	*On My Own* The answer is *not* in the text. You can answer the question without reading the text. You need to use your own experience and prior knowledge.

Source: T. E. Raphael. 1982. "Question-answering strategies for children." *The Reading Teacher* 36: 186–90.

Reflective Teaching, Reflective Learning edited by McCann, Johannessen, Kahn, Smagorinsky, and Smith (Heinemann: Portsmouth, NH); © 2005.

is to illustrate that while there are some questions with a definite right or wrong answer clearly present in the text, there are also questions that involve inferences and interpretation.

Along with Raphael's QARs, we have given students Sarah Cleghorn's (1917) short poem "The Golf Links," which is provided by Hillocks in the preface. We were introduced to this poem by Hillocks, who originally used it in a unit he designed to teach students to recognize and interpret satire and irony.

We ask students to read the poem and respond to five questions: (1) What are *golf links*? What is a *mill*? (2) Where is the mill located? (3) What do the children see when they look outside? (4) Does the author want readers to be admiring or critical of the men? How can you tell? (5) What is the central meaning or point of this poem? How do you know?

We then ask students to share their responses to the five questions and to explain where each falls on the QAR matrix. Students quickly point out that the first two questions (What are *golf links*? What is a *mill*?) can be answered without reading the text. They require knowledge outside of the text, although there are context clues suggesting their meaning. Question 2 (Where is the mill located?) is "Right There" in the text: the mill is very close to the golf links. Question 3 (What do the children see when they look outside?) is also in the text but requires examining different parts of the text ("Think and Search") in order for students to identify not just that the men are "playing" but what it is that they are playing (golf). Question 4 (Does the author want readers to be admiring or critical of the men? How can you tell?) and question 5 (What is the central meaning or point of this poem? How do you know?) are "Author and You" questions, requiring inferences and usually resulting in less agreement among students. Some students express a straight reading of the poem—it's nice that the mill is so near the golf course so that the children have something to watch while they are working, something to help them pass the time. Others recognize the irony of men playing and children working. They point out that the children are exploited by the rich men who can spend their time golfing because they are profiting from the labor of children. The next step is that we ask the class the following question: So is this a pleasant poem about children being entertained while they work or a sad poem about the injustice of child labor? After some back-and-forth between those on each side, our classes have ultimately decided that the evidence is stronger for the latter interpretation. Through the discussion, students who initially missed the irony of the poem begin to see how meaning may not be directly stated in a text.

Our purpose in conducting this kind of discussion is to illustrate for students that the answers to questions about texts aren't always "right there"—some are, but some of the most important and most worth discussing aren't; they involve interpretation. Also we hope to illustrate that for some questions there isn't just one answer, but that some ideas about a text may not hold up well on critical examination and discussion. Ultimately, we want to help them see that discussion can be a process of collaboratively "figuring out" or constructing meaning.

The Uptake Technique

The term *uptake* comes from the work of Marshall, Smagorinsky, and Smith (1995) and Nystrand (1997). It has been shown to be a powerful way to generate and sustain authentic discussion. Uptake provides an alternative to the IRE pattern.

To illustrate this strategy, we use a discussion of the poem "The Warden Said to Me" by Etheridge Knight (1968), a poem Elizabeth has used successfully with ninth- to twelfth-grade students. This eight-line poem involves a conversation between a prison warden and an African American prisoner. The prisoner, Etheridge, recounts the conversation with the warden. He begins by saying that the warden asked him, "Why come the black boys don't run off like the white boys do?" Etheridge adds that the question was an innocent one, he thinks. Etheridge then quotes his response to the warden's question in a dialect that he does not use in the rest of the poem: "I reckon it's cause we ain't got no where to run to." He also comments that he thinks his response to the question is "innocent" as well.

Uptake involves restating a student response or turning it into a question in order to encourage further elaboration. For example, as students comment on what they notice in the poem, one student says, "Etheridge isn't capitalized." Using uptake, the teacher would respond by asking, "So . . . ?" The student then adds, "It's a lack of respect for him." If the student stops here, the teacher could say, "A lack of respect?" The student might then respond, "The warden doesn't respect him because he's black."

In using uptake, the teacher does not judge or evaluate student responses by saying "good," "right," or "that's it," for example. Evaluative comments of this type tend to imply closure and shut down further discussion. They also suggest that the teacher has a particular right answer in mind. Instead, in following up a student response, the teacher can either say nothing, while conveying a look that says "That's interesting," or make a neutral comment, such as "interesting observation," "That's another viewpoint," "I hadn't thought of that," "That's a point we need to consider," and so forth. This strategy can be used with an individual student or with the whole class.

But if we as teachers accept all responses without evaluating them, then what about ideas or interpretations that are problematic? For example, what if a student says that the warden is smarter than Etheridge because Etheridge is the one who committed a crime and ended up in prison, and that's a pretty dumb thing to do? One way to handle this situation is to list all possibilities that are raised (without names attached) on the board or projector. Inevitably, we have found that students themselves will eventually question the problematic interpretations without the teacher having to do so. If no one says anything, the teacher can survey the list of possibilities and ask students whether all of them work or comment that some of them seem to contradict each other. In other words, the teacher can invite the class to evaluate the list of possibilities. Concentrating on using uptake consistently is one way that we have found to prevent us from slipping into an IRE pattern during discussions.

Questions That Focus on a Key Issue or Interpretive Problem

Uptake is most effective when used with the strategy of asking broader, more open-ended questions that focus on a key issue or interpretive problem.

Examine the following brief transcript that is also from a class discussion of Knight's "The Warden Said to Me." In this case, the transcript illustrates a recitation rather than an authentic discussion.

Teacher: Who are the characters in the poem?
Mark: The warden and Etheridge.
Teacher: Good. What question does the warden ask Etheridge?
Asra: Why don't the black boys run off?
Teacher: How does Etheridge answer that question?
Tanya: He says they "ain't got no where to run to."
Teacher: Right! What does that show?
Domi: That they don't have anywhere to go.
Teacher: Why don't they have anywhere to go?
Domi: Maybe they don't have a house? They've been in jail so they have no home any more.

As the teacher continued to press students for a reason why the African American inmates have "no where to run to," a few students offered variations on Domi's response—without any consideration of why the white inmates would have somewhere to run to—but most remained silent. Often in an IRE recitation such as this one, as the questions become more difficult ("Why don't the black boys have anywhere to run to?"), the responses begin to wane and students struggle.

One way to avoid this sort of recitation is to pose a broad, open-ended question that focuses on a significant issue or interpretive problem, give students some time to think about their responses, and perhaps have students work with others briefly in collaborative pairs or small groups before attempting to run a class discussion (see also Holden and Schmit 2002). We have used the following questions for "The Warden Said to Me" as a focus with ninth-grade students: (1) What details and patterns do you notice in the poem that seem strange, puzzling, or potentially significant? (2) What things do you learn about Etheridge in the poem?

From this foundation, a class discussion can proceed in the following manner. Notice that the teacher also uses uptake in running the discussion.

Teacher: What did you notice about the poem?
Manish: They don't speak good English.
Teacher: Who do you mean?
Manish: The warden. He says, "Why come."
Kourtney: Etheridge too. He says, "Ain't got no where."
Teacher: Okay. Anything else you noticed?
Mike: Etheridge isn't capitalized.

Teacher: What do you think that's all about?

Mike: A lack of respect for him...because he's black. The warden is racist.

Teacher: Is there anything else in the poem that suggests that the warden doesn't respect him?

Christina: Yes, he says, the black boys don't run off like the white boys do.

Teacher: Meaning?

Christina: I'm not sure...

Mike: It's like he's saying the black boys aren't as smart because they can't run off.

Teacher: So who's smarter, the warden or Etheridge?

Terry: I think the warden is smarter because he's the warden and Etheridge is in prison.

Mike: No! He doesn't know that Etheridge is kinda making fun of him. Etheridge is *acting* dumb. The warden is racist.

Teacher: Why do you say Etheridge is *acting* dumb?

At this point students may voice disagreement about who's smarter and why. Eventually someone usually mentions stereotypes and that Etheridge is intentionally fulfilling the warden's stereotype of an African American prisoner. Students examine the significance of the parenthetical phrase "innocently, I think" that is repeated in the poem. They then tackle the question of what commentary Knight is making about society. But it is the students and their responses, not a predetermined script of the teacher, that set the direction of the discussion. The teacher follows their lead, asking for elaboration and further explanation.

In selecting texts and developing focusing questions for discussion, it is important for teachers to have a good understanding of their students. For example, Elizabeth knew that for her ninth graders "The Warden Said to Me" would be a challenging poem. Elizabeth knew from using the poem in the past that a key interpretive problem for students is understanding the relationship between the speaker of the poem, Etheridge, and the warden. Most of them find the poem "easy" on the surface but consider it pointless, not much of a poem at all. They have difficulty recognizing and interpreting the irony in the poem. Elizabeth knew that a question such as "How does the poem use irony to make a point?" would not be effective in generating an authentic discussion. Most students would have nothing to say. They might say, "I forget what irony is." But most likely, even given a definition, they would not generate many ideas. One or two students might give a response and the others would probably just say, "I agree." Also, a question like this—one frequently found in textbooks—cues the students to the fact that the poem is ironic and takes away the opportunity for them to make this interpretation.

Elizabeth felt that asking students what they notice in the poem that is strange or puzzling and what they learn about Etheridge would allow all students to generate a number of different ideas and would get them to eventually confront the irony in the poem as they puzzled through the details. In order for a discussion to work, the teacher has to design key questions for the particular students and context—keeping in mind students' age, level of sophistication, interests, reading skills, social relationships, and so forth.

The Importance of Data and Time to Reflect

Larry has taught a unit on the Vietnam War in Literature (Johannessen 1992). One discussion activity he has created and used to help students develop a deeper knowledge of the issues in the literature they are going to read is the problem-based case, "A Matter of Conscience" (Figure 7–3). The Vietnam War is a watershed event in American history; however, for many of our students, it might as well be the Peloponnesian War for all they know (Christie 1989). For example, students today do not understand why the draft was such a big deal during the Vietnam period. When Larry asks students to read Tim O'Brien's (1990) *The Things They Carried,* many of them have difficulty understanding what O'Brien is conveying in his chapter "On the Way to Rainy River." Failing to comprehend meaning from this crucial chapter often prevents students from understanding or interpreting O'Brien's meaning in the work as a whole. The case provides data that gives students a way in to the knowledge they need to understand the novel.

In the chapter, Tim, the narrator, receives his draft notice at the height of the Vietnam War. Tim has been to college and has thought a great deal about the war. He has decided that the war in Vietnam is immoral. The moral question for Tim is that if he knows the war is wrong, then he has no choice but to refuse to fight, and so he reasons that he will go to Canada to avoid the draft. Tim goes to a remote lake that borders Canada and rents a cabin. After much soul searching, he discovers that he is torn between his desire to go to Canada and avoid having to fight in Vietnam and his "embarrassment" or fear of being seen as a coward by his family and the community. In the end, even though Tim believes the war is wrong, he cannot go to Canada, and he says of his decision, "I was a coward. I went to the war" (41).

Many students discount his decision, especially in light of his later actions in combat, and conclude that Tim is brave for making the decision to fight in a war that he thinks is wrong. They want to believe the popular mythology of war that anyone who fights in a war is brave, and what makes matters worse is that as a result they fail to appreciate what O'Brien is up to in later chapters, such as "The Man I Killed," and the work as a whole.

Having students wrestle with the "A Matter of Conscience" case before reading "On the Way to Rainy River" provides data to help them connect with Tim's problem in the text and activates their prior knowledge so that they develop a deeper understanding of the issue the main character confronts. It is designed to prepare students to think hard about the moral choice the narrator has to make in the novel and to get them to consider some of the consequences of having to make such a moral choice. The case is rich in details. Students are placed in a situation in which they must make a choice and for which there is no easy answer, and they must consider the consequences of that choice—nearly the same moral situation the narrator is in. As students discuss and debate whether it is ethically right for Jim Hardy, the character in the case, to go to Canada to escape the draft or to report for the draft and serve as ordered, they are engaged in the moral issue that the main character in the novel faces.

FIGURE 7–3 *A Matter of Conscience*

A Matter of Conscience

In the summer of 1969, at age twenty-one, exactly one month after graduating from a large state university in Michigan, Jim Hardy received his draft notice to fight in the war in Vietnam. He believed that the war was wrong. He could not tell for sure if it was a civil war, a war of national liberation, or simple aggression. It wasn't even clear who started the war, when, or why. He wasn't sure if Ho Chi Minh was a communist stooge, a nationalist savior of the Vietnamese people, or both, or neither. He wasn't clear about these and many other matters, especially since the debate over the war had gone from the floor of the United States Congress to the cities and towns across America. He had come to believe that when a nation goes to war it must be reasonably sure regarding the justice and necessity of its cause.

Most of all, he had been convinced that the war was wrong as a result of what he had seen it do to his older brother. Mark was two years older than Jim and had joined the Marines as soon as he turned eighteen. He had gone to Vietnam a happy-go-lucky kid and came back angry and sullen. Mark now had difficulty holding down a job, and he seemed to spend a lot of his time drinking. When Jim asked Mark about the war, if he thought it was right, he looked Jim in the eyes and said, "I don't know, Jimmy. All I know is that I saw a lot of good men die or get mangled and the only ending I see is more death and destruction. I just keep wondering, what is it going to prove?"

Jim thought about all of the reasons and decided that if he believed the war is wrong, then he could not fight in it. He had even acted on his beliefs by working on the campaign to elect Eugene McCarthy, an antiwar candidate for president. He had attended a couple of student protest rallies against the war on his college campus.

Once Jim knew that the right course of action was not to fight in this war, he did his research and decided that he was going to go to Canada. After all, he wasn't a pacifist. He believed that there were times when the right thing to do was to go to war—to stop Hitler or Mussolini. Jim got his passport and enough money to last him awhile. He boarded a bus and headed north to the nearest border crossing. He stopped in a small border town and took a room in a cheap hotel. He then wrote letters to his parents and his brother, doing his best to explain what he was doing and why.

The trouble was he couldn't make himself actually mail the letters. Something was very wrong. Jim was troubled. There was the matter of the generations of Hardy boys who had served their country without question. His father had

Continues

Reflective Teaching, Reflective Learning edited by McCann, Johannessen, Kahn, Smagorinsky, and Smith (Heinemann: Portsmouth, NH); © 2005.

FIGURE 7–3   *A Matter of Conscience* (continued)

served in the Navy in World War II. His uncle had been in the Army and lost a leg on the beaches at Normandy. His grandfather had served in the Army Air Corps in World War I. All had served with honor. How could he go against them?

He thought of his blue-collar neighborhood in the city. Most of his parents' friends and the fathers of his friends had served in the military in World War II or Korea. How could he face anyone in his community again? He would be an exile, unable to return home. His mother and father, his high school teachers and counselor, his buddies, and his community would all consider him a traitor or a coward. He even imagined the president of the United States, the Pope, and the Supreme Court all looking down at him shaking their heads at his disgrace. How could he go through the rest of his life with this embarrassment? Was going to Canada—acting on his beliefs—the brave thing to do? Was it the right thing to do?

Questions

What should Jim do: Go to Canada to escape having to fight in Vietnam or report for duty and go to Vietnam?

Why is that the right thing for him to do?

In your opinion, which course of action is an act of bravery and which is an act of cowardice and why?

Reflective Teaching, Reflective Learning edited by McCann, Johannessen, Kahn, Smagorinsky, and Smith (Heinemann: Portsmouth, NH); © 2005.

The case functions as a kind of question a teacher might ask in a class discussion, but it is much richer than a simple query like, "What should a person do when faced with the choice of being drafted to fight in a war that he or she believes is morally wrong?" Contrast this approach with how Larry might have proceeded. Before assigning students to read "On the Way to Rainy River," he could have posed the following questions to the class: If you believed the Vietnam War was morally wrong and you were drafted to serve, would you go to Canada to avoid having to serve in Vietnam or would you report to the draft board to serve your country as ordered? Why would you do that?

One difference between the case and asking a series of questions is that questions provide no data regarding the moral choice in the question. Asking the questions assumes that students have adequate knowledge of the moral dilemma a young college student might confront in the late 1960s if he were drafted to go to Vietnam. Without more data, and the context of the moral issues of the time, students have little basis for making a decision or wrestling with the moral ambiguities involved. If Larry had just asked the questions, it is very likely that what would have resulted is a brief and not nuanced discussion.

Furthermore, if Larry had approached the problem by simply posing the questions to the class, his students may not have had adequate time to think about the issues and formulate cogent responses. Therefore, when students read the case "A Matter of Conscience," he has them first write a short composition answering the questions posed at the end. This step is crucial. We have found that it is best to give students time to think about complex questions and problems if we expect them to participate effectively in authentic class discussions. As classroom teachers we sometimes forget how much time we have spent thinking about the complex questions we ask students to respond to on the spur of the moment during class discussions. That is why it is important to have students spend some time writing about the case before asking them to discuss it.

After students have written about the case, Larry typically has them meet in small groups, read their papers aloud, and try to reach a consensus about what they think Jim Hardy should do and why. Working in small groups allows students time to gain a greater understanding of other perspectives. As students' ideas or hypotheses are challenged by others, they revise and refine their thinking. Small-group collaboration provides scaffolding for students while they are learning new strategies so that ultimately they internalize procedures and are able to tackle new tasks effectively on their own (Hillocks 1995; Johannessen 2001, 2003; Johannessen and Kahn 1997; McCann 1996; Smagorinsky 1989, 1993; Smagorinsky, McCann, and Kern 1987). This, in turn, can contribute to more authentic discussions.

After students work in small groups for fifteen or twenty minutes, Larry re-forms the class for discussion. Depending on the class, he either has the groups start by reading the paper that best represents their viewpoints or has students present their solutions and discuss differences. Either way, the result is a very lively discussion.

In the small-group and whole-class discussions, students are wrestling with the same sort of problem and questions that the narrator must contend with in the novel. Students discuss and debate whether Jim should cross the border into Canada to avoid having to fight in a war that he believes is morally wrong or whether he should turn around and report for duty and serve his country as ordered. Students discuss and debate the possible consequences, such as being an outcast for the rest of his life if he avoids the draft or getting wounded or killed and having to kill if he reports for duty and goes to Vietnam. Students often even consider the emotional and psychological damage that he might experience. What is particularly striking about the nature of the discussion, and what makes it stand out as authentic, is that students are actively engaged in an inquiry into the problem posed and issues raised.

It's worth noting that the case provides data and relates to the novel without duplicating it. It is short enough for students to read several times and easily locate important details, but complex enough to give them much to dig into. The way Larry structures the activity—moving from individual writing to small-group collaboration to whole-class discussion—provides the time necessary for students to develop complex, thoughtful responses.

Students rarely agree on what Jim Hardy should do. Larry often collects student papers or has them keep their papers. Then when they finish reading and discussing "On the Way to Rainy River" or the text as a whole, he has students return to the case and, in light of the reading and discussions, reexamine what they have written and revise their papers in terms of what they have learned. This natural follow-up writing activity reinforces what students learn during class discussions.

Connecting to Students' Lives and Prior Knowledge

It is vitally important that we design our questions and problems so that they connect to the lives of our students if we hope to engage them in authentic classroom discussion. As Smith (Rabinowitz and Smith 1998) warns, the real danger is that when we focus on what we think is important, we might very well end up "torturing" our students with questions or problems that are important only to us—as he did when he had his students read Nathaniel Hawthorne's novel *The Scarlet Letter* and asked them to discuss the hat motif and other symbols and motifs in the novel (103). His students hated it, and as he indicates, they were interested in a whole set of other questions, such as, "Why the hell didn't she [Hester] just leave if they treated her that way?" (103). When we focus discussion on questions and problems that connect to the lives of our students, we show them that they matter and what they have to say matters.

In addition, as Smagorinsky (1993) and Smagorinsky, McCann, and Kern (1987) note, when we design questions or problems we need to design ones that assess our students' prior knowledge and enable them to expand their knowledge base. Furthermore, we need to make sure that we are connecting what they are learning in the instruction to the literature under consideration.

Larry has used the case "Does She Deserve Honor" (Figure 7–4) to make connections between students' lives and a novel such as *The Scarlet Letter*. This case works in much the same way as "A Matter of Conscience," described earlier. It puts the situation in the novel into a parallel but contemporary setting that is close to students' lives. The case tends to generate authentic discussion as students debate it in small groups or as a whole class. One of the issues that students debate in arguing whether Dinesen should be admitted to the National Honor Society is whether she sets a good example for others. Some students argue that having a daughter as an unwed teenager is wrong. Others argue that her decision to raise the child rather than ending the pregnancy or offering the child for adoption shows strength of character. But usually someone will reply that she would have shown more character by allowing a couple with more resources to be good parents to adopt the child. Another issue that students bring up is whether the ruling is discriminatory toward females. Some students will argue that if the student had been a male instead of female it is likely that the officials of the National Honor Society would not have known about the child and the male student would not have been kicked out of the organization, and so on.

A contemporary case can promote discussion by bringing a novel such as *The Scarlet Letter* closer to students' own experience. As students read the novel, Larry has engaged them in authentic discussion of similarities and differences between the National Honor Society case and the novel.

FIGURE 7–4   *Does She Deserve Honor?*

Does She Deserve Honor?

Jennifer Dinesen, a high school senior, was denied induction to the National Honor Society (NHS) because she is an unmarried mother. A faculty selection committee at Streamridge High School invited Jennifer to join the school's National Honor Society but then revoked the offer when it discovered that the eighteen-year-old had a daughter. Students are selected for the National Honor Society based on four criteria: character, leadership, service, and scholastic achievement. Dinesen met the academic requirements, but the committee felt that because she is an unwed mother her character is in question and she is not a good role model (leader) for other students.

The rules of the National Honor Society state that "pregnancy cannot be the basis for automatic rejection," but each school is allowed to set its own standards as long as they are applied consistently. The superintendent explained that Jennifer Dinesen is not the first student at Streamridge to be denied membership in the school's honor society because of sexual activity.

As a senior, Jennifer has a 3.8 grade point average. She has been a member of the Spanish Club since freshman year and served as secretary of the club her sophomore year. She was a starting player on the junior varsity girls' basketball team her freshman and sophomore years. During her junior year, she was in charge of decorations for the school's homecoming dance, and she also worked as a volunteer four hours a week at a local day-care center for disabled children. All her out-of-school time during her senior year has been spent caring for her baby daughter. She has not received any discipline referrals for four years.

Jennifer says, "I'm deeply hurt by the school's decision because I have worked so hard for four years."

Questions

What is at issue are two qualities the honor society demands: leadership and character. As an unwed mother, has Jennifer lost her character?

Will she lead others in the wrong direction?

Do you agree with the faculty committee's decision not to induct Jennifer Dinesen into the National Honor Society?

Why or why not?

Source: L. R. Johannessen. 2001. "Teaching Thinking and Writing for a New Century." *English Journal* 90 (July): 38–46.

Reflective Teaching, Reflective Learning edited by McCann, Johannessen, Kahn, Smagorinsky, and Smith (Heinemann: Portsmouth, NH); © 2005.

Authentic Discussion in the Classroom

The strategies we have discussed have helped us promote authentic classroom discussion in the service of helping our students construct meaning, achieve deeper understanding, and make connections to literature. At the heart of what we have argued is that we need to create a new kind of classroom, a classroom that is inquiry-driven and not dominated by teacher talk. When we think about our experiences as students in George Hillocks' MAT program, we still find ourselves using what we learned, striving to find ways to generate good authentic discussions and increase the amount of student interaction in our classrooms.

References

APPLEBEE, A. N., J. N. LANGER, M. NYSTRAND, AND A. GAMORAN. 2003. "Discussion-Based Approaches to Developing Understanding: Classroom Instruction and Student Performance in Middle and High School English." *American Educational Research Journal* 40 (3): 685–730.

BAKHTIN, M. M. 1986. *Speech Genres and Other Late Essays.* Austin: University of Texas Press.

CHRISTOPH, J. N., AND M. NYSTRAND. 2001. Taking Risks, Negotiating Relationships: One Teacher's Transition Towards a Dialogic Classroom. Report No. 14003. Albany, NY: CELA.

CHRISTIE, N. B. 1989. "Teaching Our Longest War: Constructive Lessons from Vietnam." *English Journal* 78 (2): 35–38.

CLEGHORN, S. N. 1917. "The Golf Links Lie So Near the Mill." *Portraits and Protests.* New York: Holt.

FLANDERS, N. A. 1965. *Teacher Influence, Pupil Attitudes, and Achievement.* Cooperative Research Monograph No. 12. Washington, DC: U.S. Office of Education.

———. 1970. *Analyzing Teaching Behavior.* Berkeley, CA: Addison-Wesley.

HAWTHORNE, N. (1850/1963). *The Scarlet Letter.* New York: Bobbs-Merrill.

HILLOCKS, G., JR. 1995. *Teaching Writing as Reflective Practice.* New York: Teachers College Press.

HOLDEN, J., AND J. S. SCHMIT, EDS. 2002. *Inquiry and the Literary Text: Constructing Discussions in the English Classroom.* Urbana, IL: NCTE.

JOHANNESSEN, L. R. 1992. *Illumination Rounds: Teaching the Literature of the Vietnam War.* Urbana, IL: ERIC/NCTE.

———. 2001. "Teaching Thinking and Writing for a New Century." *English Journal* 90 (6): 38–46.

———. 2003. "Strategies for Initiating Authentic Discussion." *English Journal* 93 (1): 73–79.

JOHANNESSEN, L. R., AND E. A. KAHN. 1997. "Teaching English Language Arts for a Technological Age." *The Clearing House* 70: 305–10.

KNIGHT, E. 1968. "The Warden Said to Me." *Poems from Prison.* Chicago: Broadside Press.

LANGER, J. A. 2001. "Succeeding Against the Odds in English." *English Journal* 91 (1): 37–42.

LEE, H. 1960. *To Kill a Mockingbird.* New York: Popular Library.

MARSHALL, J. D., P. SMAGORINSKY, AND M. W. SMITH. 1995. *The Language of Interpretation: Patterns of Discourse in Discussions of Literature.* Research Report No. 27. Urbana, IL: NCTE.

MCCANN, T. M. 1996. "A Pioneer Simulation for Writing and for the Study of Literature." *English Journal* 85 (3): 62–67.

NYSTRAND, M., WITH A. GAMORAN, R. KACHUR, AND C. PRENDERGAST. 1997. *Opening Dialogue: Understanding the Dynamics of Language and Learning in the English Classroom.* New York: Teachers College Press.

O'BRIEN, T. 1990. *The Things They Carried.* New York: Broadway Books.

RABINOWITZ, P. J., AND M. W. SMITH. 1998. *Authorizing Readers: Resistance and Respect in the Teaching of Literature.* New York: Teachers College Press.

RAPHAEL, T. E. 1982. "Question-Answering Strategies for Children." *The Reading Teacher* 36: 186–90.

SMAGORINSKY, P. 1989. "Small Groups: A New Dimension in Learning." *English Journal* 78 (2): 67–70.

———. 1993. "Preparing Students for Enriched Reading." In *Exploring Texts: The Role of Discussion and Writing in the Teaching and Learning of Literature,* edited by G. E. Newell and R. K. Durst, 153–74. Norwood, MA: Christopher-Gordon.

SMAGORINSKY, P., T. M. MCCANN, AND S. KERN. 1987. *Explorations: Introductory Activities for Literature and Composition, 7–12.* Urbana, IL: ERIC/NCTE.

TWAIN, M. (1884/1965). *The Adventures of Huckleberry Finn.* New York: Bantam.

8

It's Always Something
Planning for Sustained Discussion

THOMAS M. McCANN
Elmhurst Public Schools
Elmhurst, Illinois

High school teachers of first-period classes, or of second-semester seniors during any period of the day, may wonder hopelessly how to involve most of the class in a lively discussion about a topic that the students care deeply about. But even a brief casual conversation with a small group of adolescents will reveal many of the topics and issues that they all care about. Here, for example, is a scenario that I guarantee will inspire a lively discussion in any high school class:

> As Flo Reid exits the bus when it arrives at school, someone behind her gives her a shove that causes her to stumble and drop her books into the snow. When Flo looks back, she sees Bea Sauer grinning at her. As Bea and her friends exit the bus, they point at Flo and laugh. Since the beginning of the school year, Bea has been harassing Flo—by tossing food at her in the cafeteria, by spreading nasty rumors about her boyfriend, by threatening her in the hallways. On these occasions, Flo's friends have asked her, "Are you going to put up with this stuff?" As Flo bends down to retrieve her books from the snow, Bea slaps her across the top of the head. Flo has known Bea for years, and Flo knows that with little effort she can beat her tormentor up. Flo also knows that if she were to beat Bea up at this moment, she would get in equal trouble with the dean, which probably means a suspension, even though Bea was the one who started the trouble. From inside the bus, Flo's friends watch her to see what she will do in response to Bea's abuse. What do *you* think Flo should do?

This is the kind of nightmare situation that kids hate, especially because the typical high school seems incapable of granting students like Flo the protection and justice they might deserve. The situation reveals an essential unfairness that can occur in school when students are put into a vulnerable position where it would be shameful not to act and dangerous to take action. If a teacher were to introduce the scenario and provide a brief time for students to ponder it, very likely most of the students, even the drowsy, lethargic, and apathetic ones, will want to contribute some thoughts, offer some advice, recall similar instances, describe complex nuances, and even contest each other over claims about the appropriate course of action to take in such situations. It would be easy enough to prompt students to express and support opinions about the characters in the scenario. Other challenges follow: how to manage the various exchanges, how to keep the discourse civil, how to ask follow-up questions to promote rational thought, and how to bring matters to closure.

One can well imagine a classroom full of adolescents discussing and debating the scenario expansively. It is good to get students talking to each other about a compelling issue, but is it enough if the students debate one scenario in isolation, without a larger instructional context? The eager responses to the scenario with Flo and Bea would prove that it is possible to lift a group of teenagers, if even only temporarily, from their lethargy; but what does the teacher do after that? There are a number of questions that a teacher might ask in planning further: How does this discussion connect with anything else we've done this year, or with anything we will be doing? How does the participation in the lively discussion promote thinking skills that apply to any other occasion? How does the participation in the discussion prepare students for subsequent reading or writing?

Applebee and colleagues (2003) report that "when students' classroom literacy experiences emphasize high academic demands and discussion-based approaches to the development of understanding, students internalize the knowledge and skills necessary to engage in challenging literacy tasks on their own" (723). Langer (2001) reports the results of research that compares cohort schools and identifies the features that might account for students at one school outperforming students at a comparable school in measures of achievement in reading and writing. Langer and The Center on English Language and Learning (CELA) report several key features for schools that "beat the odds." In considering the important place that discussion can hold in an English classroom, I want to highlight two of the features that Langer identifies as associated with schools that beat the odds, including the type of literacy experiences just listed.

First, the curriculum is coherent. Instead of a loose collection of activities or a sequence of lessons defined by a textbook, the curriculum is supported by overarching concepts that are inherent in the field of study. Each lesson and each unit build on previous lessons and units, and prepare students for their understanding of subsequent lessons and units. Second, teachers plan strategically. Generally speaking, this is something that distinguishes experienced teachers from novice teachers. In planning strategically, a teacher thinks beyond the immediate lesson and builds toward some deep understanding or larger effect. The teachers look ahead to long-term goals and big projects and plan backward, putting the pieces of each goal or project in place so that the students have the knowledge and skills necessary to successfully achieve them. In planning strategically, the teacher assesses prior knowledge and puts in place the instructional scaffolding that is necessary for students to connect with new concepts.

In their 1971 text, Hillocks, McCabe, and McCampbell model for teachers of English how to design coherent units of instruction. They recognize the value of connecting related works of literature to plan for instructional scaffolding, facilitate students' deeper examination of concepts, and develop students' language skills in the inquiry process. They observe, "The province of the unit, then, is to arrange materials and the examination of them in such a way that the student accumulates the background necessary for knowing what and how to observe and for making appropriate inferences. If the unit is to develop the student's power to read literature, planning must be very careful" (254–55). The emphasis in their statement is on the teaching of literature, but the idea of planning coherent units of instruction applies generally to the design of curricula that integrates various language arts activities. Through subsequent publications, Hillocks (e.g., 1995, 1999) has extended this thinking and has stimulated discussion about the power of planning strategically. For decades, George Hillocks has trained and influenced teachers to think beyond isolated lessons—to combine a series of explorations, powered by discussions among peers, into an integrated coherent whole.

Smagorinsky provides detailed guidance in his methods text, *Teaching English Through Principled Practice* (2002), for designing coherent conceptual units of instruction. He emphasizes the design of each unit of instruction around a broad, overarching concept: "One consideration in planning units is the overarching concept that unifies the curriculum over the whole course. You should ask, to borrow Applebee's (1996) language, "What larger conversation should students be engaged in that in turn suggests good topics to build units around?" (40). In *Fostering the Reader's Response* (1989), Smagorinsky and Gevinson suggest a variety of conceptual units of instruction for students in middle school and high school.

The purpose of this chapter is not to attempt to repeat the capable work of Hillocks, Smagorinsky, Gevinson, and other students of Hillocks, but to refer to some of their guiding principles, which Langer's research supports, as a means to illustrate how, in a coherent curriculum, discussions build on each other. In other words, while keeping a big question or overarching concept in mind, students and their teacher can extend discussion over days and weeks to probe a significant problem in a mature and complex way.

I use a sequence of lessons here to illustrate the power of the connectedness of discussion and to show how discussions build on each other to support new learning. The sequence is, basically, this:

1. A scenario activity introduces a concept or problem.

    Example: *What does it mean to be* fair?

2. Criteria derived from discussion of the scenario serve as a framework for the analysis of a problem-based case and as warrants to develop oral and written arguments.

    Example: *To what extent is there merit to students' claims that they are being treated unfairly?*

3. The language from the discussions of the scenario and the case serves the learners in their reading and critical assessment.

Example: *To what extent does Thomas Jefferson's Declaration of Independence make a convincing argument that the colonists have been treated so unfairly that they are justified in breaking away from Great Britain?*

4   In the long term, all the activities support a broader inquiry into the original question.

Example: *Questions about fairness often return to the claim that equally entitled citizens have been treated in an uneven way. Questions about equality hark back to the claim in the Declaration of Independence that all men are created equal.*

The scenario activity in Figure 8–1 asks the students to judge in each case whether a person is correct in thinking that he or she has been treated unfairly. The activity introduces a key concept of the unit, following the practices recommended by Smagorinsky, McCann, and Kern (1987). In addition, Johannessen, Kahn, and Walter (1982) offer advice about the design of scenarios and their use in prompting discussion. Perhaps the teacher would begin the process of analysis by leading discussion of the first scenario before the students move into small groups to discuss the remaining scenarios independently.

In addition to the five scenarios listed in Figure 8–1, one could include the scenario that appears at the beginning of this chapter, because Flo's situation deals with a basic unfairness that students will recognize. In the long run, the groups share and debate their conclusions about the behavior of the characters depicted in the scenarios. Through the deliberations in small- and large-group formats, the class derives a set of "rules" or principles for determining if an action is fair and for guiding our behavior in treating others fairly. Here is a typical set of criteria that high school students might develop:

Rules for Fairness

- Everyone should have equal access to basic requirements for living.
- When there is a group vote to determine a policy, everyone in the group should be allowed to vote.
- You should get what you pay for.
- No one should be provided special privileges, unless he or she has earned them.
- People should not prejudge others on the basis of where they live or who they associate with.

There are many worthwhile aspects to the outcome of the discussions and to the process that the students experience as they develop the list of criteria. They have thought in some depth about a concept that is important to their lives. Some parents, in fact, have the impression that adolescents are preoccupied with the concept of fairness. The students have learned how to negotiate judgments with others in order to arrive at consensus. The list of criteria, while not a definitive standard,

FIGURE 8–1 *What Does It Mean to Be Fair*

What Does It Mean to Be *Fair*?

Directions: Read each of the following scenarios and determine if the central character in each case is being *fair* or is being treated *fairly*. For each decision, be prepared to explain how you arrived at your answer. There should be some rule for fairness that has guided your decision. In the end, you should have a list of rules (criteria) that define what it means to be *fair*. You will apply these rules in your analysis of a case study.

1. Ten-year-old Bennie Fitz and his seven-year-old sister, Honey, rode together in the back of their parents' sedan on the way to visit their grandparents at their home, eighty miles away. During the first forty minutes of the drive, everyone listened to Honey's tape, "Barney's Favorite Show Tunes," on the car stereo. Bennie pleaded with his parents: "Can we please listen to *my* tape now? We've been listening to that stupid Barney tape for the whole ride." His mother responded, "That's all right, Bennie. We'll listen to your tape on the way home." Was Mrs. Fitz being fair? Explain.

2. Abel Walker was stricken with chicken pox and was forced to stay home from his fourth-grade class for five days. During his absence, the class voted on where they would like to go for the class picnic at the end of the year. When the votes were counted, it was decided that the class would visit Harvest Valley Forest Preserve for their picnic. The second choice was Beaubien Pond. The vote was 12 to 11. If Abel had been there, he would have voted for Beaubien Pond. Abel was disappointed and asked his teacher, Mrs. McAnthony, to allow the class to vote again, but she refused. She said, "The class has already decided. It wouldn't be fair to vote again after you've tried to influence the decision. You'll just have to live with the decision." Was Mrs. McAnthony being fair? Explain.

3. Twenty members of the senior class at Floodrock High School have been identified as *gifted*. They qualify for the gifted program because they have IQ scores higher than 125, and they each scored above the 90th percentile in reading and mathematics. One "gifted" activity this year was to transport the twenty students to Cape Girardeau, Missouri, to see a performance of the Latvian Modern Dance Ensemble. When the gifted students missed a day of school, they were excused from any tests or homework for that day. Betty Braumeier, a senior who was not included in the gifted program this year, said, "That is so unfair. If one group of students are excused, we should all be excused." Do you agree with Betty? Why, or why not?

Continues

Reflective Teaching, Reflective Learning edited by McCann, Johannessen, Kahn, Smagorinsky, and Smith (Heinemann: Portsmouth, NH); © 2005.

FIGURE 8–1 *What Does It Mean to Be Fair* (continued)

4. When Faith McNaulty visited a convenience store in her neighborhood she looked forward to consuming a frosty Tall Swig, the store's popular twenty-ounce soft drink. The store clerk filled a container with ice, poured the soft drink inside, and took Faith's full payment. When Faith left the store and inserted a straw through the lid of the container, she noticed that the drink felt a bit light. She removed the lid and recognized that the cup was filled only half way with soda. Outraged, she stormed back into store to demand more soda or the return of her payment. However, the store clerk refused, noting the possibility that she had drunk much of the soda once she stepped outside of the store. After her attempts to receive compensation proved futile, Faith stomped out of the store, calling behind her, "I am never coming back to this store. You are so unfair!" Has Faith been treated unfairly? Why or why not?

5. Durwood Parker works as an admissions officer at Middle Border State University, where he sometimes has to make difficult decisions about which candidates will be admitted to the school. Last spring, he had to choose between two students who had almost identical academic records. One student would be a graduate of Shoreline High School, a rather famous suburban high school with a strong reputation. The other student would graduate from Metro Core High School, an inner-city school with a reputation for gang troubles, violence, and general discord. Mr. Parker selected the student from Shoreline High, figuring that a graduate of that institution would surely be a more productive contributor to the university. Has Mr. Parker been fair? Why, or why not?

Reflective Teaching, Reflective Learning edited by McCann, Johannessen, Kahn, Smagorinsky, and Smith (Heinemann: Portsmouth, NH); © 2005.

does provide a reasonable framework for making judgments about situations and human behaviors. But the discussion does not stop here. The students have an opportunity to apply the criteria to a problem-based case in order to complete a thorough analysis that supports the recommendation of a policy to correct the problems they identify. The case of "Floodrock SAVES," in Figure 8–2, recounts a situation in which students who leave their home school each day for technical and vocational training at a separate facility miss several opportunities at their home school. The affected students claim that they have been treated unfairly and petition for some redress of the wrongs they have suffered.

The process for working with the case requires that students again meet in small groups to discuss some central questions: Is there a problem at the high school? Have the students who attend the SAVES program been treated unfairly? If there are any problems, how serious are they? What attempts have already been made to correct the problems? Obviously, these questions follow a model for academic debate. In the end, the students will recommend a policy; that is, a course of action for the school

FIGURE 8–2 *Floodrock SAVES*

Floodrock SAVES
(Saline Area Vocational Education Satellite)

Background

The curriculum at Floodrock High School is most accommodating to those students who plan to enter college or some field of business after graduation. There are no "shop" classes held at the school; instead, students who wish to receive technical or vocational training must attend a separate facility for half of the school day. The technical/vocational students attend core curriculum classes (English, math, social studies, science) at Floodrock in the morning and then attend the Saline Area Vocational Education Satellite (SAVES) facility in the afternoon. At SAVES, students study cosmetology, woodworking, electronics, metal working, printing, auto mechanics, and/or auto body. There are a variety of courses available in each vocational field. Approximately 10 percent of the Floodrock enrollment attends afternoon classes at SAVES. In addition, students from four other area schools attend SAVES: some in the morning and some in the afternoon. See the table on page 128 for enrollment data.

Problem

Many of the students who attend SAVES have complained that they have been treated *unfairly*; that is, that the practices and policies of the school and the major population have denied them the rights and opportunities that have been available to students who do not attend SAVES. Here are the central questions: *To what extent do the SAVES students have reasonable complaints when they claim that they have been treated unfairly? If the SAVES students have been treated unfairly, how can they influence the school administration and their peers to change the policies and practices?*

Questions for Reflection:

- Is there actually a *major* problem at Floodrock High School?
- Is the school already acting adequately and appropriately to be *fair* to all students?
- What does it mean to be *fair*?
- What has been done already in an attempt to change policies?
- Should the school adopt any *new* procedures?
- Will any new procedures cause additional problems? Are new procedures likely to produce benefits for the school?

Continues

Reflective Teaching, Reflective Learning edited by McCann, Johannessen, Kahn, Smagorinsky, and Smith (Heinemann: Portsmouth, NH); © 2005.

FIGURE 8–2 *Floodrock SAVES* (continued)

The Data

Examine the following data to determine the nature and seriousness of the problems at Floodrock High School. The data are available in four forms: reports of incidents and practices at the high school, testimonies from interviews; a descriptive fact sheet for the SAVES program; and tables showing enrollment figures, graduation rates, and the school's bell schedule.

Complaints

Although the SAVES students from Floodrock High School receive a quality education, many of them have complained over the last five years about being denied the full opportunity that other students at Floodrock High School enjoy. The main source of irritation is that the school's designated period for announcements, assemblies, and balloting is ninth period, when SAVES students are away from the building. The ninth period has traditionally been the designated time for announcements, meetings, balloting, and assemblies. According to the school bell schedule, the ninth period is five minutes longer than other periods so that activities do not consume too much instructional time. Any change to the bell schedule would be a significant change from tradition and would cause some expense and inconvenience. The complainants point to the following:

- Student announcements are read during ninth period at Floodrock, when SAVES students are not present. The SAVES students miss important announcements about clubs, sports, scholarships, school events, and community activities.

- Special school assemblies are commonly held during ninth period. Assemblies include events such as introducing the Homecoming Court candidates and the Student Council candidates, but also the appearance of motivational speakers and artistic performers such as musicians, magicians, and actors.

- All students pay an activity fee of $12.50 per year. The money from this fee goes toward paying for the special assemblies. The SAVES students pay the fee even though they cannot participate in the assemblies.

Continues

Reflective Teaching, Reflective Learning edited by McCann, Johannessen, Kahn, Smagorinsky, and Smith (Heinemann: Portsmouth, NH); © 2005.

FIGURE 8–2 *Floodrock SAVES* (continued)

- Student Council, the official representative body of the student population, meets during the afternoon. The time rotates around periods 8, 9, and 10. SAVES students cannot serve on the Student Council because they are never available to attend meetings. The Student Council does determine some policy for the school, including issues that affect parking, Homecoming activities, the prom, and graduation speakers. SAVES students have little say in these decisions.

- A committee of Student Council members recommends the attractions for special assemblies. SAVES students have no voice in these decisions, yet they are required to pay the student activity fee.

- Pep assemblies are held at the end of the last period, on days when the school runs a modified schedule. The SAVES students never return to Floodrock in time to participate. Even athletes who attend SAVES never return to school in time to be included in the pep assemblies. One extreme case occurred two years ago, when state wrestling champion Thug Armour was not present at the assembly to honor winter sports participants.

- SAVES students believe that the administrators, teachers, and students at Floodrock view them as second-class members of the school population. They worry that students who are not in a college prep track of classes are viewed as dumb and undesirable. In fact, there is some evidence that deans have encouraged troublemakers to enroll in SAVES so that they are away from Floodrock for at least part of the day.

- Over the last five years, students from SAVES have met with the principal and the superintendent on several occasions to complain about the way they have been disenfranchised. The administrators have taken no action to change school policy.

- Over the last five years, students from SAVES have pleaded with their fellow students to change the hour for announcements and assemblies, but the Student Council has ignored their requests.

- SAVES students have attempted to circulate a petition among the student body to protest their ill treatment, but they collected only a few signatures of students who did not attend SAVES.

Continues

Reflective Teaching, Reflective Learning edited by McCann, Johannessen, Kahn, Smagorinsky, and Smith (Heinemann: Portsmouth, NH); © 2005.

FIGURE 8–2 *Floodrock SAVES* (continued)

TESTIMONIES

- Adam Samuels, an eleventh-grade student who attends SAVES, observes, "We have to be more aggressive in getting what we want. Instead of just asking for fair treatment, we have to *demand* it. If the administration does not accommodate our reasonable demands, we need to take action. Petitions have done no good. We need to picket, boycott, and even sabotage some school events. These suggestions may seem pretty radical, but extreme circumstances call for extreme measures."

- Cornelius Wallace, the athletic director, notes, "Every student at SAVES chooses the program. No one forced any student to attend SAVES. Although students attend SAVES, they still participate fully in clubs and sports. The SAVES students have nothing to complain about. They have just what they want. In many ways, they enjoy advantages that the rest of the Floodrock students don't have."

- Dr. George King, the assistant principal, claims, "The students at SAVES have always been complaining. They have the same opportunities that all the other students at Floodrock have. They enjoy the benefit of our wonderful staff. We have to extend our resources to provide them with additional services in another facility. In many ways they have more benefits than the Floodrock student who doesn't go to SAVES."

- Beth Ross, a twelfth-grade student, says, "We might just as well have our own school at SAVES. I think most students take more pride in being associated with SAVES than with Floodrock. The education is probably better at SAVES because the facility is newer, the staff is younger, and the attitude is more progressive."

- Ms. Regina Smuggs, senior class advisor, points out, "I'm glad that a lot of the school's troublemakers go to SAVES. They don't contribute anything to the school. We are better off having them out of the building for at least part of the day. As far as I'm concerned, the kids who go to SAVES are losers."

- Jeff Thomessen insists, "We've done everything that a person could reasonably expect us to do to secure our rights as students at Floodrock. We've complained. We petitioned. We've protested. In every instance,

Continues

FIGURE 8–2 *Floodrock SAVES* (continued)

we were ignored by the administrators, the teachers, and the other students. The most disturbing thing is that our fellow students don't support us. We are *Floodrock* students, just like everyone else at the school. We should have as much say in the Student Council and how our money is spent as anyone else."

SALINE AREA VOCATIONAL EDUCATION SATELLITE FACT SHEET

- SAVES provides students with the use of state-of-the-art technology to train for careers in technical or vocational fields.

- SAVES serves students in a modern building, with attractive rooms and labs, in a comfortable, climate controlled environment.

- SAVES emphasizes learning by *doing*, which means that students are involved in hands-on experiences in their chosen field of study.

- SAVES provides a welcome environment for students, because it allows students to study areas about which they have a keen interest.

- SAVES serves 476 students from five area high schools.

- SAVES immerses students in a realistic and rich multicultural environment, with students representing sixty-seven nationalities and forty-three language groups.

- SAVES values diversity among the student population.

- SAVES attracts students who want to apply their learning in a particular career area: Students apply mathematics and science in metalworking, cosmetology, electronics, and woodworking. Students read in order to solve problems in printing, auto body, and auto mechanics. The students strengthen their understanding in core curriculum areas because they have immediate application for their learning.

- SAVES invites students to study the areas in which they plan to work: The training is practical and relevant.

- SAVES graduates enjoy a high rate of employment after graduation. Employers in the area recognize the value of training in the SAVES environment.

Reflective Teaching, Reflective Learning edited by McCann, Johannessen, Kahn, Smagorinsky, and Smith (Heinemann: Portsmouth, NH); © 2005.

FIGURE 8–2 *Floodrock SAVES* (continued)

TABLE 1
Enrollment Figures

	TOTAL	SAVES A.M.	SAVES P.M.
Floodrock High School	2027	——	203
Austin McGreal Memorial High School	1843	151	——
Elsah Heights High School	1254	147	——
Cypress Hills High School	2190	207	——
Williamson High School	2892	——	312

TABLE 2
Graduation Rates
Previous School Year

Floodrock H.S. Total	91%
Floodrock non-SAVES	93%
Floodrock SAVES	79%
SAVES Total	78%

TABLE 3
Floodrock High School
Bell Schedule

Period 1	7:50–8:40	
Period 2	8:45–9:35	
Period 3	9:40–10:30	
Period 4	10:35–11:00	Lunch
Period 5	11:05–11:30	Periods
Period 6	11:35–12:00	
Period 7	12:05–12:30	
Period 8	12:35–1:00	
Period 9	1:05–2:00	
Period 10	2:05–2:55	

Reflective Teaching, Reflective Learning edited by McCann, Johannessen, Kahn, Smagorinsky, and Smith (Heinemann: Portsmouth, NH); © 2005.

to follow. In order to support the recommendation, each speaker or writer will analyze the data to determine if there are any compelling problems that need to be corrected and if the problems can be corrected with minor adjustments within the system that is already in place. Here is a typical discussion that focuses on the case:

Teacher: Is there a problem at Floodrock High?

Bernice: Yeah.

Teacher: What's the problem?

Bernice: The SAVES kids don't get to hear the announcements.

Teacher: Why is that a problem? I know a lot of students here who don't pay any attention to announcements.

Russell: But if you want to listen to announcements and you can't, you could miss a lot of important stuff.

Teacher: What could be that important?

June: Like there might be some announcement about scholarships, and if you don't know you can't apply.

Teacher: So somebody might miss a scholarship opportunity. In some cases, this might make a difference in going to college. But is this *unfair*, like the students are claiming?

June: Yeah, it's unfair.

Teacher: But, *why*?

Emilio: Because everybody should have a chance to apply for the scholarship if it is available.

Teacher: So, you are insisting that as a general rule all students should have equal opportunity to learn about scholarships so that they can apply for the scholarships if they are eligible?

June: That's right. They are denied the opportunity to hear the information, and everyone should be able to get the information. And another thing, there could be announcements about practices or meetings, or about practice being canceled. They wouldn't know and could miss a ride or something.

The discussion continues to explore the many problems at the school. The students repeat various claims that the Floodrock students make about unfair treatment, they cite the available data, and they quote from the testimonies of the characters involved in the case as a means to provide details and substance to support the claims. As the discussion progresses, the teacher acknowledges the "facts" of the case but insists on some interpretation by asking the students to explain what the facts mean. As Smith (1984) points out, in prompting students to develop their arguments, the recurring questions are "Why?" and "So what?" One question asks the speaker to provide the *grounds* for making a claim. The other question asks the speaker to provide the *warrant* that interprets the data and links the data to the claim. In the discussion of the Floodrock case, students draw from their previous discussion of fairness for warrants that they use to interpret their claims. For example, if we put together the contributions of two or three speakers in the discussion, an argument looks like the following:

The SAVES students are being treated unfairly (claim). Every day they miss announcements. The announcements could provide valuable information about scholarships and could convey important messages about meetings and practices (data). This is wrong, because everyone should have equal access to the opportunities that are available in school (warrant).

While this argument is an essential part of the whole case analysis, the thinking about the case is not complete. Students also note the steps that the SAVES students took in the past to attempt to correct the problem (i.e., meetings, appeals, petitions), and they explore the set of contingencies that they might follow to try to correct the problems now. The recommendations for action range from picketing and boycotts to the ultimate action of separating from Floodrock and attending SAVES full time.

When students write their responses to the case, they typically include the following elements: the identification and interpretation of the grievances that the SAVES students have against the leadership of the school, the review of the previous attempts to correct the problems, and an assessment of the various courses of action the SAVES students might yet take to improve their situation. So the students have engaged in several discussions, large and small, and they have written a persuasive composition to argue for a particular policy. How then do these activities prepare students to write, discuss, and analyze the Declaration of Independence? Another question one might ask is this: Why would you want students to read the Declaration of Independence?

Let me answer the second question first. The reading of the Declaration of Independence would be particularly important in the context of an integrated, coherent unit of instruction that invites students to study several related works of literature organized around some broad overarching question, such as "What does it mean to be equal?" or "What does it mean to be fair?" In the context of the unit of instruction, the reading of the Declaration of Independence and the subsequent discussion about it can serve as a point of entry for the broader inquiry process.

Having worked through the fairness scenarios and having discussed the "Floodrock SAVES" case, students are equipped to discuss the Declaration of Independence from several angles. As Flanagan (1998) points out, it is useful to infuse the investigation of literature with conflict that suggests the importance of how we construct meaning from a text. One focus of discussion might be this question: If Jefferson offers the Declaration as a rationale for illegal action in breaking away from the established authority, to what extent are his arguments legitimate? With the appropriate preparation, students do refer to the specific abuses that Jefferson lists and note that the king's actions were unfair, according to their framework for judging fairness. Under another line of inquiry, the students can examine Jefferson's rhetorical strategy, because they have used a similar strategy in arguing for changes in the policies at Floodrock High School. Specifically, students note that Jefferson offers descriptions of the king's actions as evidence of the harms he has imposed on the colonists. The principles of fairness serve as warrants in interpreting the impact of the harms that Jefferson lists. In addition, students note the steps that the colonists have taken within the current conditions to correct the abuses before they have been moved to the radical action of revolution. Just as important, when the students empathize with the feelings of the SAVES students from Floodrock High, in a sense they have felt to some degree the outrage that the colonists would have felt in the time of Jefferson. It is not unusual for students to observe that Jefferson has written something like the documents that they have written themselves, and that his reasoning is similar to their own.

I have offered sample instructional activities here as a means to illustrate the idea that discussions in English classes are not necessarily disparate, unconnected experiences. In some classrooms, the discussions about complex concepts and significant texts build on one another, with each discussion serving as a scaffold for subsequent discussions, and with each discussion deepening and broadening students' understanding of concepts and texts. Enabling students to develop some habits of thinking analytically about what they have read and about the critical issues that derive from the literature is the result of teachers' strategic planning, which provides the connections between many discussions, all contributing to one big conversation.

References

APPLEBEE, A. 1996. *The Curriculum as Conversation.* Chicago: University of Chicago Press.

APPLEBEE, A., J. A. LANGER, M. NYSTRAND, AND A. GAMORAN. 2003. "Discussion-Based Approaches to Developing Understanding: Classroom Instruction and Student Performance in Middle and High School English." *American Educational Research Journal* 40 (3): 685–730.

FLANAGAN, J. 1998. "Using Multiple Perspectives to Foster Civil and Rational Discourse." *Illinois English Bulletin* 85 (Spring): 82–93.

HILLOCKS, G., JR. 1995. *Teaching Writing as Reflective Practice.* New York: Teachers College Press.

———. 1999. *Ways of Thinking, Ways of Teaching.* New York: Teachers College Press.

HILLOCKS, G., B. MCCABE, AND J. MCCAMPBELL, J. 1971. *The Dynamics of English Instruction: Grades 7–12.* New York: Random House.

JOHANNESSEN, L. R., E. KAHN, AND C. C. WALTER. 1982. *Designing and Sequencing Prewriting Activities.* Urbana, IL: ERIC/NCTE.

LANGER, JUDITH A. 2001. "Beating the Odds: Teaching Middle and High School Students to Read and Write Well." *American Educational Research Journal* 38 (4): 837–80.

MCCANN, T. M. 2003. "Imagine This: Using Scenarios to Promote Authentic Discussion." *English Journal* 92 (6): 31–39.

SMAGORINSKY, P. 2002. *Teaching English Through Principled Practice.* Upper Saddle River, NJ: Prentice Hall.

SMAGORINSKY, P., AND S. GEVINSON. 1989. *Fostering the Reader's Response: Rethinking the Literature Curriculum, Grades 7–12.* Palo Alto, CA: Dale Seymour.

SMAGORINSKY, P., T. MCCANN, AND S. KERN. 1987. *Explorations: Introductory Activities for Literature and Composition, 7–12.* Urbana, IL: ERIC/NCTE.

SMITH, M. W. 1984. *Reducing Writing Apprehension.* Urbana, IL: NCTE.

LITERATURE INSTRUCTION

9 Accepting the Challenge of Chevys
What My Research Means for My Teaching

MICHAEL W. SMITH
Temple University
Philadelphia, Pennsylvania

When I was coeditor of *Research in the Teaching of English*, I sent an issue of a journal, made up of studies set in elementary-school classrooms, to my daughter Rachel's third-grade teacher. I meant it as a collegial gesture, but I'm afraid Rachel's teacher didn't regard it as such. As I found out from a phone call the night she received the journal, she took it as an implied criticism of her teaching. She wondered what it was in her teaching that I wanted to change. If I didn't want her to change, she reasoned, why would I send her those studies?

I was initially surprised that Rachel's teacher took my gesture as criticism. But on reflection, I have to admit that I did hope that the research in that issue would lead to changes in how she thought about literacy education. This incident caused me to consider just how much my scholarly work has been motivated by the desire to change the things in schools that I think need changing; I write articles and give talks in the hope of fostering reform.

My most recent study on the literate lives of young men both in and out of school was undertaken for just that reason. My coauthor, Jeff Wilhelm, and I (Smith and Wilhelm 2002) undertook our project in response to a large body of research clearly establishing that boys underperform girls in academic literacy measures. In fact, as Newkirk (2000) points out, the gap between girls and boys in the United States is "comparable to the difference between whites and racial/ethnic groups that have suffered systematic social and economic discrimination in this country" (295). Newkirk's contention was borne out by our experience: When Jeff and I taught in our schools' lowest tracks, our classes were dominated by boys. But although those young men might have been in trouble in school, we knew that there were areas of their lives in which they were very surely not in trouble. They may have been athletes or gamers or mechanics or skaters or hunters, but they all were engaged in some activity in a way that would almost surely have brought them success in school had they been comparably engaged in their schoolwork. We wanted to understand why the boys were passionate about what they were passionate about and to see how that related to their literate activity both in and out of school. We suspected that our findings would challenge at least some of the conventional ways of doing business in schools. What we didn't suspect was how our discoveries would challenge our own practice.

Having done the research on young men, I find myself in the uncomfortable position Rachel's teacher was in. Although our findings provide support for much of what I have done as a teacher and a teacher-educator, they have also challenged my teaching practices in important ways. In this chapter I explore both those areas of support and those challenges in the hope that it will be helpful to others who are thinking about their own curricular and instructional decisions. Because George Hillocks' work is the foundation for so much of my own, I'll use his writing as a touchstone when I describe our study and what it means for me as a teacher.

A Quick Description

We worked with forty-nine boys in four very different sites: an urban high school made up almost entirely of African American and Puerto Rican students; a diverse comprehensive regional suburban high school; a rural school; and a private all-boys school. About one-third of our boys had been high achievers in school, one-third had been average achievers, and one-third had had a more troubled school history.

We collected four different kinds of data. First, we asked the boys to rank their favorite activities using the survey in Figure 9–1. Then we interviewed them about their responses. This interview was designed to help us understand the qualities of activities that boys find pleasurable and the extent to which they attribute those qualities to reading. We collected activity interviews from all forty-nine boys. Second, we asked them to keep a log of all of their reading, writing, listening, and viewing, both in school and out, for three months. Although not all our boys kept the log for all three months, we conducted reading log interviews with forty-six boys. Third, we asked them to read and respond to profiles of young men who took up or rejected literate activity in different ways: for example, a rapper who loved word play but who avoided schoolwork, a fix-it man who read manuals as needed, a committed reader who took regular trips to the library. Finally, we also asked them to do think-aloud protocols on four stories. We used stories of a similar theme that vary in terms of the gender of the main character and whether the story is more plot-driven or character-driven.

What We Discovered

Because we were interested in understanding why the boys enjoyed what they enjoyed outside school, we had to look beyond educational research for a lens that might have explanatory power. Our searching for work that explained passionate engagements led us to the research of Mihalyi Csikszentmihalyi (1990) and his discussion of *flow* experiences—those experiences that are so fulfilling that one loses track of time while one is engaged in them. We found that the features of flow

FIGURE 9-1 *Activity Ranking Sheet*

Activity Ranking Sheet

Please rank the following activities in the order of your liking of them. Put a 1 next to the activity you like most, down to a 14 for the activity you like least.

_____ Listening to music

_____ Hanging out with friends

_____ Playing sports

_____ Playing video games

_____ Doing something mechanical, like fixing an engine

_____ Drawing, painting, or cartooning

_____ Reading a good book

_____ Watching a favorite sports team on TV or at the stadium

_____ Surfing the Net

_____ Learning something new about a topic that interests me

_____ Working on a hobby (Please specify your hobby_____
_____)

_____ Going to school

_____ Watching television or going to the movies

_____ Other (Please specify_____)

Reflective Teaching, Reflective Learning edited by McCann, Johannessen, Kahn, Smagorinsky, and Smith (Heinemann: Portsmouth, NH); © 2005.

experiences described by Csikszentmihalyi resonated both with the boys' and with our own personal experience.

Csikszentmihalyi provides eight characteristics of flow experiences that we think can be usefully collapsed into four themes: the importance of competence and control; the importance of an appropriate challenge; the importance of clear goals and immediate feedback, and the importance of focusing on the immediate. These four themes—as well as one additional theme that emerged from our conversations with the boys, the importance of the social—go a long way to explain why boys like to do what they like to do and why they embrace some literate activities and reject other literate activities. As a consequence, they have been an extremely useful guide for me as I have examined my own teaching.

The Importance of Competence and Control

Csikszentmihalyi (1990) argues that people in the modern world are often buffeted by forces that are beyond them. That's why people gravitate to those activities in which they feel competent and over which they feel they have control, activities during which "entropy is suspended" (61). That's true for me. I love to play tennis because I'm pretty good at it. I've given up playing golf because I just can't manage to hit the ball straight.

We saw a similar dynamic at work when the boys talked about what they liked to do. One of them put the theme in a nutshell when he explained why lacrosse was his favorite sport: "I just like being good at it." The boys' literate activity outside of school was marked by a similar desire for competence. For example, the boys in our study read to deepen an area of existing competence rather than to develop new ones. Reading may be able to take you anywhere, but the boys in our study read to return to familiar destinations. This is how one of them put it: "I just like to learn about stuff that, you know, I kinda like to learn a little more about. I already know something, so I want to know more."

Again, their experience resonates with mine and I suspect it will with yours as well. I turn to the sports page first thing every morning because I enjoy sports and know about them. I know that it would be good for me to know more about financial issues but I never read the business page. When I'm reading about sports, I'm an expert. When I'm reading about business, I'm a novice. Like the boys, I much prefer being an expert.

What was true for boys in their out-of-school reading was also true for their in-school reading, and their desire for competence had unfortunate consequences. Most notably, the young men in our study tended to reject activities if they didn't feel competent in them. One young man put it this way: "I'd rather say reading is stupid than maybe have to admit that I might be stupid."

Sadly, only one of the forty-nine boys in our study talked about how a teacher helped him become more competent:

> I haven't started reading until this year pretty much.... I have been starting novels this year because of Mrs._____ kinda like assigns the homework and this is the only time it's really been due so I've been reading pretty good novels now and I like John Steinbeck and stuff. A lot of novels like that get to me and Mrs. _____ 's been kinda showing me the road and the path. I kinda thought reading was dumb, but now I'm kinda getting more into it.

This sad state of affairs is something that George Hillocks has been working against for his entire professional career. This is how he put it more than thirty years ago (Hillocks, McCabe, and McCampbell 1971):

> Assigning tasks is appropriate only when the students already know how to do those tasks.... The real question is how we can teach so that the students can learn how to do the tasks they cannot already do. How can the English teacher

create an environment and a sequence of experiences in which the student becomes increasingly sophisticated as reader, writer, listener, speaker, and above all, thinker? (xi–xii)

As this book indicates, Hillocks and his students, myself among them, have been seeking answers to this question through the development of prereading and prewriting instruction and through the use of sensible sequencing that encourages students to develop increasingly sophisticated understandings and abilities as they engage in similar issues over time.

Although Hillocks has been a leading figure, perhaps *the* leading figure, in literacy education when it comes to understanding how to help students develop their competence before assigning academic tasks, he seems to me to have paid less attention to the other half of our first major finding: the importance of control. As a student of his, I thought it was my job to create contexts that would help students to perform better on and to enjoy more the reading and writing I assigned. Our research pointed out that I need to think harder about how to create contexts that would allow students to exercise more choice in the work we did.

The young men in our study embraced those few occasions in which they could exercise even limited choice in their literate activity in school. For the most part, this choice was relegated to choosing a particular topic on which to write within a very circumscribed topic area: for example, choosing what animal to research in a unit on animals. None of the boys reported being allowed to choose reading materials as part of the curricula for their English/Language Arts classes. This state of affairs, I'm afraid to say, would have been true in my classes as well.

Ironically, it would have been true for good reason. Because I was interested in developing students' competence, I built my units around a set of strategies, tools, or key questions that they could employ again and again with increasingly sophisticated texts. For example, I embedded our reading of *Julius Caesar*, a required text in our tenth-grade curriculum, into a unit on *power*. My students and I asked the following key questions in a number of short stories that we read before we began the play: What was the person's goal in seeking power? What were the means by which the person came to power? What was the effect of the person's having been in power? I thought that asking these questions would encourage students to think broadly about the texts in the unit and give them a focus for their reading of Shakespeare. Indeed, their consideration of these questions fostered engaging discussions about, for example, whether the ends justified the means in a story we were reading or who was the most admirable character in the play.

My experience jibes with research by Applebee, Burroughs, and Stevens (2000) that establishes the importance of what they call coherence. They argue that the most powerful (and rarest) curricula are those in which students' knowledge can be carried from one textual experience to the next, curricula designed to promote learning across a sequence that can be seen as a coherent whole. The question then becomes, How can we tap the power of choice while maintaining the power of coherence?

Jeff has used our research to urge me to think about unit questions in a different way. Instead of building a unit around a set of key questions, he believes that teachers should build units around inquiry questions. By inquiry questions he means questions that address human issues of fundamental import. Such big questions are necessarily messy and complicated and one can only think hard about them by employing a wide range of information. And here's where control comes in. Imagine what would have happened had my unit been built around this question: "Does power corrupt?" My class and I could have taken up that question through our reading of *Julius Caesar* and the short stories and poems that we read. But students would have been able to enlist other texts in their inquiries: news stories about the trial of Dennis Kozlowski, Tyco's chief executive, or about Bill Gates' philanthropy; an interview in *Vibe* with Suge Knight, the head of Death Row records; and on and on. As Jeff points out, to engage such a question, class members would have to be invited to bring in texts of their own choosing.

But that doesn't mean I would have had to give up my desire to give students something they could take from text to text. Making room for students to choose doesn't mean I can't exercise choice as well. I could still have created a framework that sequenced those texts I chose so that students could build their understanding from text to text. But if that framework had room for texts the students selected, and if their selections would tend to come from newspapers, magazines, movies, songs, and so on, I could have enhanced their appreciation for reading even as my students and I thought seriously about the issue of transfer. We could have coupled our inquiry on power with an inquiry on reading strategies and asked, "Which strategies work across texts and which ones seem specific to reading literature?" We could have worked together to determine whether it means the same thing to read between the lines in a news story as it does in a short story. We could have tested whether our understanding of subtext was equally applicable to the dialogue in a play as it was to an interview.

My point here is simply this: I thought it was my job to foster students' engagement in and understanding of texts I had selected. Our data have helped me see that as well-intentioned as my efforts were, I should have taken them a step further by creating a context that encouraged students to bring in texts of their choice as our class pursued its common project.

The Importance of an Appropriate Challenge

Csikszentmihalyi (1990) argues that flow experiences come "at a very specific point: when the opportunities for action perceived by the individual are equal to his or her capabilities" (52). We think this characteristic of flow explains the attraction of video games. Video games are designed so that as the player gets better the game gets harder. As one of the young men in our study explained, that's the source of their enjoyment:

> James Bond, when you first play, um, it's OK and then I think the thing that really sucks you into it is there is a lot of hard levels and there are a lot of things that you can do.

Once again, the boys' experience resonates with mine. My kids received a driving video game for a Christmas present. I'm completely overmatched by it. I can't even get the car to go forward. So I feel no impulse to play it. On the other hand, they enjoy it and delight in seeing their scores improve. But if they were to master it, they'd quickly get bored. (When's the last time you enjoyed playing a game of tic-tac-toe?)

What is true for video games seems equally true for the boys reading in school. The challenge that a book provides has to be appropriate. The boys didn't want easy books, but they wanted ones they felt they had a chance to understand. Here's how one of them put it:

> I like a book that isn't, isn't easy but is not so difficult that you don't under-stand what is going on. Because if you are reading a book that doesn't make sense to you then you just, you know, "Well I don't know how to read this" and then you have negative attitude and you don't concentrate and you don't really gain anything from the experience.

Unfortunately, school, especially in the upper grades, frequently offers students challenges that may well be beyond them. Think, for example, of the traditional chronological arrangement of American and British literature classes in which many of the most difficult texts come at the beginning of the semester. Starting a semester with *Beowulf* seems somewhat akin to a ski guide encouraging a novice skier to start with the Black Diamond run.

I am a good reader. I have "the ability to translate words into images, to empathize with fictional characters, to recognize historical and cultural contexts, to anticipate turns of the plot, to criticize and evaluate the author's style, and so on" (Csikszentmihalyi 1990, 50). But I know the frustration I feel when I encounter a text that I feel is beyond me. My book club read Ralph Ellison's *Juneteenth*. And as much as I loved *Invisible Man*, throughout my reading of *Juneteenth*, I was thinking that that book was written for someone much smarter than me. Had it not been something we were going to talk about in the book club I would have put it down and I'll admit that much of my reading was perfunctory at best. The book was simply too hard.

Hillocks has long recognized the importance of providing students with an appropriate challenge. Here's how he put it back at a time when some schools had Thackeray in the curriculum (Hillocks, McCabe, and McCampbell 1971):

> Selections used to introduce concepts should be relatively free of problems that the students have not learned to handle previously. If the teacher can think of no other vehicle for the introduction of imagery than *King Lear*, he [or she] should probably abandon the idea of teaching imagery. Fortunately, in most of the conceptual areas of literature there is a wealth of simple mate-rial available. . . .

If we ask poor readers to fight through *The Return of the Native*, they are likely to have little reward for their efforts despite whatever critical and pedagogical stature it might have. Although *Johnny Tremain* and *The Bronze Bow* are not such great historical fiction as *A Tale of Two Cities* or *Henry Esmond*, they undoubtedly will offer a great deal more to certain students at certain points in their development than will novels by Dickens or Thackeray. (292)

The principle of creating sensible sequences that move from the familiar to the less familiar and from the simpler to the more complex resounds throughout Hillocks' writing. He convinced me of the importance of sensible sequencing, so as a teacher I worked to include literary texts in my units that were appropriately challenging. I think my students benefited from my efforts.

But what I didn't do was question the primacy of literature. Our study made it clear that the texts the boys found most engaging tended not to be literary. The boys read newspapers and magazines and comics and Internet sites. These were the texts they found appropriately challenging. I didn't include them in my classes, or if I did, I used them not as objects of study and discussion in their own right but rather as bridges to the literature with which I was more concerned. Our study has caused me to think harder about employing a far wider array of texts than I had in the past.

For example, when I taught American literature, we developed a unit on the American dream. My thinking went something like this: "We have *The Autobiography of Benjamin Franklin*, and *The Great Gatsby*, and *Death of a Salesman* in the book room. Hmm, maybe I could put these texts together into a unit on the American dream." But what if I started differently, something like this: "My kids are thinking about going to college or starting a career. Might be a good time for them to think hard about their dreams for the future. Let me see, what texts speak to the issue of the dreams people have, what they do to achieve them, and what might keep those dreams from being achieved?" If I started that way, I'd quickly think of a much wider array of texts: hip-hop songs; recent movies such as *Working Girl*, a comedy that focuses on a secretary's efforts to join the ranks of heavy hitters in mergers and acquisitions; episodes of *Family Ties*; nonfiction such as *A Hope in the Unseen: An American Odyssey from the Inner City to the Ivy League*. Maybe John Edwards' stump speech. And *Ben*. And *Gatsby*. And *Death*. Just by changing my starting point, I'd be likely to provide my students a much wider variety of texts.

Clear Goals and Immediate Feedback

Csikszentmihalyi puts it simply: "The reason it is possible to achieve such complete involvement in a flow experience is that goals are usually clear, and feedback immediate" (1990, 54). Once again, Csikszentmihalyi's research resonates with my experience. One reason that cooking is appealing to me is that it provides the kind of immediate feedback that my writing does not. I make a dish and it either tastes good or it doesn't. I don't have to wait months for a judgment as I do with my scholarly writing.

Similarly, the boys gravitated toward activities that provided them clear goals and immediate feedback, as one of them explains in his discussion of why he likes weightlifting:

> Yeah, like, I mean, no pain, no gain. There has been times when I work out so hard that I can barely pick up an apple to eat. I'm in so much pain, but I like the way I look at the end. I look all pumped up and everything, and uh, I feel good. And actually, I feel, I look bigger. I like that.

This young man was alone among the boys in being a weightlifter, but many of the boys were actively involved in sports and games. By their very nature, sports and games provide clear goals and immediate feedback: You win a point or lose it, get to the next level of a video game or crash and burn. Even those boys who were not involved in sports or games enjoyed activities that provided goals and feedback of a similar sort. Several of the boys were musicians. Some were artists. In each of these cases the activity provides the same kind of goals and feedback that sports and games do.

The boys' literate activity was also often informed by clear goals and often provided immediate feedback. Many of the boys read to gain information. When Mark checked the Internet to get a hockey score, simply finding out the score was a clear measure of his success. When the boys got a joke in *The Simpsons* or figured out whodunit in the latest thriller, their viewing was successful.

But the boys didn't see the purpose of their reading and writing in school. Here's an exchange that Jeff had with one of them:

Jeff: Why do you have to [read Shakespeare]? Why do schools make you do it, if everybody's frustrated, and nobody gets it?
Young Man: I really—there's really no answer to that question I can think of right now. They have us do it, but I really have no idea, but they're obviously doing it for a reason; I'm not going to just sit here with a grudge and not do it.

There has to be a reason. He's just not sure what it could be.

Hillocks has long been a champion of clear goals and immediate feedback. In *Teaching Writing as Reflective Practice* (1995), he offers a succinct explanation of one of the major features of the kind of instruction he endorses: "The approaches to teaching that seemed to have the most powerful effects on student writing, as revealed by the synthesis mentioned earlier... always had clear, specific objectives" (58). He offers an equally compelling argument for the importance of clear objectives in the teaching of literature. As any of his students will tell you, he constantly pushed us to offer a rationale both for the texts we selected and the way that we taught those texts.

But because our emphasis was literature, we often did not select texts that provided immediate feedback by their very nature. Rabinowitz (1987) offers a compelling argument that works of literature are canonized by virtue of the kind of interpretive activity they invite and reward. Densely structured, highly nuanced texts call for a kind of close reading that we as English majors both enjoy and are good at. These texts let us do a certain kind of teacherly work as we help students come to grips with their interpretive demands.

But reading texts that are informational, or angry, or funny, or visual doesn't allow that kind of teacherly work. As a consequence, I didn't include much of it when I taught. I've said, "Well, if I let them read (you can fill in the blank), they wouldn't need me." And as a teacher I wanted to help. What our research has helped me to see is that my desire to play the teacher may have kept my students from experiencing the kinds of texts that made me a reader.

A Focus on the Immediate

Csikszentmihalyi (1990) notes that when an "activity is thoroughly engrossing, there is not enough attention left over to allow a person to consider either the past or the future" (62). Here's how one yachtsman explained his enjoyment of his sport: "So one forgets oneself, one forgets everything, seeing only the play of the boat with the sea" (62).

One of our informants offered a startlingly similar description of the allure of video games:

> Say you're having a problem with someone or whatever. You play a video game or it's like a shooting game or airplane flying game. You have to take the mission. That helps you take your mind off the stuff that's going on in your life, and you just, for that ten or twenty—for however long you play the game—it helps you forget that. It helps you relieve your mind from that and focus yourself on the game.

Having a flow experience means being in the moment. We seek flow experiences not for what they will bring us but rather for the quality of experience we enjoy while we are having them. I play tennis because I love to play tennis not because it will make me fit. I might choose to exercise to become more fit in order to improve my tennis game. But while I have flow experiences playing tennis, I never have them while exercising.

Hillocks has long been an advocate for focusing on the moment. He wants teachers to help students become better readers and writers in the future. But he doesn't lose sight of the importance of the here and now. He puts it quite simply: "Perhaps the most important principle in designing and sequencing is to ensure that the students enjoy doing the work" (1995, 180).

In my own teaching I'm afraid I sometimes lost track of the here and now. In my efforts to design carefully sequenced units, I'm afraid that sometimes I sacrificed the fun of reading a text for its instrumental value in advancing a unit concept. Rather than, say, enjoying the delicious moment at which a reader recognizes the irony in a text, I'm afraid that I may have worried too much that students articulated the strategies that informed their understanding (cf. Smith 1989, 1992). The desire to write a coherent and carefully sequenced curriculum may not have to stand in conflict with the enjoyment of a text for its own sake; for me, at least, it sometimes did.

The Importance of the Social

Although Csikszentmihalyi (1990) mentions that socializing is "universally enjoyable" (50), he doesn't develop this line of thought throughout his book and indeed many of his examples are drawn from solitary activities. But for the boys in our study, being social was critically important. Far from the alienated figure portrayed in the boys-in-trouble genre of the popular press, every one of our participants was part of a circle of one or two or three or sometimes more intimate friends. And their relationships with these friends were of the utmost importance to them. One of them put it this way: "It's always better with friends—always."

The boys' literate activity outside of school was profoundly affected by their socialness. One young man shared his poems with a group of friends. Another was engaged with his friends in elaborate role-playing games that took enormous amounts of reading and writing. One read only one book a year: *Of Mice and Men*. He read it because his older brother, with whom he lived, gave it to him. One hated to volunteer in school but was willing to speak in front of his whole church congregation because in school it "seemed like nobody's really paying attention. They're talking to somebody else. And in church, it seems like more people pay attention to what you're doing."

Hillocks has again been in the forefront of promoting instruction that is in line with what the young men in our study seemed to be looking for, instruction designed both to take advantage of and to foster students' social relationships. He put it this way (Hillocks 1995): "Peer-group discussion or collaborative talk, usually in small groups, is the second essential feature, perhaps the *sine qua non*, of what I have called environmental teaching" (64). The other chapters in this volume provide ample illustration of how central small-group discussion is to his approach.

There were very few days in my classes in which students were not engaged with each other in small-group discussions. And I worked hard to build a social dimension into other work that we did. We sent our writing to other classes. I tried to make the author we read come alive so that we could talk back to them. I designed activities that helped make students at least provisionally regard the characters about whom they read as people worthy of their attention and concern.

But there was one set of social relationships that I didn't sufficiently draw on: the students' relationships to their families. To be sure I kept in close touch with families. I sent home letters introducing myself and my curricula. I made more than my share of phone calls, both to share congratulations and worries. But I didn't mine students' funds of knowledge (Moll and Greenberg 1990) the way I might have.

Imagine how much it would add to a discussion of *Pygmalion* to have first-generation Americans interview their immigrant parents about how their language use has affected their social mobility. Imagine how much it would have enriched my unit on power to have students interview their parents about how they encountered power in their workplaces or what qualities they thought made for a good boss. The possibilities are endless. I wish I had taken better advantage of them.

When I test my teaching against what we learned from our study, I realize I can't be content with what I've done. I've been thinking of how to strike a balance between helping students become more competent and offering them a greater degree of control. I've been questioning more and more the primacy of the kind of literature I tended to teach. I've been working with the preservice teachers I teach to devise ways to make parents a more valued resource than I made them.

Change is hard. When I taught, I had anthologies filled with canonical literature and years of lesson plans that I would have to leave behind to put the research we did into practice. I still have lesson plans and my university students are going out to teach in schools that have updated versions of those same anthologies to work with. I have to work against the very title of one of my courses, Teaching Literature, to enact the expanded conception of textuality the young men in our study taught us. But those young men's passionate engagement in literate activity when the conditions of flow were present convinces me that that hard work will be well worth the effort.

References

APPLEBEE, A. N., R. BURROUGHS, AND A. S. STEVENS. 2000. "Shaping Conversations: A Study of Continuity and Coherence in High School Literature Curricula." *Research in the Teaching of English* 34: 396–429.

CSIKSZENTMIHALYI, M. 1990. *Flow: The Psychology of Optimal Experience.* New York: Harper & Row.

HILLOCKS, G., JR. 1995. *Teaching Writing as Reflective Practice.* New York: Teachers College Press.

HILLOCKS, G., JR., B. MCCABE, AND J. MCCAMPBELL. 1971. *The Dynamics of English Instruction, Grades 7–12.* New York: Random House.

MOLL, L. C., AND J. B. GREENBERG. 1990. "Creating Zones of Possibilities: Combining Social Contexts for Instruction." In *Vygotsky and Education: Instructional Implications and Applications of Sociohistorical Psychology*, edited by L. C. Moll, 319–48. New York: Cambridge University Press.

NEWKIRK, T. 2000. "Misreading Masculinity: Speculations on the Great Gender Gap in Writing." *Language Arts* 77 (8): 294–300.

RABINOWITZ, P. 1987. *Before Reading: Narrative Conventions and the Politics of Interpretation.* Ithaca, NY: Cornell University Press.

SMITH, M. W. 1989. "Teaching the Interpretation of Irony in Poetry." *Research in the Teaching of English* 23: 254–72.

———. 1992. "The Effects of Direct Instruction in Understanding Unreliable Narrators." *Journal of Educational Research* 85: 339–47.

SMITH, M. W., AND J. WILHELM. 2002. *"Reading Don't Fix No Chevys": Literacy in the Lives of Young Men.* Portsmouth, NH: Heinemann.

10

Reading Level Response
Helping Students Write About Literature

DECLAN FITZPATRICK
Ladue Horton Watkins High School
St. Louis, Missouri

It was my first year in the classroom and the long-awaited Chicago spring had finally arrived. Faced with teaching *Lord of the Flies* to my sophomore English students, I felt overwhelmed and frustrated. How could I get them to *want* to write about this novel in ways that would help them grow as readers and writers? After trying many different approaches, I turned to "reading inventories," a set of questions developed by Hillocks (1980; Hillocks and Ludlow 1984) to reveal how well students make inferences and generalizations in relation to their reading. These questions begin with requests for literal information and go on to ask students for more difficult inferences and abstractions.

For instance, take Kurt Vonnegut's short story "Harrison Bergeron," set in a dystopian future America in which everyone is made equal by forcing those with advantages to assume physical and mental "handicaps." Here's the first paragraph:

> The year was 2081, and everybody was finally equal. They weren't only equal before God and the law. They were equal in every which way. Nobody was smarter than anybody else. Nobody was better looking than anybody else. Nobody was stronger or quicker than anybody else. All this equality was due to the 211th, 212th, and 213th Amendments to the Constitution, and to the unceasing vigilance of agents of the United States Handicapper General.

The main characters, George and Hazel Bergeron, wearing heavy weights and distracted by radios implanted in their ears, watch television impassively while their son, Harrison, breaks into the TV station. Harrison proceeds to throw off his handicaps on live television and rebel against Diana Moon Glampers, the Handicapper General, and her H-G enforcers by dancing with a ballerina. An early question in the sequence might ask for basic stated information: "How intelligent are George and Hazel?" A mid-level inference might be required in a question about a complex implied relationship: "What does George and Hazel's reaction to what Diana Moon Glampers does to Harrison tell you about the government's influence on their thinking?" A more sophisticated structural generalization is sought in the question, "How do George and Hazel change from the beginning of the story to the end? What is the author saying through the development of these characters?" (Smagorinsky and Gevinson 1989, 78).

Hillocks encourages teachers to use responses to a reading inventory to evaluate students' ability to make inferences. This knowledge can suggest both the kinds of texts that are appropriate to read and the kinds of instruction that would benefit students most. I decided to adapt the reading inventory as a tool for guiding writing in response to literature. My goal was to provide all students with meaningful ways to write about fiction, no matter their current level of readiness. I wanted students to be able to judge the complexity of their own ideas about a story and to suggest "next steps" for developing and deepening those ideas. I wanted students to focus on a specific passage and to explain how that passage was significant to their understanding of the story. Since a passage may be significant to a student for very simple or very complex reasons, any response supported with evidence from the text was a good response.

Since that first year in the classroom, I have continued to tinker with this response tool, which I have named Reading Level Response (RLR). The RLR prompts give students a way to assess and increase the complexity of their responses without directing them toward a specific reading of the text. My goals are to validate my students' personal responses and to help them articulate those responses at increasingly complicated levels.

RLR comprises seven types of prompts representing seven levels of interpretation (see Figure 10–1). The first three levels are based on information directly stated in the text. Levels 4 through 7 are based on information that has not been directly stated. All seven levels are important for a rich response to the story, but each level requires more information, more abstraction, and a greater ability to make an inference.

Context for Using RLR

The RLR is a means to many of the things English teachers are asked to do: use portfolios for assessment; differentiate instruction based on student readiness; allow students to self-select and guide their own progress; challenge every student; provide every student with opportunities for success; provide fast, meaningful feedback; assess whether students are learning what they've been taught; teach strategies for coping with different levels of difficulty; help students learn to learn; encourage independent performance; and gather data to guide professional development.

I use RLR in the context of thematic units designed around issues I think are relevant to my students' lives. (See Hillocks, McCabe, and McCambell 1971, Smagorinsky and Gevinson 1989, and Smagorinsky 2002 for extended discussions and illustrations of thematic or "conceptual" units of instruction.) It is important to understand that RLR is *not* the centerpiece of my teaching. Rather, it is a device I use to help students engage with the unit themes and feel competent about their analytical abilities. In other words, RLR works *in service of* more satisfying, better

FIGURE 10–1 *Reading Level Response Guide*

Reading Level Response Guide

LEVEL	READING INVENTORY PROMPTS	WHAT RESPONSES AT THIS LEVEL DO
1 Basic Stated Information	How well does the doctor know this family? How long has the child been sick? What does the doctor need to do to find out if the child has diphtheria?	Restate important information: • Who, what, where, or when • Character information • Action
2 Key Details	Why do they suspect she has diphtheria? What does the doctor's exam reveal? What are the effects of diphtheria infection?	Distinguish between important and irrelevant information. Identify facts that have the greatest impact on the plot: • Change the course of the story • Big revelations
3 Stated Relationships	Why don't the parents speak much at first? Why does the father's participation make it hard to complete the exam? What does the narrator say are his reasons for continuing with the exam?	Reexplain a connection stated in the text: • Cause or effect • Similarity or contrast • Reason why
4 Simple Implied Relationships	Why is the child so resistant to being examined? How does the mother contribute to the child's fear and discomfort?	Explain the implication of a particular statement in the text: • Unstated cause or effect • Unstated judgment of a character • Motivation for a single action
5 Complex Implied Relationships	How does the doctor's attitude toward the child change throughout the story? Use details and/or examples from the story in your answer.	Demonstrate the implied connection between several details from various places in the text. Generalize about a major change in a character. Generalize about implied comparisons or contrasts.
6 Author's Generalization	How does the story suggest what causes might bring otherwise reasonable people to use violence against a child? Use details and/or examples from the story in your answer.	Support a generalization about the world using evidence from the text. Apply the generalizations suggested in the text to the world. Demonstrate the implications of the author's representation of the world.
7 Structural Generalization	Explain the significance of the title of the story. Use details and/or examples from the story in your answer.	Support a generalization about the purpose of literary elements used in the story. Explain how the author's generalization is supported by the structure of the story. Connect literary techniques to the generalization about the world.

Note: The illustrative prompts pertain to William Carlos Williams' "The Use of Force."

Reflective Teaching, Reflective Learning edited by McCann, Johannessen, Kahn, Smagorinsky, and Smith (Heinemann: Portsmouth, NH); © 2005.

informed reading experiences with texts selected to resonate with important life themes: the journey, coming of age, peer pressure, self-reliance, courageous action, and many more. Furthermore, I'm aware that the literary analysis elicited by RLR, while central to the college prep curriculum, is only one in a range of response possibilities. Students' personal, creative, and constructive responses are also important.

RLR in the Classroom

Whenever I give students a reading assignment, I ask them to respond in writing. Writing about reading nearly every day encourages *active* reading. The guidelines I provide relative to this daily writing are shown in Figure 10–2.

I do not grade every response every time. When I tried to, I was crushed under the weight of the daily grading. I find that I can keep track of students' progress by skimming each student's response each day. I want the students to think of their responses as works in progress that do not have to look polished. When I want to evaluate an entire set of responses, I give the students some time to peer-edit and write a more polished draft that reflects both their initial responses and any additional insights gained from class activities.

The entire process is designed to encourage students to use textual support in their writing and in their discussions. I find RLR useful both when everyone is reading the same text and when students are reading self-selected novels—especially ones I have never read myself. Although I may not be aware of the specific details, I can judge whether a student is using them to support judgments, inferences, and generalizations at an appropriate level.

Preparing Students for RLR

I model all the response levels using a story we have read together and with which students are therefore familiar. I teach them about the increasing complexity demanded at each level by using the analogy that reading and understanding a story is like putting together a puzzle. The illustrations that follow are for the story "Snow," from *How the Garcia Girls Lost Their Accents* by Julia Alvarez (1991).

Level 1: Basic Stated Information

Goal: To demonstrate knowledge of the basic facts (who, what, where, and when) of the story.

A Good Response Will: Repeat the basics of the story, such as character information, action, setting, who, what, where.

Sample RLR Beginnings

"What we know so far is..."

"The setting of the story is..."

FIGURE 10–2 *Reading Level Response Guidelines*

Reading Level Response Guidelines

FREQUENCY

Every time you have an independent reading assignment in this class, you also have a writing assignment. The goal is for you to begin to develop your ideas about what is important or worth paying attention to by writing a focused response to the reading before you come to class. I hope our class discussions will be better developed and more focused because you will each have prepared a response for class each day.

BASIC REQUIREMENTS

- At least one-hundred words
- Name, class, date
- Title of response
- Title of work read
- (Attempted) reading level

COMMON ELEMENTS

Each response must:

- *Identify a focus*—focus on a single specific passage. The tighter the focus, the better the response is likely to be.
- *Create a context*—provide information about the circumstances surrounding the focus of the response. You must find a way to indicate:
  - Who, what, where
  - Where the passage fits in the plot
  - Source of any specific information
- *Express an opinion*—state your own opinion about the significance of the passage on which you focus.
- *Include a quotation*—use a quotation to support your opinion about the significance.

COMPLEXITY

The complexity of your response must be appropriate to your analytical reading level. Your responses should get more complex as the quarter continues.

EXAMPLE

Level 3 Response: pp. 20–35 of *Lord of the Flies*—At the beginning of the chapter, "Beast from Water," the boys have been on the island for several weeks. A ship has passed the island without finding them, because the fire went out. While he is planning what to say at the meeting, Ralph notices that his clothes are dirty and his hair keeps getting in his eyes. This is important, because it emphasizes that things are starting to fall apart. Their meetings are more chaotic, and the boys aren't following the rules that they set anymore. "With a convulsion of the mind, Ralph discovered dirt and decay, understood how much he disliked perpetually flicking the tangled hair out of his eyes..." (77). Ralph is beginning to notice how much effort it takes to maintain the normal civilization that we take for granted.

"The main characters are..."

"What happened in the story was..."

"The narrator of the story is..."

Reading Level 1 Kernels from "Snow"

Yolanda is an immigrant.

Yolanda is the narrator.

The story is set in New York City.

Yolanda is learning to speak English.

Information about the characters, their actions, and the setting helps readers construct the story in their heads and follow what is going on. I ask students working on this type of response to emphasize information that is important no matter which part of the story is being considered: If they were to draw a single picture to illustrate the central action of the story, who would be doing what? where? In the following example, a student provides the basic information necessary to follow the story "Raymond's Run" by Toni Cade Bambara:

> Throughout the story a boy name Raymond gets taken care of by his big sister. Her and Raymond goes for a run..."she takes her running seriously..." (p. 49). She runs with Raymond beside her. She doesn't mind Raymond playing like he is driving a stage coach, she just hopes that he doesn't interrupt her breathing exercises. Raymond gets annoying sometimes for his sister for what she has to put up with when it comes to him. It's a lot of responsibility and it causes Raymond's sister to get frustrated and agrivated.

Many students working at this level are tempted to summarize everything they know about the story. Even the process of identifying and selecting a specific moment within the text is a complex skill that requires practice. In the preceding response the student describes the relationship between the narrator and her brother as revealed in the beginning paragraphs of the story.

Level 2: Key Details

Goal: To distinguish between more important and less important information; to identify the information that has the greatest impact on the plot of the story.

A Good Response Will: Identify the information that is essential to the plot; this information is clearly stated and obvious, changes the course of the story, or provides a big revelation.

Sample RLR Beginnings

"The main event in the story so far is ..."

"The event that got the story moving was . . ."

"One detail that is important is . . ."

"An important thing to remember about the main character is . . ."

Reading Level 2 Kernels from "Snow"

Russian missiles are being assembled in Cuba.

Yolanda thinks the snow is nuclear fallout.

When I introduce this level of response, I ask the students to think of the information required as the corner pieces of the puzzle: There are very few of them, but they mark out the boundaries of the picture being created. In the same way, a response of this type focuses on an event that is fundamental to the outcome of the plot. Questions that might prompt a response of this type include *what events change the course of the story?* and *what information changes the reader's understanding of the story?*

When students struggle with this level of response, I ask them to begin with the conclusion of the story and decide which events had to happen in order to arrive at that point. I have them read a text that has a very specific ending or outcome, often a fable or a story with a surprise ending, and ask them to list all the events that must happen in order to arrive at that conclusion. For the story of the turtle and the banquet in the sky, retold in Chinua Achebe's *Things Fall Apart* (1958), students might create a list like this:

- Turtle has to convince the birds to take him with them.

- He has to convince them to each give him a feather.

- He has to convince them that they should all take new names for this special event.

- He has to choose the name "All of You."

- He has to be elected speaker for the group.

- He has to ask the people of the sky, "For whom is this food offered?"

- They have to reply, "For all of you."

- The birds have to realize they have been tricked.

- The birds have to take their feathers back.

Each of the events on the list is a key detail, worthy of being featured in a response of this level.

Students writing this type of response need to distinguish between more and less important information in the story. Students who cannot make such distinctions tend to write summaries that list details in the order in which they recall them. The prompt asks students to look for events or details that clearly change the rest of the story. I advise students to look for moments that are so significant that if overlooked, a reader would have trouble following the story. The following example is a response to "American History" by Judith Ortiz Cofer:

> This story is about a girl Elena, who lives in a Spanish/Mexican building. Right below her building she can see a house. When a new boy, Eugene, moves in they become good friends. The day that JFK died the two had a study date. So that night when Elena goes over Eugene's mom opens the door and on page 45 she says, "We won't be in this place much longer, no need for him to get close to people—it'll just make it harder for him later." I think Eugene's family moves a lot and he doesn't ever know when it happens.

This response focuses on the climax of the story. Although the writer doesn't use one of the suggested sentence openers (e.g., *everything changes when* or *the most important event in the story is when*), she has distinguished this event as one worthy of attention. This level of response does not require students to organize and relate specific moments in the text; all that is required is to identify an event that is clearly essential to following the plot.

Level 3: Stated Relationships

Goal: To recognize the connections, explanations, and comparisons that the narrator makes; to comment on the connections the narrator makes between details.

A Good Response Will: Explain a connection stated in the text, or reexplain what the narrator says about a cause-and-effect relationship, a comparison (similarity or contrast), or a reason something happened.

Sample RLR Beginnings

"The narrator claims that [X] happened because of [Y]."

"One event that reminds the narrator of another is . . ."

"The narrator thinks that if [X] happens then [Y] will follow."

"The narrator points out the difference between . . ."

"The author uses a simile to describe . . ."

Reading Level 3 Kernels from "Snow"

Yolanda is put in a special seat because the nun wants to tutor her without bothering the other students.

Yolanda thinks the snow looks like the dots that Sister Zoe drew on the blackboard to represent nuclear fallout.

Writing a response of this type requires following a connection made by the narrator. I illustrate the kind of connection required with a "barbell" chart:

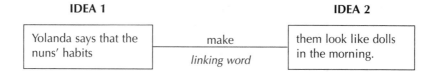

	IDEA 1		IDEA 2

Yolanda says that the nuns' habits	make	them look like dolls in the morning.
	linking word	

To prepare students to provide this level of response, I give them sentences that contain stated relationships and ask them to break them into two parts connected by a word describing how the two parts are linked.

This is the first level at which students are required to manage discrete bits of information. I often refer to this ability as "recognizing relationships pointed out for you." Any time a narrator specifically points out cause, effect, similarity, or difference, it must be important; the author is directing the reader to note these pieces of information. At this level a student only needs to reiterate the information, not express an opinion about it. Ideally, students will translate the narrator's words into their own and yet express the same relationship.

In the example that follows the student satisfies the expectations of a level 3 response except that she does not restate the relationship. I include it here because the student clearly understands the stated relationship between Elena and Eugene in "American History," even if she doesn't quite make it the focus of the response.

> She was very fond of a boy named Eugene; seeing him was the only thing that really mattered to her. One day she went to his home for a study session. His mother answers the door, shunning Elana away. "Listen. Honey. Eugene doesn't want to study with you. He is a smart boy. Doesn't need help. You understand me. I am truly sorry if he told you you could come over. He cannot study with you. It's nothing personal. You understand?" As a white American, growing up in the community that I do, it is extremely difficult for me to relate to her in a situation like this one.

Level 4: Simple Implied Relationships

Goal: To recognize suggested connections that are not overtly stated in the text; to explain the implied link between two related details.

A Good Response Will: Explain the implication of a particular statement in the text; examine a statement and explain what it suggests in terms of:

- an unstated cause or effect;
- an unstated judgment about a character;
- the mood;
- the motivation for a single action;
- the meaning of a single obvious symbol;
- a metaphor;
- an unstated comparison

Sample RLR Beginnings

"You know [X] because [Y]."

"The character did this because..."

"[X] is just like [Y] because..."

"The real reason that [X] happened is..."

"This detail is a symbol of..."

"The real cause of [X] was..."

"The metaphor the author uses to describe [X] helps to..."

Reading Level 4 Kernel from "Snow"

The kids take the air-raid drills seriously. When they go through the drills, they really think about what will happen if there is a nuclear attack.

This level of response is most aptly illustrated with a puzzle analogy. A simple implied relationship requires that a student recognize information suggested by other details in the text, in the same way that one can see the shape of a missing puzzle piece suggested by the pieces around it. I introduce this idea to my students by drawing three pieces of a four-piece puzzle and asking them if they have enough information to draw the necessary shape of the fourth piece. Of course, they do. I suggest that it works the same way with information in a story. Certain pieces of information will suggest some other pieces of information. A passage in which this happens is worthy of an RLR.

While working with students on this level of response, I use a modified bar-bell chart:

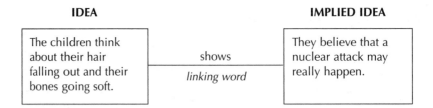

The left side of the chart shows the information stated in the text, the right side, what one can infer from it. For practice, I give students a list of several statements from the text that suggest an inference. They write things that can be inferred from the statements and check them against their understanding of the story.

Being able to write this level of response requires reading the text carefully and weighing the information in terms of the context in which it is presented. A response should identify a specific passage, sentence, phrase, or word and explain what it implies. Making this connection can be difficult: the inference must not be directly stated anywhere in the text. There is a huge difference between what students say based on unsupported general recollection and what they say based on careful reading. Based on general recollection a student may write, "You can tell this character is a bad person because she hurts people," but not be able to identify a single specific instance. Responses at this level benefit from using specific passages as evidence. Although the following student does not provide direct quotes, she nonetheless provides appropriate evidence:

> The real reason Eugene's mom told the girl to leave is most likely because she's Puerto Rican. It was because of her skin color... The detail about the green door is a symbol of new starts or possibilities. This is very significant, because it is opened for a short time before it is closed on the girl, which represents options closing.

Level 5: Complex Implied Relationships

Goal: To demonstrate the connection between several details from various places in the text; to construct an understanding of change within the text; to gather details to support a generalization; to recognize repeated ideas, issues, or images.

A Good Response Will: Support a generalization with evidence in the text concerning:

- a character, setting, situation, tone, or focus;
- a change in character, setting, situation, tone, or focus;
- the similarities between two characters, settings, or situations;
- a recurring symbol;
- recurring images.

Sample RLR Beginnings

"Throughout the story..."

"This character is always..."

"The changes since the beginning of the story have been caused by..."

"These two characters are different throughout the story because..."

"The children in the story all..."

"The author repeats the image of [X] to suggest..."

Reading Level 5 Kernel from "Snow"
(as supported with details or examples from the story)

Throughout the story the author emphasizes the morbid atmosphere of Yolanda's fourth-grade class. The narrator makes it seem as if the students accept the terrifying images of radiation sickness as just another part of school.

At this level the puzzle analogy starts to break down. It is analogous to noticing a pattern in the way the pieces are cut, but putting together a puzzle rarely requires that kind of awareness. Nevertheless, writing complex arguments about fiction does. I emphasize to my students that writing a response at this level requires that they recognize a *pattern* of inference within the text.

When introducing this type of response, I use a chart to help my students visualize the amount and type of information required to support an implied generalization. Later, students use charts like this to capture enough information to support a generalization.

Generalization: "Throughout the story the author emphasizes..."

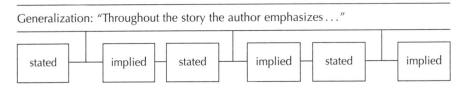

To write a response at this level, students need to do more than simply lump together bits of information from different parts of the text. Rather, they need to make sure that the details all support a particular point or generalization and are *warranted*; that is, the student should be able to explain clearly why the evidence provided demonstrates or supports the point. Here is one student's response to "Raymond's Run":

> The changes since the beginning of the story have been caused by Squeaky's ability to win that final race, and to use the race as a connector between two people and not a divider. In the beginning of this story, Squeaky thinks she is the fastest thing on two feet, and uses that to put her above everybody else. Near the end, Squeaky and Gretchen are at the race, and they both plan on winning because of bragging rights. Just before the race is when you can start to see a character change in Squeaky. When she is setting up, she sees Raymond and starts to see the potential he has as a runner, and she wants to be able to coach him. After Squeaky wins the race, she sees Gretchen as a friend because she used the race as a connector instead of using it to put herself above her opponent as she did in the past. Throughout the story, you can see change in Squeaky from being an attention-grabbing show off switching to a helpful person by using her abilities to help others and make friends as opposed to using her talents to raise herself on a pedestal to let everybody know she is the best.

This student has made a generalization that the act of competing has changed Squeaky's attitude toward both her brother and her closest competitor. The number of implications required by this response emphasizes how much more complex this response is than the one at the previous level.

Level 6: Author's Generalization

Goal: To support a generalization about the world outside of the book; to demonstrate the implications of the author's representation.

A Good Response Will: Apply the generalizations from the text to the world; explain how the generalization suggests a truth about life, the world, or human behavior. It may:

- illustrate a universal law ("In a world where...");
- demonstrate a judgment about a certain group of people ("People who [X] must [Y].");
- generalize the results of a particular kind of struggle ("When a person tries to...").

Sample Beginnings

"The author suggests that when people [X], the result is [Y]."

"The problem in the world that the author is focusing on is..."

"Whenever an [X] kind of person tries to [Y] the outcome is always [Z]."

"The character's tendency to [X] implies that the author thinks..."

"The generalization about [X] that is suggested in the story is..."

Reading Level 6 Kernel from "Snow" (as supported with details or examples from the story)

The author suggests that children unquestioningly accept the attitudes that the adults around them express. The children in the story take in the information that the nun gives them about nuclear attack and accept it as part of their everyday reality.

To explain the requirements of this level of response, I have to abandon the puzzle analogy. I explain to students that a response at this level requires the awareness of several generalizations suggested throughout the story and the ability to arrange those generalizations in a way that produces a broad generalization about life, the world, or human experience. Most often when working at this level, I ask the students to look for an implied generalization about the kind of people in the story, the situation they face or the context in which they exist, and the outcome of putting that kind of person in that kind of situation. Again I use a chart:

What kind of people	Children
In what context	When surrounded by ideas of death and destruction
Get what results	Accept without question the reality of impending doom

To satisfy expectations for this level of response, students have to be able to examine the real–world implications of generalizations suggested by the text: They have to be able to extrapolate. Doing so often requires stating a theme or a generalization about the world or human experience that can be supported by the text. To write a response like this, a reader needs to be able to make inferences and generalizations based on the stated relationships at the lower levels of response that support a particular reading of a text, as in this response to "Raymond's Run":

> The author suggests that when people care about each other deeply they learn to act selflessly in order to benefit the other individual. In this story, Squeaky realized that things are not all about winning and learns that making others happy is more important. This is showed when, at the beginning of the story Squeaky states that "I always win cause I'm the best" (pg 51). She believes that winning is everything and that is the reason why she runs. At the end, she says that "if I've lost the race or if me and Gretchen tied or even if I've won, I can always retire as a runner and begin a whole new career as a coach with Raymond as my champion."

This student is able to extrapolate the changes in this specific character to a generalization about human experience.

Level 7: Structural Generalization

Goal: To explain how the author's use of literary techniques emphasizes or contributes to the generalization supported by the story; to support a generalization about the form or style of the story; to explain how the author's purposes are met by the use of literary techniques.

A Good Response Will: Connect literary techniques to the generalizations about the world; explain how the author structured the story for a particular effect. In doing so, it might:

- explain the impact of a symbol used at a particular moment for a particular purpose;
- explain the effect of the juxtaposition of characters, setting, symbols, or plot elements;
- describe the purpose of the narrator's point of view;
- explain how the plot sequence or design helps create the impact of the story.

Sample RLR Beginnings

"The author uses [technical element] to emphasize that when people [X] they find [Y]."

"The repetition of [image] emphasizes the idea that when . . ."

"The author sets up [generalization X] at the beginning of the story so that . . ."

"The author contrasts these two characters in order to emphasize [generalization]."

Reading Level 7 Kernel from "Snow"
(as supported with details or examples from the story)

Although Yolanda obviously likes the nuns at school, the narrator characterizes them as images of death in order to emphasize how children accept the morbid images that they are fed. Sister Zoe becomes a sort of benevolent angel of death, combining the everyday presence of routine and horrifying extermination.

I explain this level of response as requiring a student to keep in mind a clearly articulated author's generalization and look for elements of structure or literary technique that suggest or support that generalization. At this point my exhausted students usually say something like, "No wonder it's so hard." And that difficulty should be emphasized, to both students and teachers. The process of literary analysis at this level is incredibly complex and technical. It is not something that one can or should drag students to, no matter their demonstrated level of readiness. There are many forms of worthy response to literature that do not require this level of abstraction, this degree of familiarity with literary techniques. For me, understanding this level of response reassures me that literary analysis is not the be-all and end-all. Indeed, for many students work of this type is irrelevant to their experience and their academic goals.

Once students have begun to grasp how to write theme statements, they often begin to notice literary devices as they are reading. They can begin with the theme and look for literary devices that suggest and support it, or they can notice things that are likely literary devices and look for the theme. Here is one student's response at this level:

> In the end of the story, Elena sees the snow through the window falling in the sky, but she doesn't look down as it touches the ground and turns gray. The white pure snow is the symbolism of Elena's dream of a better life in America. The gray ground is the symbolism of the real world that is racially divided. The author uses the snow turning gray as it touches the ground to emphasize that Elena's dream is impossible in real life.

Although this student does not use the term correctly, she does explain the effect that complex symbolism has on her understanding of the change that Elena has gone through. This response represents a complex generalization about the way the author has used a literary device in several places in the story.

The Process

I follow the sequence of procedures outlined below when using RLR in my analytical reading class. This process can be used in a single unit or throughout a course.

1. I pretest students using a reading inventory.

2. I rate the results, using three categories:

   - Comfort level (one level below highest-level response).

   - Mastery level (highest-level response).

   - Developing level (one level above highest-level response).

3. I introduce and teach the significance of every level in the RLR sequence.

4. I teach how to provide appropriate responses at each level.

5. I ask students to respond in writing to every reading assignment.

6. Students discuss what they have written in small groups and help one another identify reading kernels at the next level.

7. I see, skim, and date-stamp every response every day.

8. After the first opportunity to write a response (and occasionally thereafter), students turn in an edited response for detailed grading and feedback.

9. I give written feedback to one person's entire collection of responses as often as possible.

10. Students create a portfolio of their responses each quarter and semester.

11. Students take another reading inventory at midterm.

12. Students' final unit/project includes an RLR.

13. Students are posttested.

I do not label or pigeonhole my students. I tell them their pretest results, introduce them to the entire set of response options, and encourage them to adjust their responses to match their own sense of readiness. I don't believe that improvement in a complex skill happens in a linear progression from one step to the next. Rather, students tend to stretch for more complex skills and fall back to simpler levels as a result of many factors.

Most often the pretest reassures me that I have a heterogeneous class with a wide range of reading experiences and abilities. However, on occasion, I have discovered that I have a class of students whose response levels are remarkably similar. Knowing more about how my students read, at least as revealed through the inventory, allows me to tailor my instruction to the needs of all learners in the class, rather than relying on preconceived notions of "typical" grade-level competencies.

Effects of RLR on Instruction

Impact on Class Discussion

How do you get to an analysis if students are still struggling with plot? Or how do you get every student involved in the discussion of a text if some of them are struggling with plot and others have learned tools for analysis? I find that having students write an RLR before we talk empowers more students to join the discussion, because the prompts provide a structure. While students are examining one another's responses in small groups, I put a list of questions on the board, beginning with the literal (*what events change the course of the story?*) and moving toward the abstract (*what inferences can you make about this character? what generalizations about this issue can you support from this text?*). The small groups prepare responses to the questions using ideas and details from their RLRs.

This way I can use flexible grouping—either heterogeneous or homogeneous —and still prepare everyone to participate in large-group discussions. I can trust that conversations will be fruitful and I will not feel compelled to direct the comments toward a specific reading of the text. Focusing on the RLR prompts creates an environment in which every student can comfortably contribute even when there are vastly divergent reading levels in the room.

Class discussion then has a specific, immediate purpose. Students use it to improve, refine, and combine ideas they have developed in order to increase the complexity of a response. A simple but effective concluding activity asks students to add something to their responses in order to make them more complex. By commenting on the responses orally, occasionally grading them, and giving a posttest, I constantly reassess my students' performance of these skills.

Impact on Student Writing

I see RLR writing both as daily reinforcement of the kind of careful reading that will help students with their analytical essays and as preparation for the independent reading required in college literature classes. The prompts help students read literature carefully and guide them toward ways of making and supporting generalizations and other inferences about the text. In their responses students are encouraged to use quotes, analyze text, and support generalizations. Although I do not require it, as students move to the more inferential levels, they tend to embed their quotes into formal paragraphs.

I also teach minilessons that bridge the gap between response writing and formal analytical essays. Students practice selecting quotes and presenting them within an appropriate context every day. Although students' abilities vary dramatically, every assignment, every discussion further prepares the students for writing literary analysis essays.

When I added portfolios to the process, the practice was transformed. In my alternate-day ninety-minute classes, students normally generate between twelve and fifteen responses in a grading period. At the end of the first quarter, I have them gather five of their responses and rewrite each one. They then assemble the originals and the rewrites in a portfolio and label evidence of their improvement. At the end of the second quarter, students assemble a ten-entry portfolio (the five first-quarter-portfolio responses plus five new ones, ten newly rewritten responses, or any combination thereof) that includes an introduction for an outside reader and a reflection on the process.

Focusing on portfolios enables students to pay more attention to their RLR. Students gather and exchange ideas about each level of response. They confer with me often and complete several drafts of individual responses to ensure significant improvement. Many students develop successful portfolio responses three and sometimes four levels higher than they originally demonstrated on the pretest. Although improvement is rarely as significant on the posttest, posttest responses are longer than pretest ones and more likely to use direct evidence from the text. My students are able to assess their own reading by seeing how many levels in the RLR they can respond to, a good sign that they are learning to learn how to transform their reading experiences for the better.

Impact on Teaching

I can use reading level responses to figure out where I need to focus my instruction. For example, recently a class of sophomores discussing Poe's "The Cask of Amontillado" could not agree on the author's attitude toward the murderous main character. Listening to their conversations, I realized that they had vastly different interpretations of not only Montressor's motivation but even what really happened. I sent them back to the text to make a list of the steps in Montressor's plan using the level 2 prompt: *find the events that change the course of the story, those that have to happen to get to the end result.* Once they had a clear picture of the plan, I asked them to look for the level 3 explanation that Montressor gives for seeking his revenge. These efforts cleared up their disagreements considerably.

As a result of learning to trust RLR writing, I have been able to add more independent reading assignments. I am much more comfortable than I used to be letting every student in my class read a different novel, even if I haven't read most of them. I used to find that despite my lesson plans and goals, I would resort to lecturing if class discussion got stymied or if I felt we were getting off the track. Now I am much more likely to refer to the RLR prompts as a way to get the discussion back to the text. Instead of trying to design the perfect set of questions to raise and develop issues inherent in a particular text, I have a framework I can apply to any text. I'm much more comfortable accepting and promoting divergent readings of a text: I can rely on the complexity of the reading instead of being troubled by interpretations I did not expect.

Other writing opportunities can be built on the RLR. Once students have sorted out the sequence of action and understood characters and their motives, for instance, they can add creative-writing exercises such as rewriting a particular scene or event from a different character's perspective. After making inferences about characters and the broader narrative structure, students can make cross-discipline inferential leaps by interpreting the literature through art. Reading level response is a useful tool for teaching students how to think about their reading and writing in ways that serve a variety of purposes, for both the conventional analytical writing found in virtually every school curriculum and the more imaginative work that makes literacy come alive.

References

ACHEBE, C. 1958. *Things Fall Apart.* London: Heinemann.

ALVAREZ, J. 1991. *How the Garcia Girls Lost Their Accents.* Chapel Hill, NC: Algonquin Books.

HILLOCKS, G., JR., 1980. "Toward a Hierarchy of Skills in the Comprehension of Literature." *English Journal* 69 (3): 54–59.

HILLOCKS, G., AND L. H. LUDLOW. 1984. "A Taxonomy of Skills in Reading and Interpreting Fiction." *American Educational Research Journal* 21: 7–24.

HILLOCKS, G., B. J. McCABE, AND J. F. McCAMPBELL. 1971. *The Dynamics of English Instruction, Grades 7–12.* New York: Random House. Available at www.coe.uga.edu/~smago/Books/Dynamics/Dynamics_home.htm.

SMAGORINSKY, P. 2002. *Teaching English Through Principled Practice.* Upper Saddle River, NJ: Merrill/Prentice Hall.

SMAGORINSKY, P., AND S. GEVINSON. 1989. *Fostering the Reader's Response: Rethinking the Literature Curriculum, Grades 7–12.* Palo Alto, CA: Dale Seymour.

11   *Cultural Modeling in the Hillocks Tradition*

CAROL D. LEE
Northwestern University
Evanston, Illinois

I began my doctoral studies with George Hillocks after twenty-two years as an educator: fifteen as an administrator and teacher in an independent African-centered elementary school (Lee 1992) and seven as an English teacher in a high school and community college. Upon entering graduate school, I knew I wanted to combine my formal training in the teaching of secondary school English Language Arts with what I knew about African American culture from my life experience and teaching and helping to design the African-centered elementary school. Several sources influenced how I came to study connections among African American culture, response to literature, and composition. Most fundamental to the evolution of my thinking was the work of George Hillocks, my PhD advisor, whose work with writing has influenced my beliefs about how to teach literature.

Hillocks and the Teaching of Writing

George Hillocks (1986, 1995) argues that simply being able to identify the elements of any written form, which is the way writing is typically presented in textbooks and taught in schools, is not enough. Rather, students have to know *how* to produce the elements that are expected in particular kinds of writing. As Smagorinsky (1991) has shown, simply providing students with models of writing forms does little to teach them how to produce those forms. Instead, students need experience with the kinds of procedures and strategies that they can use during the process of writing. Hillocks recommends that activities designed to help students learn *task-specific strategies*—for instance, learning how to generate evidence to support claims in argumentation, and then learning how to explain the connection between evidence and claims by using warrants—ought to be at the center of writing instruction.

Since the 1970s, the "models" approach has been complemented or replaced—at least in educational writing—with a general writing process involving prewriting and planning, composing, and revising. While Hillocks acknowledges that writing includes these stages, he also believes that writing involves constructive processes that are not adequately captured by simply asking students to use these steps. In contrast, he describes what he calls an *environmental* approach to the teaching of composition. This environmental approach requires (1) a rethinking of written genres and (2) the careful planning of activities that would provide students with guided practice in the production and evaluation of the elements of each genre.

Hillocks states that three genres are the most appropriate for K–12 school-based writing instruction: narrative, extended definition, and argument. He says that expository writing is really a form of argumentation. Perhaps among his most important contributions is the conceptualization of what he calls gateway activities (Hillocks 1995, 1999; Smagorinsky, McCann, and Kern 1987). Hillocks (1995, 1999) sees gateway activities as opportunities for students to learn strategies for producing good descriptions or good dialogue in narratives; or to learn how to evaluate claims, evidence, and warrants as well as how to produce them in argument.

For more than twenty years, Hillocks worked tirelessly with Master of Arts (MAT) in Teaching and PhD students in English Education to produce a series of publications for teachers with practical lessons on how to design such activities. These included publications in the TRIP (Theory and Research into Practice) series of the National Council of Teachers of English. One influential book in that series is *Observing and Writing*, in which Hillocks (1975) offers activities for describing sounds such as running water, describing smells such as lavender, creating dialogue, as well as many others. Similarly, Johannessen, Kahn, and Walter (1982) offer activities that help students determine criteria for defining concepts such as courage. These activities include scenarios of different situations in which a person exhibits what appears to be a particular trait, but by comparing contrasting cases, students come to make distinctions and outline the criteria that distinguish one situation from the other. By working with these gateway activities, students begin to engage in the kinds of reasoning required to produce well-formed narratives, extended definitions, and arguments.

Hillocks and the Teaching of Literature

I was profoundly influenced by this work as I thought about the implications of clearly defining which key concepts and problem-solving processes students need to learn in response to literature (akin to Hillocks' shifting emphasis from exposition to argument and extended definition). The question for me was, how can one think about gateway activities in relation to response to literature? I wanted to design gateway activities that would help African American students who speak African American English (AAE) tap their knowledge of ways of using language. In thinking about this question in relation to AAE speakers, I also wanted to learn the implications of this knowledge for students from other ethnically diverse backgrounds and students living in low-income communities. Without Hillocks' prompting, I most certainly would never have imagined what I call *Cultural Modeling* (Lee 2001).

While most of Hillocks' research has been in the area of composition, he had also done substantive thinking about the teaching of response to literature. He and his then PhD student Michael Smith (Smith and Hillocks 1988) argued that in order for students to construct rich interpretations of literature, they need to develop conceptual knowledge, knowledge of genres, and interpretive strategies. They believed that more expert-like literary explanations involved use of "noting details, identifying salient similarities, [and] drawing inferences on the basis of the details" (48). Two other former students of Hillocks, Peter Smagorinsky and Steve Gevinson (Smagorinsky and Gevinson 1989), made similar claims, illustrating them with examples from their own teaching and instructional design. They expanded the earlier line of reasoning by Smith and Hillocks with arguments about how middle to high school instruction needed to meet the developmental needs of adolescents. There was also a publication in the TRIP series by another group of Hillocks' students (Smagorinsky, McCann, and Kern 1987). Using classroom-tested examples, they illustrated the importance of drawing on students' prior knowledge to help prepare them for reading canonical literature: knowledge of themes, extended definitions (such as criteria for what makes a good parent as preparation for thinking about Atticus Finch in *To Kill a Mockingbird*), dilemmas (contemporary examples of the issues with which Romeo and Juliet wrestled), and other relevant knowledge.

There are two important points to be made here. First, Hillocks clearly provided the intellectual cornerstone around which a significant body of teaching practice and research revolved, carried out by prior students—both PhD and MAT students—all of whom have gone on to make significant contributions in both universities and secondary schools. Each extended the fundamental propositions that arose from Hillocks' own groundbreaking work in unique ways. Second, it is clear that Hillocks provided an intellectual community for the incubation of studies about what it means to learn and to teach novices to read literature and to write and otherwise respond to literature. While this body of work provided the foundation for the evolution of my own research, I tried to find a unique place in that community of thought by focusing on what all this meant for ethnically and linguistically diverse populations.

Cultural Modeling

Basic Propositions

To address my interests, I developed two lines of inquiry: What is meant by culture, and how is this work useful for thinking about everyday social practices? From an examination of both cultural-historical activity and cognitive anthropology theory (Cole 1996, 1998; Lave 1988; Rogoff and Lave 1984; Scribner and Cole 1981), I arrived at the following propositions that undergird the framework of Cultural Modeling.

1. Culture is not an amorphous box into which we can easily place individuals and groups (Lee, Spencer, and Harpalani 2003; Rogoff 2003). Rather, culture is found in routine practices from which emerge belief systems, ways of using

language, and forms of social organization (Gutierrez and Rogoff 2003). Through participation in these routines people signal membership and construct important aspects of their identities (Nasir and Saxe 2003). Historically in the United States (and in other countries), members of identifiable minority groups have been stigmatized. As a result, cultural practices that are typically associated with these groups have been viewed as deficits that interfere with students' opportunities to learn.

2. Language is one of the clearest indicators of difference in schools, especially when others assign low status to those who speak in a dialect, accent, or language that departs from the norm (Wolfram, et al. 1999). So, for example, if a students' first dialect is the version of English associated with the White middle and upper middle class, that language use is marked as not only acceptable, but prestigious. If, on the other hand, the students' first dialect is AAE or Appalachian English, that language use is perceived as unacceptable or nonstandard. These evaluations are based on relationships of power, not on sound linguistic knowledge. There are many dialects of English, each with situations where it is the most appropriate to use (Wolfram and Schilling-Estes 1998). What we call Standard English is the medium of communication in school. Some version of it is the medium of communication in the mainstream world of business. By this I mean that within what most people would identify as Standard English, there are examples of language patterns that are acceptable in business that would be considered unacceptable in school. Weaver (1996) constructed a letter with several categories of grammatical "errors" and sent it to business people to locate the errors. Patterns associated with AAE, for example, were identified as errors, while other errors were not even recognized as such. This examination of language practices was informed by sociolinguistic research. Research on AAE over many decades had documented both the consistent nature of the grammar of AAE and its creative ways of using language (Baugh 1983; Labov 1972; Mufwene, et al. 1998).

African American English as a Resource

One genre of talk in AAE is called *signifying* (Mitchell-Kernan 1981; Smitherman 1977). Signifying involves ritual insult. It is a practice that has been maintained across generations. Signifying always involves a high use of figurative language, especially metaphor, symbolism, irony, and satire. It always involves double entendre and an appreciation of language play as an aesthetically pleasing end in itself (Lee 1997).

Based on this research and my own life experiences, I have observed that youth who are AAE speakers may enter literature classrooms and not adequately participate or achieve; yet as soon as they walk outside the classroom door, these students will comprehend and produce the imaginative qualities I have described. Please note that I have not equated being Black as a racial category with being a speaker of AAE, although significant proportions of African Americans speak AAE, even if they switch into Standard English as they move across settings. I thus concluded that these students were engaging in the forms of reasoning and habits of mind required to participate in literary reasoning. However, that knowledge was tacit and was not being tapped in typical classrooms (Lee 1993, 1995a, b, 2000).

There are other everyday practices in which African American and other minority youth engage that may productively be drawn on to support novices learning to employ literary reasoning. My understanding of the role of everyday practices in learning was enhanced by the research on poor children who sold candy on the streets of an urban center in Brazil (Nunes et al. 1993; Saxe 1991, 1992). These children typically had little or no schooling, but learned to buy wholesale, price, and sell candy in an underground economy. Schools, however, did not build on the competencies the children developed, such as the ability to estimate, and so the achievement of those who attended school did not reflect the abilities they showed on the street. Hillocks' work in both composition and literature encouraged me to look for knowledge and competencies that my students already had and to think about ways to use that knowledge and those competencies to help them develop deep understandings of subject matter.

Because literature is largely about narratives, I began to look for everyday practices that involved the comprehension and interpretation of narratives as sites for everyday literary reasoning. Youth culture proved a rich untapped source. Hip-hop as a subset of contemporary youth culture was an important site of investigation. While hip-hop crosses racial, ethnic, and even national borders, it is still largely rooted in and influenced by African American youth culture (Kitwana 2002; Rose 1994). Many of the lyrics are highly literary in quality, requiring listeners to interpret symbols, irony, satire, and use of unreliable narration (D'Andrad 1995; Mahiri 2004; Meacham 2000; Morrell 2002). In addition, videos are produced to advertise new songs. These videos can be seen on BET (Black Entertainment Television) and other channels or on the Internet but are not available for purchase. The videos are rarely a simple enactment of the plot line of rap lyrics. Rather, they often serve as reinterpretations of the lyrics themselves, and as such are another interesting source for viewing implicit knowledge of literary reasoning in the everyday practices of youth, specifically hip-hop culture.

I illustrate with one example, the rap called "I Used to Love H.E.R." by Common. The song was highly successful and its metaphor was taken up in a movie called *Brown Sugar*. In each stanza, the narrator describes the characteristics of a girl and his evolving relationship with her as she grew up. Each stanza provides vivid details about this young woman. It is not until the final stanza that Common reveals that the woman to whom he refers is Hip-Hop itself. The listener as reader must make judgments all along the way about the reliability of the narrator (see Smith 1991) who proves to be unreliable to the extent that he tries to entice the reader into thinking one thing and then at the end undermines the conclusions he has led the reader to believe.

The woman as a character is an extended metaphor that Common exploits in order to satirize the evolution of Hip-Hop. In order to understand Common's metaphor, the reader must compare Common's lyrics to his or her own knowledge of the history of Hip-Hop. The reader must note patterns across the details describing the actions of the woman in each stanza in order to construct generalizations both about the woman from Common's point of view, and, by extension, about hip-hop. Thus, I argue that these lyrics demand that the listener as reader engage in forms of reasoning and habits of mind that we know are similarly demanded by canonical works of literature.

The question then arises, how is this recognition of the evidence of literary reasoning in everyday practices of African American youth who are speakers of AAE (and others) taken up in both instruction and in overall curriculum design? In Cultural Modeling, I attempt to design both classroom instruction and curricula that connect these forms of everyday reasoning with reasoning about canonical works of literature.

In daily classroom instruction, Cultural Modeling identifies what I call cultural data sets. In the study of literature, these cultural data sets are everyday texts with which students are very familiar. They may be of a variety of media (written texts, oral texts such as music, multimedia texts such as film or television, or pictorial texts such as advertising that may include both images as well as words). The act of making sense of these texts requires the kind of reasoning that students will need to understand a series of canonical texts that will follow in instruction. There should be a common kind of interpretive problem in the canonical texts that is similar to that in the everyday text. The following interpretive problems serve as an important foundation for learning to engage in literary reasoning about canonical texts: symbolism, irony, satire, and use of unreliable narration.

The Cultural Modeling Project designed and implemented several interventions in a large urban high school. The Cultural Modeling in Literature curriculum was used in freshman through senior literature classes. In a unit on symbolism, cultural data sets included rap songs such as "The Mask" by the Fugees, rap videos such as the one designed to complement the rap song "Retrospect of Life" by Common, and television films such as *Sax, Cantor Riff* by African American director Julie Dash, among other multiple-media everyday texts.

In each of these, symbolism is central to understanding the text. In the Fugees' song, the mask serves as a symbol through which the group makes political commentary on human duplicity as a form of both self-protection and aggression. In *Sax, Cantor Riff,* multiple images serve symbolic functions with local meanings as well as thematic meanings across the film. While symbolism is privileged in each text, each cultural data set also provides opportunities to explore other literary problems. For example, "The Mask" involves multiple narrators, each of whom embodies unique as well as complementary points of view. *Sax, Cantor Riff* allows for the investigation of authorial intent. It also requires the viewer/reader/interpreter to impose coherence on events that on the surface seem unrelated. This problem is akin to the challenge posed by Toni Morrison in *The Bluest Eye* (1970) when, in an early chapter, the narrator begins, "The nuns walked by quiet as lust." There are no nuns to be found anywhere else in the chapter or the novel; and nuns and lust do seem to be an odd combination.

The canonical texts that followed included

- the chapter titled "Damballah" from John Edgar Wideman's novel by the same name;

  Toni Morrison's novel *Beloved*;

- short stories "Rice Husband" and "Ying Yang" by Amy Tan (from *The Joy Luck Club*);

- "Wash" and "A Rose for Emily" by William Faulkner;

- poetry, including Robert Hayden's "Runnagate," Frances Harper's "The Slave Mother," Emily Dickinson's "Because I could not stop for death," Robert Frost's "The Road Not Taken," Dylan Thomas' "Do not go gentle into that good night," and selections from Milton's *Paradise Lost* and Dante's *Inferno*;

- readings on the history of the African Holocaust of Enslavement to provide background knowledge for the first two texts, Wideman's "Damballah" and Morrison's *Beloved*; and

- Shakespeare's *Macbeth*.

There are several important points to be made about this unit of instruction on symbolism. First, each text requires special attention to symbolism. Second, each also involves other related problems of point of view. Third, while each text requires attention to a key interpretive problem, the texts cross traditional definitions of genre. Cultural Modeling's focus on designing units of instruction that address an interpretive problem is important for novice learning.

Symbolism, for example, is a kind of problem that presents itself across traditional genre boundaries (e.g., poems, novels, short stories, plays) and across historical and national traditions as well as literary movements. There is no question that additional knowledge of authors, of a range of related texts, and of the social and historical world embodied in the text are required to construct powerful interpretations. However, if a reader can detect when a literal interpretation is not enough, when patterns point to symbolism as the kind of problem being tackled, and can construct a warrantable interpretation, that reader is in a strong position to wrestle with a nineteenth-century Russian novel such as Dostoevsky's *Crime and Punishment*, an Elizabethan sonnet by Shakespeare, a twentieth-century play such as August Wilson's *Fences*, or a twenty-first-century rap or film.

This principle stands in contrast to the typical organization in commercial anthologies by chronology or by genre of literature units. This is a multicultural unit, but its orientation is different in several ways. Here the texts from non-European traditions are not added on to augment the unit. Rather, the non-European texts are the center. Also, these texts from different ethnic traditions cohere not only around loosely related themes, but, equally important, around common interpretive problems they pose.

Instruction moves from investigations of cultural data sets to canonical literature. The canonical literature is sequenced according to the following principles: The first literature in the sequence is accessible to students in terms of both form and the characters' behavior. At the same time, students are beginning to experiment with using literary strategies that they have learned through their examinations of culturally familiar texts. In subsequent literature, we presume that students may have less direct knowledge of the social codes operating in the texts, but now have more experience in using literary strategies.

Talk in these classrooms, especially during the modeling phase, is focused on how students go about detecting and making sense of the problems in culturally familiar texts. This discussion is then less about what a student understands and more about how a student comes to understand. The purpose of such talk is twofold. First, it allows the students to make public the strategies they use in everyday contexts. The teacher plays a critical role of translating students' observations about problem solving in their own worlds into broader statements of principles and strategies that apply beyond the individual text before them. Second, from the beginning of instruction, these conversations socialize students into understanding the importance of reasoning in literary analysis. Third, because these texts are familiar to the students, they are more likely to engage in deep reasoning, producing complex and nuanced literary explanations.

Also, because there is a fundamental shift in access to knowledge, the power relations around speaking roles are turned around. Students are more likely to assume teaching roles (for both the teacher and other students). The fact that this role reversal happens at the beginning of instruction helps establish a culture of inquiry in the classroom that extends to talk about the more difficult canonical texts that follow. The modeling that occurs during this phase of instruction differs from more traditional forms of modeling during which the teacher is presumed to be the source of authoritative knowledge who models expertise for students. Instead, both students and the teacher are jointly the experts in ways that are not artificial, but emerge naturally from the tasks.

Discussion

Besides an understanding of the potential of everyday practices of students, Cultural Modeling requires a basic reorganization of the literature curriculum. These proposed changes are very much influenced by the Hillocks tradition. However, there are differences. I propose that an important point for teaching students literary reasoning is helping them understand what I call generative interpretive problems. These problems are generative—as I attempted to describe in the case of symbolism—because knowledge of them allows one to tackle a wide range of literary texts. The literary problems around which Cultural Modeling is organized include symbolism, irony, satire, and use of unreliable narration. Each of these problems has a family of related subtypes. For example, there is verbal irony, dramatic irony, and situational irony. There are multiple forms of satire. Unreliable narration is a particular instance of problems of point of view (Booth 1974, 1983; Smith 1991). Typically, these interpretive problems are referenced in school-based literature anthologies, but rarely is there any explicit instruction as to how one goes about figuring out when the problem presents itself as symbolism versus satire. Students at best get anecdotal experience with these problems.

In Cultural Modeling, I propose that irony, satire, and use of unreliable narration are a related family of interpretive problems. Each requires a rejection of the literal and a reconstruction of meanings that stand in contrast to the literal (Ortony 1979; Winner 1988). By comparison, symbolism requires a rejection of the literal and a reconstruction of meanings that stand in addition to, as amplification and extension of, the literal. Thus it is useful to think about sequencing instruction on symbolism first and then satire, irony, and unreliable narration. The purpose here is to help students distinguish among the patterned ways that non-literal interpretations, which stand in contrast to or in tension with the literal, present themselves.

In addition, we have begun in Cultural Modeling to try to capture strategies that are useful—in noticing the details signaling this kind of reading between the lines; in recognizing that a pattern of details signals particular interpretive problems; and in reconstructing interpretations that can be strongly warranted. The problems of noticing, imposing meaning on patterns, and reconstructing interpretations are strongly influenced by other sources of knowledge that readers need (Rabinowitz 1987). I have mentioned these earlier. They include knowledge of authors, of other texts, of literary traditions. This knowledge is most often used to warrant claims made about literary texts. For example, a reader might argue that an interpretation makes sense because it is consistent with other works by the same author, with works exemplifying similar themes, or produced within similar literary traditions.

While I absolutely recognize the importance of this kind of literary knowledge, I argue that knowledge about authors, other texts, and literary traditions is insufficient, especially for novice readers, to construct rich and nuanced interpretations. Our work in Cultural Modeling has been effective, providing students with guided practice in understanding how they reason about these key interpretive problems in everyday experience and then how these same strategies can be used to dig deeply into the innards of canonical literature (Lee 1993, 1995a, b, 2001). This work has been done primarily with high school students with low scores on standardized reading tests and histories of low academic achievement.

While in this chapter I discuss the application of this everyday knowledge to response to literature, I have found that students' use of AAE can be tapped to help them produce rich written narratives (Lee, Rosenfeld, et al. 2003). In a similar vein, Smitherman (1994, 2000) examined essays from 1969 to 1988 from the National Assessment of Educational Progress and found positive correlations between the overall quality of essays as judged by NAEP raters and the presence of what she calls African American English discourse features. My work with Cultural Modeling in the teaching of literature and composition supports

Vygotsky's (1981) belief that what students can do with support is greater than what they can do by themselves. Thus, modeling with cultural data sets as a transition to canonical problems has proven fruitful for students who typically are underachieving in our nation's schools.

References

BAUGH, J. 1983. *Black Street Speech: Its History, Structure and Survival*. Austin: University of Texas Press.

BOOTH, W. C. 1974. *A Rhetoric of Irony*. Chicago: University of Chicago Press.

————. 1983. *A Rhetoric of Fiction*. Chicago: University of Chicago Press.

COLE, M. 1996. *Cultural Psychology, A Once and Future Discipline*. Cambridge, MA: The Belknap Press of Harvard University Press.

————. 1998. "Can Cultural Psychology Help Us Think About Diversity?" *Mind, Culture, and Activity* 56 (4): 291–304.

D'ANDRADE, R. G. 1995. *The Development of Cognitive Anthropology*. New York: Cambridge University Press.

GUTIERREZ, K., AND B. ROGOFF. 2003. "Cultural Ways of Learning: Individual Traits or Repertoires of Practice." *Educational Researcher* 32 (5): 19–25.

HILLOCKS, G., JR. 1975. *Observing and Writing*. Urbana, IL: National Council of Teachers of English.

————. 1986. *Research on Written Composition: New Directions for Teaching*. Urbana, IL: National Conference on Research in English/ERIC Clearninghouse on Reading and Communication Skills.

————. 1995. *Teaching Writing as Reflective Practice*. New York: Teachers College Press.

————. 1999. *Ways of Thinking, Ways of Teaching*. New York: Teachers College Press.

HILLOCKS, G., B. J. McCABE, AND J. F. McCAMPBELL. 1971. *The Dynamics of English Instruction, Grades 7–12*. New York: Random House

JOHANNESSEN, L.R., E. KAHN, AND C. WALTER. 1982. *Designing and Sequencing Prewriting Activities*. Urbana, IL: National Council of Teachers of English.

KITWANA, B. 2002. *The Hip Hop Generation: Young Blacks and the Crisis in African American Culture*. New York: Basic Civitas.

LABOV, W. 1972. *Language in the Inner City: Studies in the Black English Vernacular*. Philadelphia: University of Pennsylvania Press.

LAVE, J. 1988. *Cognition in Practice: Mind, Mathematics and Culture in Everyday Life*. Cambridge: Cambridge University Press.

LEE, C. D. 1992. "Profile of an Independent Black Institution: African-Centered Education at Work." *Journal of Negro Education* 61 (2): 160–77.

————. 1993. *Signifying as a Scaffold for Literary Interpretation: The Pedagogical Implications of an African American Discourse Genre*. NCTE Research Report No. 26. Urbana, IL: National Council of Teachers of English.

————. 1995a. "A Culturally Based Cognitive Apprenticeship: Teaching African American High School Students' Skills in Literary Interpretation." *Reading Research Quarterly* 30 (4): 608–31.

————. 1995b. "Signifying as a Scaffold for Literary Interpretation." *Journal of Black Psychology* 21 (4): 357–81.

————. 1997. "Bridging Home and School Literacies: A Model of Culturally Responsive Teaching." In *A Handbook for Literacy Educators: Research on Teaching the Communicative and Visual Arts*, edited by J. Flood, S. B. Heath, and D. Lapp, 330–41. New York: Macmillan.

————. 2000. "Signifying in the Zone of Proximal Development." In *Vygotskian Perspectives on Literacy Research: Constructing Meaning Through Collaborative Inquiry*, edited by C. D. Lee and P. Smagorinsky, 191–225. New York: Cambridge University Press.

————. 2001. "Is October Brown Chinese? A Cultural Modeling Activity System for Underachieving Students." *American Educational Research Journal* 38 (1): 97–142.

LEE, C. D., E. ROSENFELD, R. MENDENHALL, A. RIVERS, AND B. TYNES. 2003. "Cultural Modeling as a Framework for Narrative Analysis." In *Narrative Analysis: Studying the Development of Individuals in Society*, edited by C. L. Dauite. Thousand Oaks CA: Sage.

LEE, C. D., M. B. SPENCER, AND V. HARPALANI. 2003. "Every Shut Eye Ain't Sleep: Studying How People Live Culturally." *Educational Researcher* 32 (5): 6–13.

MAHIRI, J., ED. 2004. *What They Don't Learn in School: Literacy in the Lives of Urban Youths.* New York: Peter Lang.

MEACHAM, S. J. 2000. "Black Self-Love, Language, and the Teacher Education Dilemma: The Cultural Denial and Cultural Limbo of African American Preservice Teachers." *Urban Education* 34: 571–96.

MITCHELL-KERNAN, C. 1981. "Signifying, Loud-Talking and Marking." In *Mother Wit from the Laughing Barrel*, edited by A. Dundes, 310–28. Englewood, Cliffs, NJ: Prentice-Hall:

MORRELL, E. 2002. "Toward a Critical Pedagogy of Popular Culture: Literacy Development Among Urban Youth." *Journal of Adolescent and Adult Literacy* 46 (1): 72–77.

MORRISON, T. 1970. *The Bluest Eye.* New York: Random House.

MUFWENE, S., J. RICKFORD, ET AL. 1998. *African-American English: Structure, History and Use.* New York: Routledge.

NASIR, N., AND G. SAXE 2003. "Emerging Tensions and Their Management in the Lives of Minority Students." *Educational Researcher* 32 (5): 14–18.

NUNES, T., A. D. SCHLIEMANN AND D. W. CAFRAHER. 1993. *Street Mathematics and School Mathematics.* New York: Cambridge University Press.

ORTONY, A. 1979. *Metaphor and Thought.* New York: Cambridge University Press.

RABINOWITZ, P. 1987. *Before Reading: Narrative Conventions and the Politics of Interpretation.* Ithaca, NY: Cornell University Press.

ROGOFF, B. 2003. *The Cultural Nature of Human Development.* New York: Oxford University Press.

ROGOFF, B., AND J. LAVE 1984. *Everyday Cognition: Its development in Social Context.* Cambridge, MA: Harvard University Press.

ROSE, T. 1994. *Black Noise: Rap Music and Black Culture in Contemporary America.* Hanover, NH: University Press of New England.

SAXE, D. W. 1992. "Framing a Theory for Social Studies Foundations." *Review of Educational Research* 62 (3): 259–77.

SAXE, G. 1991. *Culture and Cognitive Development: Studies in Mathematical Understanding.* Hillsdale, NJ: Lawrence Erlbaum Associates.

SCRIBNER, S., AND M. COLE 1981. *The Psychology of Literacy.* Cambridge, MA: Harvard University Press.

SMAGORINSKY, P. 1991. "The Writer's Knowledge and the Writing Process: A Protocol Analysis." *Research in the Teaching of English* 25: 339–64.

SMAGORINKSY, P., T. MCCANN, AND S. KERN. 1987. *Explorations: Introductory Activities for Literature and Composition, 7–12.* Urbana, IL: National Council of Teachers of English.

SMAGORINSKY, P., AND S. GEVINSON 1989. *Fostering the Reader's Response: Rethinking the Literature Curriculum, Grades 7–12.* Palo Alto, CA: Dale Seymour.

SMITH, M. 1991. "Constructing Meaning from Text: An Analysis of Ninth-Grade Reader Responses." *Journal of Educational Research* 84 (5): 263–71.

SMITH, M., AND G. HILLOCKS. 1988. "Sensible Sequencing: Developing Knowledge About Literature Text by Text." *English Journal* 77 (October): 44–49.

SMITHERMAN, G. 1977. *Talkin and Testifyin: The Language of Black America.* Boston: Houghton Mifflin.

———. 1994. "The Blacker the Berry, the Sweeter the Juice: African American Student Writers." In *The Need for Story: Cultural Diversity in Classroom and Community*, edited by A. Dyson and C. Genishi, 80–101. Urbana, IL: National Council of Teachers of English.

SMITHERMAN, G., ED. 2000. "African American Student Writers in the NAEP, 1969–1988/89" and "The Blacker the Berry, the Sweeter the Juice." In *Talkin That Talk: Language, Culture and Education in African America*, 163–94. New York: Routledge.

VYGOTSKY, L. 1981. "The Genesis of Higher Mental Functions." In *The Concept of Activity in Soviet Psychology*, edited by J. Wertsch. Armonk, NY: M. E. Sharpe.

WEAVER, C. 1996. *Teaching Grammar in Context.* Portsmouth, NH: Heinemann.

WINNER, E. 1988. *The Point of Words: Children's Understanding of Metaphor and Irony.* Cambridge, MA: Harvard University Press.

WOLFRAM, W., C. ADGER, AND D. CHRISTIAN. 1999. *Dialects in Schools and Communities.* Mahwah, NJ: Lawrence Erlbaum Associates.

WOLFRAM, W., AND N. SCHILLING-ESTES. 1998. *American English: Dialects and Variation.* Oxford, England: Basil Blackwell.

12

Critically Thinking About Harry Potter
Applying a Hillocksian Inquiry Framework to Controversial Works in the English Classroom

JOANNE M. MARSHALL
Iowa State University
Ames, Iowa

An Inquiry Framework for Controversial Works

Other authors in this book have delineated the way in which Hillocks' conception of *inquiry* can be applied to literature in the English classroom. Teachers can design introductory activities and assignments that encourage students to utilize a "strategy of inquiry" (Hillocks 1982), whereby students are presented with a set of data—often a work of literature itself—and asked to identify patterns and to come to some conclusions about, for example, its themes, characters, or imagery. Once they have come to some conclusions, usually during small- and large-group discussion, they can present those conclusions in a coherent written or verbal argument, using their data as evidence to support a thesis. Hillocks' work as well as that of others has established that an inquiry process is beneficial for improving both students' discussion and written work (Hillocks 1986, 1987; Johannessen 1989, 2001; Smith and Hillocks 1989).

This kind of inquiry process can be especially beneficial when teaching controversial works of literature, because the process can encourage teachers and students to acknowledge and analyze the controversy itself. Students can engage the work on a meta-analytical level, asking themselves and each other what it is about this work that makes it controversial, providing evidence from the work to support their opinions, and ultimately coming to a statement about whether the work is "worth" reading. An example of this inquiry process as applied to controversial works is provided in this chapter using the Harry Potter series.

Harry Potter as Test Case

Since J. K. Rowling's Harry Potter series was first published in 1997, parents, teachers, and readers of all ages have been fans of the boy wizard, enthusiastically standing in bookstore lines at midnight to purchase the next installment, or flocking to the movies, or rushing to buy the DVD. Previously reluctant readers, including young adult readers (MacRae 2000), are suddenly enthralled with a book, and the adults who care for those readers are equally enthralled with its results. Magic, indeed.

However, not everyone has been under Harry's spell. The American Library Association reported in 2004 that from 1999 to 2003 the Harry Potter series were either the most-challenged or the second most-challenged books on their Challenged Books List, and there have even been reports of the books' public burning (Goldberg 2002b) or cutting (Goldberg 2002a). These rejections of Harry have been largely from a few conservative Christian groups who feel that the Bible's many admonitions against the practice of witchcraft and sorcery (see Deuteronomy 18:9–14, for example) are to be taken seriously (Abanes 2001). Other critics feel that the books are often violent and scary, and note that sometimes its characters disobey or disregard authority. These parents, therefore, both religious and nonreligious, are concerned about the negative influence such a story, especially such an extremely popular story, could have on their children. It is important to note, therefore, both that Harry Potter's critics are not limited to conservative Christians and that not all conservative Christians condemn the books. Some authors in Christian publications view the books as morally positive and uplifting (see, for example, Jacobs 2000; Maudlin 2000; Granger 2004), while others have written thoughtful, if not completely accepting, analyses (see, for example, Faries 2000; Neal 2001).

Regardless of the source of people's discontent with Harry and his friends, the popularity of the books, when combined with the vociferous objections to their use in English classrooms, serves to make Harry Potter an ideal test case for how teachers and media specialists can handle controversial works using Hillocksian inquiry.

A Framework for Discussing Controversial Works

The most important step in bridging ideological gaps is to open discussion. As *Educational Leadership* editor Alex Molnar writes, "Educators too often do a poor job of reaching out to diverse groups of parents and community members and drawing them into the life of their schools" (1994, 5). At the school level and in the classroom, English educators can lead the way in open discussion, particularly discussion about books such as the Harry Potter series. I offer the following seven-step framework as a way to begin that discussion, having tested it in three young-adult literature college classrooms and one adult-education church classroom. While my experience has been with college-age or older adults, I am confident that young adults in high school or middle school classrooms would also benefit from this exercise, which is at its heart an exercise in critical thinking. Although the Harry Potter books are of immediate interest because of their current buzz, the framework could be adapted to any other work of media.

First, I ask students (a) if they have read any of the Harry Potter books or (b) if they have seen the movie. I count the people to get an idea of my audience. I ask people to keep their hands up for a moment so that those who haven't read the books or seen a movie can find the Harry Potter readers or movie-watchers later when answering group questions that require some in-depth knowledge of the stories.

Second, I summarize the story very briefly. My summary, which I put on a slide, is:

> Harry, an orphan living with his mean aunt and uncle, discovers at age eleven, when summoned to Hogwarts School of Witchcraft and Wizardry, that he has magical powers and is famous in the magical world—a sort of parallel England—for surviving evil Lord Voldemort's attack on his parents. Adventures at school ensue as Harry learns more.

I ask the group if there are any questions or if anyone would like to add any other key details.

Third, I draw "for Harry" and "against Harry" columns on a chalkboard and ask the class to quickly fill in the arguments for reading the Harry Potter books and against reading them. As a group, people have been quite good at filling in both sides, even when it is obvious that they wholeheartedly agree with only one side.

Fourth, I introduce the concept of finding common ground by thinking critically about the book, calling the group to a democratic ideal of open discussion and asking them to try to see the other side's point of view, complimenting them on a good beginning by their success in fulfilling step three. I also introduce the concepts of ascertainment and discernment, modified from Ted Baehr's work (1998). Ascertainment is simply the idea of figuring out what happens, as in ascertaining the facts about something—in this case, what happens in the Harry Potter story. Discernment is the personal application of that ascertainment, or how what happens affects you as a reader, if at all. For most readers, the *Oxford English Dictionary*'s definition of discernment as "The act of discerning or perceiving by the intellect; intellectual perception or apprehension" suffices. In other words, discernment is about thinking critically. In conservative Christian theology, discernment is also a spiritual gift, the ability to tell good from evil, or to "discern between the spirits" (I Corinthians 12:10; Thomson and Elwell 1996). So in Christian theology, discernment is also about thinking, or perhaps feeling, critically. There is, therefore, some common ground available around these ideas of ascertainment and discernment. While everyone might agree on what happens in the book, there is room to disagree about how what happens might affect the reader. Regardless of the opinions, however, the application of ascertainment and discernment requires readers to discuss the book critically. I emphasize that the point of this exercise is not to tell people *what* to think about reading the Harry Potter series, but to provide an opportunity for people—whether adults, young adults, or younger students—to practice *how* to think about books or other media.

Fifth, I provide a handout (see Figure 12–1) based on the work of Baehr (1998) and Romanowski (2001), a media professor. There are three columns. The first column provides two sets of questions in eight categories for readers to answer about the Harry Potter series, providing evidence for their responses in the second column. One set of questions is intended to help the reader ascertain the facts of what's going on in the Harry Potter books; the other set is intended to help the reader discern the impact of those facts. Readers use the third column to indicate whether they think, given their answers to the questions and evidence from the books or movies, Harry Potter is a positive, negative, or neutral influence. I break the audience into small groups, asking them to make sure they have at least one Harry Potter reader or viewer in the group, and then I assign each group one of the eight categories to discuss. Categories include questions about how the hero, the villain, violence, sex, Christianity/religion, worldview/culture, moral lessons, and authority are addressed in the book. Category number four, sex, is not really relevant to the Harry Potter series—yet—but it is included here so that the framework might be applied to other media.

Sixth, I compile column three responses from each group, writing each positive, negative, or neutral evaluation on the board. When finished, I ask the group if they are surprised by any of the ratings, if they have questions for any group, and if there are any group's ratings they would like to discuss. These questions lead to some lively discussion, as groups ask questions of others, defend their answers, and provide textual evidence for their responses.

Finally, I ask the audience to make an overall statement about whether they think these particular books are worth reading, and if there are any limits they would place on their being read. These questions provoke interesting discussion about the value of the books as well as age-appropriateness. If I were using this framework in a high school or middle school classroom, I would ask students to write a short persuasive essay outlining their position about the appropriateness of Harry Potter, in keeping with research on the positive effects that inquiry-based activities such as this one have on student writing (Hillocks 1986; Johannessen 2001). Or I might ask them to apply the framework to another piece of literature. The framework is intentionally broad enough to be used for any work of literature or movie and with any group of people, from young adults to concerned parents.

Working with Controversy

As readers and educators, we tacitly acknowledge the power that books have on us. We fall in love with stories, can't stop talking about books, and hope that we share some of that love with younger readers as we teach and model reading. We teach books by diverse authors so that our students can learn about others' experiences and points of view, perhaps even feeling something in response, and our literary theory acknowledges the power of experience and reader response (Rosenblatt 1991; Scholes 1989). So it should not be completely surprising to us that parents are concerned about their own children's affective response to a particular set of

FIGURE 12–1 *Questioning Framework: Ascertainment and Discernment*

Questioning Framework: Ascertainment and Discernment

Ascertaining/Discerning Questions	Answers/Evidence from Harry Potter	How does Harry rate? (positive, negative, or neutral)

1. The Hero
 	
▪ Ascertain:
  ▪ Who is the hero?
  ▪ Why does he or she succeed?
▪ Discern:
  ▪ Who is the hero?
    ▪ Heroes fight man, nature, self, supernatural
    ▪ What kind of role model is that hero?		

2. The Villain
 	
▪ Ascertain:
  ▪ Who is the villain?
    ▪ Villains fight man, nature, self, supernatural
▪ Discern:
  ▪ What is the message behind the villain's role?
    ▪ Is the villain sympathetic?
    ▪ What's the source of evil?		

3. Violence
 	
▪ Ascertain:
  ▪ How much violence is there?
▪ Discern:
  ▪ How is the violence portrayed?
    ▪ Necessary? Fun? Normal?
    ▪ Shock factor?		

Continues

Reflective Teaching, Reflective Learning edited by McCann, Johannessen, Kahn, Smagorinsky, and Smith (Heinemann: Portsmouth, NH); © 2005.

FIGURE 12–1 *Questioning Framework: Ascertainment and Discernment* (continued)

Questioning Framework: Ascertainment and Discernment

Ascertaining/Discerning Questions	Answers/Evidence from Harry Potter	How does Harry rate? (positive, negative, or neutral)

4. Sex
• Ascertain:
 ▪ How much sex is there?
• Discern:
 ▪ How is the sex portrayed?
  ▪ Loving and glorious in marriage or a committed relationship?
  ▪ Fun and frequent goal outside marriage or a committed relationship?		

5. Christianity/Religion
• Ascertain:
 ▪ What's the role of religion, the church, God, Christians, or other religions in this story?
• Discern:
 ▪ How is religion, etc., portrayed?
  ▪ Foolish, weak?
  ▪ Admirable?		

6. The Worldview/Culture
• Ascertain:
 ▪ What is the worldview or the culture like in the book/movie?
• Discern:
 ▪ How is the worldview or culture portrayed?
  ▪ Gloomy, hopeless, violent, exotic, everyday?
  ▪ What's the value of life? Worth living?		

Continues

Reflective Teaching, Reflective Learning edited by McCann, Johannessen, Kahn, Smagorinsky, and Smith (Heinemann: Portsmouth, NH); © 2005.

Questioning Framework: Ascertainment and Discernment

Ascertaining/Discerning Questions	Answers/Evidence from Harry Potter	How does Harry rate? (positive, negative, or neutral)

7. **Moral Lessons**
■ Ascertain:
  ▪ What are the moral lessons of the piece?
■ Discern:
  ▪ How do those lessons compare with typical moral or religious lessons		

8. **Authority**
■ Ascertain:
  ▪ Who or what are authorities? (adults, government, tradition, God, etc.)
■ Discern:
  ▪ Are the authorities worth respect? Do they make good decisions? How do they compare with real-life authorities?		

Source: Adapted from T. Baehr. 1998. *The Media-Wise Family*. Colorado Springs, CO: ChariotVictor/Cook; and W. D. Romanowski. 2001. *Eyes Wide Open: Looking for God in Popular Culture*. Grand Rapids, MI: Brazos/Baker.

Reflective Teaching, Reflective Learning edited by McCann, Johannessen, Kahn, Smagorinsky, and Smith (Heinemann: Portsmouth, NH); © 2005.

stories. Rather than dismissing those concerns as ridiculous or crying "censorship!" we should instead work to try to understand them. The advantage of the framework provided here is that it acknowledges those concerns and provides a voice for them while also demanding that readers think critically about what they are reading. In that sense, then, we can use controversy to make our classrooms places devoted to diverse and well-reasoned voices, and we can encourage students to be better thinkers and writers.

References

ABANES, R. 2001. *Harry Potter and the Bible: The Menace Behind the Magick.* Camp Hill, PA: Horizon.

AMERICAN LIBRARY ASSOCIATION. 2004. "Alice Beats Harry Potter as Most-Challenged Series." Retrieved October 1, 2004, from www.ala.org/ala/alonline/currentnews/newsarchive/alnews2004/february2004/challenged.htm.

BAEHR, T. 1998. *The Media-Wise Family.* Colorado Springs, CO: Chariot Victor/Cook.

FARIES, K. 2000. "Why Harry Potter Is Not the Chronicles of Narnia." *Radix* 27: 18–21.

GOLDBERG, B. 2002a. "Harry Potter Bewitches Fans, Foes at the Library, Movies." *American Libraries* 33 (1): 27.

———. 2002b. "Pastor's Potter Book Fire Inflames New Mexican Town." *American Libraries* 33 (2): 19.

GRANGER, J. 2004. *Looking for God in Harry Potter.* Carol Stream, IL: Tyndale.

HILLOCKS G., JR. 1982. "Inquiry and the Composing Process: Theory and Research." *College English* 44 (7): 659–73.

———. 1986. *Research on Written Composition: New Directions for Teaching.* Urbana, IL: ERIC/NCRE.

———. 1987. "Synthesis of Research on Teaching Writing." *Educational Leadership* 44 (8): 71–82.

JACOBS, A. 2000. "Harry Potter's Magic." *First Things* 99 (January): 35–38.

JOHANNESSEN, L. R. 1989. "Teaching Writing: Motivating Inquiry." *English Journal* 78: 64–66.

———. 2001. "Teaching Thinking and Writing for a New Century." *English Journal* 90 (6): 38–46.

MACRAE, C. D. 2000. "Harry Potter Update: Is It for YAs?" *English Journal* 89 (4): 137–38.

MAUDLIN, M. G. 2000. "Virtue on a Broomstick." *Christianity Today* 44 (September): 117.

MOLNAR, A. 1994. "Fundamental Differences?" *Educational Leadership* 51 (4): 4–5.

NEAL, C. 2001. *What's a Christian to Do with Harry Potter?* Colorado Springs, CO: Waterbrook.

ROMANOWSKI, W. D. 2001. *Eyes Wide Open: Looking for God in Popular Culture.* Grand Rapids, MI: Brazos/Baker.

ROSENBLATT, L. M. 1991. "Literary Theory." In *Handbook of Research on Teaching the English Language Arts*, edited by J. Flood, J. M. Jensen, D. Lapp, and J. R. Squire. New York: Maxwell Macmillan.

SCHOLES, R. 1989. *Protocols of Reading*. New Haven, CT: Yale University Press.

SMITH, M. W., AND G. J. HILLOCKS. 1989. "What Inquiring Writers Need to Know." *English Journal* 78 (2): 58–63.

THOMSON, J. G. S. S., AND W. A. ELWELL. 1996. "Spiritual Gifts." In *Evangelical Dictionary of Theology*, 1042–46. Grand Rapids, MI: Baker.

INQUIRY, LEARNING, AND REFLECTION

13

From What to How
Developing Procedural Knowledge in the English Classroom

KIERSTIN THOMPSON
Downers Grove South High School
Downers Grove, Illinois

JENNIFER ROLOFF WELCH
Harvard Graduate School of Education
Cambridge, Massachusetts

As teachers we're well aware that knowing what we're supposed to do is not the same as being able to do it. Realizing, for example, that we want our evaluation to support our instruction or that we want our classroom rules to foster the creation of a learning community or that we want students to be able to do a critical analysis of texts doesn't mean that we have mastered the means by which to achieve those goals. What is true for us as teachers is also true for our students. If we teach them by, say, only presenting model readings of texts or analyzing the features of model papers, we are merely presenting them with goals for their learning. We are not helping them develop the knowledge they need to achieve those goals. In this chapter, we argue that teachers need to go beyond helping students understand *what* they need to do by helping them understand *how* they can do it, and we share a series of lessons that exemplifies our approach.

Our work has its foundation in two strands of literature connected to teaching English. The first is George Hillocks' inquiry-based learning, from which we are drawing the concept of procedural knowledge, or teaching students *how* to complete a task such as writing an argument. The second strand of literature is related to metacognition in the classroom, or teaching students to be mindful of their own actions as learners.

Procedural Knowledge

George Hillocks, Jr. talks frequently about the differences between declarative knowledge and procedural knowledge. As he explains, the difference lies with how thinking and knowing take place. Declarative knowledge is knowledge that can be spoken. Students hear information, record it, perhaps memorize it, and then retell it in almost the same form in a test or essay. Procedural knowledge is knowledge of doing. To get it, students have to engage in thinking about information together, process it with the help of the teacher and their peers, and use the new information to process new knowledge. Hillocks (1999) summarizes in this way: "The essence of procedural knowledge lies in what the students do in class. It is learning *how*" (28). And, he explains, procedural knowledge ought to be the essence of classroom instruction:

> Curiously, though the level of declarative [the *what*] and procedural knowledge [the *how*] in classrooms varies from teacher to teacher, all of our writing teachers evaluate their students on the basis of their written products, products that necessarily reflect the acquisition of procedural knowledge.... Some teachers tell their classes that they want them to learn *how* to perform the operations involved in various types of writing and help them to do so. (28)

As students of George Hillocks, Jr. we learned that teaching students to think critically involves the *how* of learning.

Peter Smagorinsky's (1991) research provides a compelling rationale for focusing on the procedural. In his study, high school students were assessed after they experienced three different kinds of teaching about writing: teaching that focused on declarative knowledge of form in which writing models were shown to students as exemplars; teaching that focused on general procedures for writing, in which students learned to freewrite; and teaching that focused on task-specific procedural knowledge in which students were given problems that required them to apply the strategies needed to write extended definitions. Based on two measures that included writing and critical thinking, students who had been taught the task-specific procedural knowledge scored highest. Next were students who were taught general procedural knowledge, and lowest were students who were taught only with declarative models or exemplars.

The research of Hillocks (1986, 1995, 1999) and Smagorinsky (1991) provides a powerful argument that teachers have the best results with their students when they make goals and criteria explicit and when they engage them in activities to help them develop procedures for meeting those goals and criteria. When we help students develop the procedures, we are not declaring what students should write. Rather, we are giving them tools to think and write on their own.

Instead of focusing our attention on the content of what students will write about—for example, by developing discussion questions that can lead students to a particular interpretation of a literary work—we think teachers will be well served by focusing on a different set of questions: What are the processes that writers follow? How does one produce solid writing? How does one assess one's own work? These are questions that we want students to internalize and be able to answer by the time they leave our classrooms. These are the processes of thinking about one's own thinking and writing that we think will stay with students long after they have left our classrooms.

Metacognition

Knowing the content and learning the process of understanding that content are the first steps toward a classroom whose students succeed in learning *how* to learn and know. The second step is "thinking about thinking" (Fogarty 1994, vii) and considering how one is an actor in the process of learning. Sitko (1998) writes about the research in metacognition and writing instruction and shows the link between "process knowledge" and "product knowledge" (94). She explains that in the research by Flavell and Wellman (1977) and Brown (1987), definitions and explanations of metacognition were developed and described. She writes, "These definitions include knowledge of the task and one's own cognitive resources, and monitoring, or the ability to control and regulate one's own thinking." When we teach students material, we think it is also our job to teach them how to think about the materials, and then how to think about their thinking. Central to metacognition is thinking about one's thought processes. According to Hacker (1998), "Thinking can be of what one knows (i.e., metacognitive knowledge), what one is currently doing (i.e., metacognitive skill), or what one's current cognitive or affective state is (i.e., metacognitive experience)" (3). He asserts:

> Thus, the promise of metacognitive theory is that it focuses precisely on those characteristics of thinking that can contribute to students' awareness and understanding of being self-regulatory organisms, that is, of being agents in their own thinking. (20)

We encourage students to develop these three aspects of metacognition because in so doing, students are not using the teacher as an external source for reassurance and recognition. Rather, they are using themselves and their awareness of their own thinking processes to gauge their understanding of materials. Teaching metacognition is a way to empower students, to let them know that while information may come from outside them, the ability to process it, use it, and remember it lies within them. Teaching metacognition in the classroom encourages "deliberate, planful, and goal-oriented thinking" (Hacker 1998, 3).

To show these steps in action in an English classroom, we are presenting a unit of instruction that begins by focusing on the theme of *what it means to be a good student* and that later addresses *what it means to be a good writer*. Students in this unit learn about good student habits through a series of inquiry-based activities. Students in turn look inward at themselves to assess where they are in terms of good student habits. Later, students engage in activities related to writing processes, and then use the criteria they set for good writing to judge their own written work. In this way, students look outward at materials and then inward at themselves to assess and monitor their own work and progress. We hope that this process helps students to learn to trust themselves and their own authentic understanding of themselves as learners rather than relying on what teachers tell them is good and right about the work they produce. Thus, our work in this unit is guided by the following two fundamental beliefs:

1. Students should have both an understanding of the content material and learn the process of critically thinking through that material.

2. Students should get to know themselves as learners and follow up that knowledge with activities aimed at self-assessment—a look back at their writing and look forward to what they will do to progress as writers.

What Is a Good Student?

Establishing a culture of serious academic study is a difficult task in the average ninth-grade English class. As new teachers, we were surprised at the inconsistency in students' beliefs and habits with regard to academic honesty and the work ethic. Perhaps the surprise was a result of naïveté. After all, our students come to our classes having experienced different teachers, different texts, different rules, different technologies, and different standards.

We knew that in order to accomplish our goal of creating a culture of serious study, we would first have to work to align our students' expectations with our own. As any classroom teacher knows, this is easier said than done. In the first place, it requires that we clearly delineate our own expectations, something we realized we hadn't done. After much discussion, we determined that we wanted our students to look beyond grades in their assessment of what made a good student and to at least consider the following characteristics:

- Good students manage their time

- Good students take pride in their own ideas

- Good students always try to improve

- Good students contribute to the learning environment

- Good students take positive risks

But delineating our own expectations is only half the battle. It takes only a few years of teaching experience to develop an arsenal of examples of expectations that are misconstrued or misinterpreted by students. And while after-the-fact discussions of where things went wrong are present in every teacher's workroom, we wanted to establish methods that would alter our students' practices so that their work would satisfy not only our expectations, but, more important, their own. In order to accomplish this goal we needed to raise our students' awareness about themselves as students through inquiry. Inquiry-based activities would help them develop an articulated understanding of their goals in a way that direct lecture never could.

As students of George Hillocks, we were both familiar with using scenario-based activities for the purposes of introducing literature and preparing written compositions (Johannessen, Kahn, and Walter 1982; Smagorinsky, McCann, and Kern 1987). We knew that scenarios provide students with controversial situations that promote inquiry as students discuss those controversies (Hillocks 1995). Controversial situations compel students to offer opinions and to solve problems through negotiation. If we could use controversial scenarios to raise questions about what it means to be a good student and then ask students to discuss and resolve those questions, we would be enabling them to articulate and defend their expectations and to assess how their expectations might promote or hinder their success. In effect we would help them become good students.

To determine the subjects of the scenarios, we simply recalled challenging or troubling situations we had dealt with as teachers of public high school students. We thought that if the situations challenged us, they'd challenge our students as well. We wrote brief scenes narrating those situations and presented them to our classes.

In our minds, the best way to introduce an inquiry-based activity is to set the stage for debate by inviting the entire class to discuss a scenario together before releasing them into small-group discussion. To kick off the activity we chose a scenario that focuses on a potentially controversial though time-honored tradition: exploiting an older sibling's experience and knowledge for personal achievement.

Anya is a student in Mr. Harpster's physical science class. As part of an assignment the students are required to weigh and measure different household substances and write a report on their findings. Anya's older sister, Bev, had to do the same assignment two years ago so Anya asks for Bev's help. Bev hands her sister her graded report. Anya records her sister's measurements and then writes her own original lab report. Is Anya a good student?

We allow students to respond openly without much intervening. At first they are a little shocked by the fact that a teacher has knowledge of this tradition and wants to discuss it publicly. But after the shock wears off, they seem intrigued enough to offer their perspective. As the students offer their opinions, we ask probing questions in order to encourage them to elucidate the reasoning behind their assessment. It is extremely important that the students persuade each other, even in this whole-class example, as the large-group discussion sets the stage for the small-group discussions. Once a few different viewpoints are expressed, we explain that they should participate in similar conversations in small groups and emphasize that their conversation is important because they are going to determine the classroom expectations regarding being a good student.

We then put the students into small groups and distribute a handout entitled "What Makes a Good Student" that includes various other Good Student scenarios we developed (see Figure 13–1). While students discuss the scenes, we walk around, mostly listening, asking questions only if a group falls silent. Often students ask the question, "What if we don't agree?" The candid answer is, "Perfect! That's how the activity was designed," but students are typically more satisfied with, "It's okay to disagree, but you must defend your opinions to determine the best answer."

The small-group discussion of the scenarios generally takes about thirty minutes. When most groups have finished their discussions, we ask them to return to their seats for a whole-class discussion. In leading this discussion we try to intervene only

FIGURE 13–1 *What Makes a Good Student*

What Makes a Good Student?

Directions: Read the scenarios below. Discuss each one at length in your group. Determine whether or not the person in the scenario is a good student. Then offer rules for good students that the person either meets or does not meet.

1. Dahlia has been assigned to do an expository paper on the state of civil rights today. She needs a good grade on this project to raise her C+ to a B in Mr. Enriquez' current issues class. Dahlia starts her research early. She finds some magazine articles and takes notes on them for the report. She also finds a college student's paper titled, What the U.S. Needs Now Is a New Civil Rights Leader. The introduction to the paper states exactly what she wants to say so she uses some of the same ideas in her introduction. The paper was a huge success; it received an A. Is Dahlia a good student? How could she be a better student?

   YES   NO

   Rule: _____

2. Preston doesn't mind going to Mr. Plimpton's English class. Often, he just sits in his seat listening carefully to what the other students have to say. He is never quite sure what Mr. Plimpton's expectations are on a paper. For every paper he's turned in he's gotten a D. But that is a passing grade so Preston doesn't bother to read the comments. He's never really been good at English and he accepts it as his one weakness. Is Preston a good student? How could he be a better student?

   YES   NO

   Rule: _____

3. Maria is a popular student whom everyone seems to like. She is especially helpful to one particular disabled student whom Maria helps with homework almost every day after school. Maria and this student, Joey, sit outside the cafeteria working on math problems. Maria likes to sit where teachers and students can see her so that they know how helpful she's being to another student. Is Maria a good student? Why or why not? How could she be a better student?

   YES   NO

   Rule: _____

Continues

FIGURE 13–1 *What Makes a Good Student* (continued)

4. Marc sits in algebra class and knows he can answer Mrs. Canto's questions, but he is afraid to get the answer wrong in front of the class and possibly be made fun of by his classmates. He feels like Mrs. Canto doesn't think he's smart because he never raises his hand and looks away when she makes eye contact with him. When other students answer in class and get the answer wrong, Marc joins in with others who make fun of the students. Is Marc a good student? Why or why not? How could he be a better student?

YES   NO

Rule: _____

5. Lucia has to study twice as long as some of her friends to earn the same grades that they get. Now that it's softball season, she knows she won't have a lot of time to study. With scouts visiting the team this year, she knows she has to be doing well in school and softball to get a scholarship. Her parents make her go to the school's resource center three mornings a week for extra homework help and ask her to quit two extracurricular clubs that she belongs to. She decides to do what her parents tell her. Is she a good student? Why or why not? How could she be a better student?

YES   NO

Rule: _____

6. Jack is an athlete and an expert on the computer. He already has a scholarship to one of the best Big Ten schools. In history class, he gives Mrs. Moore a hard time because they are studying the plight of the Native Americans and the loss of their land to the Europeans. Jack tells the teacher that this stuff isn't important because it took place so long ago and "Nobody cares about those people and what happened to them anyway." Is Jack a good student? Why or why not? How could he be a better student?

YES   NO

Rule: _____

7. In English class Jeannine decides to do a speech on mental illness. Jeannine's twenty-five-year-old sister has just been diagnosed with bipolar disorder, and Jeannine wants to understand this illness better. In her presentation Jeannine feels it's important to explain why she chose this project and how depression and mental illness have affected her family as well as a millions of Americans. She decides to include this in her speech even if it means that some of the students might judge her or her family. Is Jeannine a good student? Why or why not? How could she be a better student?

YES   NO

Rule: _____

Continues

Reflective Teaching, Reflective Learning edited by McCann, Johannessen, Kahn, Smagorinsky, and Smith (Heinemann: Portsmouth, NH); © 2005.

FIGURE 13–1 *What Makes a Good Student* (continued)

8. Terrence and Anita are lab partners in Mr. Orozco's chemistry class. Every week they are assigned a project that must be completed by the week's end. For the first month of school Terrence and Anita worked diligently during class time to complete their lab tests. Both would then show up with their individual homework the following day and continue their tests. Every Thursday they would meet after-school and compare their results and write their lab report in the library. Terrence particularly liked the Thursday after-school sessions; they gave him a chance to learn from Anita. He admired her precision and accuracy. As the year progressed, the lab assignments got more and more difficult. Terrence frequently asked for help from Anita. The partners started to fall behind a little in their lab tests and now had to meet Wednesday and Thursday nights to compensate for all of Terrence's questions. They both still hand their work in on time, but their grades have slipped a little. Are Terrence and Anita good students? How could they be better students?

    YES   NO

    Rule: _____

9. José chuckles to himself when he sees his peers rush home to do their home-work. José is enrolled in all honors courses and has the highest G.P.A. at Blake-Davis High School. Honors classes are a lot of work, but José has fig-ured out a surefire system for getting all the work done. José starts his home-work on the bus ride home. He skims the chapters he has to read for English and takes notes. At 11 o'clock after a few hours of TV and Internet, he starts his honors history. He reads the chapters and does half of the homework; he'll finish the rest in sociology. Science is next; he'll read the assigned packet, but the questions can wait until tomorrow. In the morning before school starts, José runs into Martina, who will give him the answers to the science questions because she has a crush on him. Another day is done and José Olamina is still at the top of his game. Is José a good student? How could he be a better student?

    YES   NO

    Rule: _____

    Continues

Reflective Teaching, Reflective Learning edited by McCann, Johannessen, Kahn, Smagorinsky, and Smith (Heinemann: Portsmouth, NH); © 2005.

FIGURE 13–1 *What Makes a Good Student* (continued)

10. Olivia sits quietly at the back of Mrs. Merkowitz' classroom. She dreads coming to this Algebra II class because the students are constantly asked to show their work on the blackboard. Mrs. Merkowitz is a devilish woman who calls on students who don't volunteer. Olivia has an A- in Algebra II, but hates showing off in front of the other students. She'd much rather just sit in her seat without drawing much attention. Mrs. Merkowitz isn't nearly as bad as Mr. Palmer. In his political science class there's always group work to be done and he never lets his students select the groups. Olivia doesn't say much in the group. She is afraid of being called a know-it-all if she gives too good of an answer. A lot of times she'll agree to do the writing for the group so that she can still get her participation points without saying a word. After all, she wants to keep her B. Is Olivia a good student? How could she be a better student?

YES NO

Rule: _____

11. Ari comes to class every day with his homework completed (and all the answers are normally correct!), but when he pulls it out of his backpack, the papers are usually ripped and crumpled. When he turns it in, he says he worked on it for hours and knows it's good work, but he always has an excuse for why the homework looks such a mess. His teachers have asked him to get a folder to keep his work neat and presentable, but Ari figures as long as he does the homework, what does the appearance matter? Sometimes, though, Ari is missing pages of his homework because they have ripped off the original packet. Is Ari a good student? Why or why not? How could he be a better student?

YES NO

Rule: _____

Reflective Teaching, Reflective Learning edited by McCann, Johannessen, Kahn, Smagorinsky, and Smith (Heinemann: Portsmouth, NH); © 2005.

with questions that ask students to substantiate their thinking. It is critical for students to feel as if they are in control of the decision making. Once some consensus is reached, we record the various rules on an overhead or the board. Some rules and criteria will be repeated because there are many rules that can be determined from each scenario. So our final activity is to reread the rules on the board and eliminate any repetition. Once the rules for a good student are established, we hang a poster of the rules as a reminder of the class's expectations for good student practice.

Knowledge of Self: Students' Examining and Setting Goals

We hoped that our students would measure themselves against the poster of rules. When Jennifer worked with a class of urban students in summer school, she wanted to make sure that students' self-measuring took place. So she drew on the work of Sean Covey, whose father, Stephen Covey (1989), wrote the best-selling *Seven Habits of Highly Effective People.* Sean Covey's (1998) book, *The Seven Habits of Highly Effective Teens,* is a tremendous resource for high school teachers and students, for it has many activities to engage students in thinking about themselves and their goals. The students enrolled in this summer school program did not need to be reminded of what their goal was (not very often at least—many of them needed this class in order to graduate or play ball the next year). Rather, they needed to learn how to set specific goals for themselves. This is where the Sean Covey book was extremely helpful and timely. Jennifer used many of the activities, especially those related to getting to know oneself, as introductory activities, then led the students through a series of activities, including one in which the students wrote their own mission statements. The students loved writing mission statements, but learned even more by coming back to those mission statements midsummer to assess how they were doing.

In order to write a mission statement, students had to be aware of themselves as active agents in the classroom. To help them plan, Jennifer gave them a handout that paraphrases the questions Covey poses:

- Name the qualities of a person you admire.

- Which people do you want around you in twenty years?

- What would you cross a steel beam between two skyscrapers for?

- Describe a time when you were inspired.

- What do you love to do?

- What would you study if given all day in a library?

- What would you want people in the future to say about you?

- Which animal represents you and why?

- Who would you like to spend an afternoon with if you could spend it with anyone?

The handout also included questions regarding their learning styles; for example: Would you claim to have talents such as "being good with numbers, words, creative thinking, accepting others, listening, singing, trivia?" (Covey 1998, 85–89). After students finished writing about themselves on this handout, Jennifer moved to the next part of the lesson: the mission statement.

The first step in this lesson is to acquaint students with what a mission statement is. Jennifer used the following definition: A statement of one's guiding beliefs and goals. In the spirit of what the summer school academy had created as its philosophy of teaching for the summer, each teacher and teaching team wrote individual mission statements. Sharing these statements allowed students to see models of what they would be doing as they embarked on writing, sharing, and presenting their own individual mission statements and then the mission statements that they and their small team created together.

Students began by writing for ten minutes or so to brainstorm individually and proceeded to write ideas for their own mission statements, which could be original or something they had heard previously (a slogan, song lyrics, or combinations of their own original ideas and what they were borrowing from somewhere). Students wrote one to five statements that they would like to consider as their mission statements for the semester or school year.

At this point, students moved from individual brainstorming to group work. After students shared their individual mission statements, they worked together to create one mission statement for the group, the way the teachers had. Students then made a poster of the collaborative efforts.

During the regular school year, Kierstin also followed this lesson plan with her suburban students. As the following mission statements from her class attest, students used the assignment to do some real soul searching:

I recognize the hardships school will bring and I am willing to work hard to overcome them. Lindsay, 14

My mission: I will take notes, and work hard to keep my grades at the best they can be. I will learn to accept my flaws, whether or not others don't. I will try to find new strengths, to make the flaws less obvious. Losing will no longer be a problem to me, I will accept it, and work harder to achieve victory in my next challenge. Being wrong is not a big deal, I will open my thoughts to others, and if they are wrong, then so be it, I've learned something new. Should I choose to accept it, I will be happier. Scott, 14

I will always stand up to tell what I believe in. I will never be offended if other people make fun of me when I say something. Also, I will become more social to meet new people and friends. I want to participate in all class activities. John, 14

This year in English, my goal is to improve on my reading and writing skills. I also want to improve on my verbal speaking abilities; this includes being in small groups and in front of the class. Lastly, I just want to become an all-around better student to make it easier and funner for me and everyone else. Brian, 15

Some of my goals are to one, get good grades, but I really don't think of that as a goal, more like an expectation that I set for myself. Another goal that I have set for myself is to go to college and then maybe law school, maybe not. I also feel that I have like, a feel for music, so I'm really not sure what I want to do in my life so I really can't set a goal for this, but I think I'll be good at acting, or maybe in the music business. My goal for life is to try the hardest I can and be the best I can be at anything and everything I do. Brittani, 14

Through discussion of the good student scenarios and the writing of mission statements, the class is beginning the process of metacognitive reflection that is so important to learning. At that point we turn to making a bridge between their considerations of themselves as students and their academic writing.

Writing Practice Through the *What Makes a Good Student?* Activity

Both the good student scenarios and the mission statement require students to create and apply criteria—crucially important skills in the writing of certain kinds of arguments. In order to help students transfer the verbal skills they developed to their writing, we introduced them to criteria-based writing. Assigning an encomium, an argument of praise for a controversial figure (you may be familiar with Gorgias's "Encomium of Helen"), seemed like an ideal way to incorporate the criteria of being a good student into a grounded argument.

While the encomium is perhaps not as commonly used in the English classroom, it still accomplishes a major goal of the English curriculum: writing to defend a point of view. The other great aspect of the encomium is that it requires students to defend a controversial point of view. We feel that writing on a controversy fosters good writing because students must defend their point of view in anticipation of the arguments of others. An argument praising, say, Mother Teresa is far easier than one praising the pop star Madonna. Because most people readily agree that Mother Teresa was a great humanitarian, a writer would not need to exert much energy to persuade his or her audience. And less exertion means less work, less evidence, and a less appealing writing product.

If students are to defend controversial points of view, they need to understand the basic components of argument. In our classrooms, we teach Toulmin's (1958) model of argument. Toulmin delineates three essentials to a grounded argument: a claim (a statement of opinion), reason/evidence (facts or observations in support of an opinion), and a warrant (a general rule that explains how the reason offered supports the claim) (Lunsford, Ruszkiewicz, and Walters 2001). The third component, the rule, is the most challenging aspect of the argument for the student. As many teachers have experienced, students can readily offer an answer or opinion in writing, but they rarely explain how they reached that opinion without some prompting.

Having established rules for a good student, however, means that students have already engaged in writing general rules to link evidence to a claim. Asking students to write a short essay identifying the best student from the What Makes a Good Student? activity allows them to transfer their ability to make arguments during a conversation to a writing situation in which their conversational partners are imagined. Because creating arguments that reflect Toulmin's model is a new concept for most students, we suggest that you provide a graphic organizer (e.g., Figure 13–2, Organizing My Good Student Encomium) to help students arrange their body paragraphs. The organizer also makes it more likely that students will provide concrete evidence to support their claims.

The assignment of an encomium praising a student from the scenarios accomplished our two major goals. Students developed procedural knowledge because they had to apply what they had learned to do in a new situation. Students developed metacognitive understandings because they had to make their ideas about what makes a good student explicit, which required them to think about their thinking. This assignment may be challenging enough for young writers, but in a more sophisticated classroom the encomium praising a good student could simply be a stepping stone, a precursor to a much more detailed research essay praising an individual or object. Ultimately, the goal of using metacognitive and reflective practices in the English classroom is to familiarize students with a process so that they can recall and apply that process in other situations. In keeping with this goal, we ask students to write a second encomium, this time praising someone the student selects for a reason other than being a good student. For younger students, it might be best to suggest a topic with which students are familiar. High school students deal with issues of friendship, loyalty, and leadership enough that these would be "definable." For a senior elective writing course, we ask students to identify and research an individual, then determine why this person deserves praise. Essential to both versions of the assignment is the student's determination of justifiable criteria independent of classmates or teacher-supplied scenarios.

We prepare for this assignment by identifying a celebrity who has been the subject of some controversy. Again, modeling through a discussion establishes a process similar to the written process the student will complete during the assignment. For the past several years, we have used Bart Simpson for this model encomium topic. Most students are familiar with Bart and, because of their familiarity, offer rich information about him. Showing a short clip of an episode of *The Simpsons* is typically enough to allow even students who are less familiar with him to participate in the discussion.

In our initial discussion we determine what Bart's praiseworthy and blameworthy qualities are and list them on an overheard. (See Figure 13–3.) We also use this list to discuss whether the admirable qualities outweigh his negative qualities or vice versa. At that point we ask students to take on the role of a defender of Bart and ask, *What does Bart offer to society that makes him unique, unlike anyone or anything else?* The answer to this question could likely be turned into a thesis for an encomium praising Bart Simpson.

FIGURE 13–2 *Organizing My Good Student Encomium*

Organizing My Good Student Encomium

_____deserves praise for being a good student.

Why?

CRITERIA for a good student	EVIDENCE that proves my nominee meets the criteria	EXPLANATION of how my evidence meets the criteria

Reflective Teaching, Reflective Learning edited by McCann, Johannessen, Kahn, Smagorinsky, and Smith (Heinemann: Portsmouth, NH); © 2005.

FIGURE 13–3 *To Praise or Blame Bart?*

To Praise or Blame Bart?

Who would praise Bart Simpson?	Why?

Who would condemn Bart Simpson?	Why?

Reflective Teaching, Reflective Learning edited by McCann, Johannessen, Kahn, Smagorinsky, and Smith (Heinemann: Portsmouth, NH); © 2005.

As a class, students generate evidence to prove that Bart makes a unique contribution to society because of the admirable qualities students identified. To aid students in this search for evidence we use an article by Richard Corliss (1998), entitled "Bart Simpson." Be warned that some of the vocabulary in the article is a little sophisticated for a ninth grader.

Once the class has established reasons why Bart should be praised and evidence to support those reasons, we ask, "What about the reasons why some people might despise Bart? We can't forget about these people. What group of people do you believe most often criticizes Bart?" Typically, "parents" is the response. We then encourage the class to think about how they can overcome that criticism by asking, "How can you prove to parents that these admirable qualities you have listed are really important?" This last question is simply a way of encouraging the students to defend their criteria, since they will have to do this in their individual encomiums.

Writing the encomium on a controversial figure requires students to do everything they did when they wrote about the good students and more. Since the student is the first to establish the rules on which to base his or her judgment, he or she must justify the logic behind each rule. Therefore, the final encomium should have an introduction, a major claim (statement of opinion), several criteria (warrants) for why the subject deserves praise, reasons (backing) why those criteria are important, evidence that the individual has fulfilled the criteria, and a conclusion.

Reading the final encomium assignment helped us determine how much knowledge each student had of Toulmin's model of argument. However, in keeping with our interest in metacognition, we also asked students to complete a postwriting reflection. This postwriting reflection required students not only to describe the process they used in writing the encomium, but also to consider what parts of the process and product were particularly challenging or particularly enjoyable. (See Figure 13–4 for the reflection assignment.)

In summary, in our classes we try to help students develop procedural knowledge they can transfer to new learning situations and metacognitive knowledge about themselves that will help them determine their learning goals. We have found these activities invaluable in achieving our goal of helping students learn content, process, and purpose. In essence, we hope to help students learn not only the *what* but also the *how* and the *why*.

FIGURE 13–4 *Reflection on Persuasive Writing*

Reflection on Persuasive Writing

Directions: You have completed a first draft of an encomium. Consider the methods you used to write this assignment and the thoughts you used to compose the argument. Reflect on this process by answering the questions below.

Identify one issue or problem you struggled with while writing this paper.

What did you do to try to solve this issue/problem?

What one idea/thought do you want your audience to remember after reading your argument?

What did you do to emphasize this idea/thought?

If you had to do this assignment a second time, what steps would you take to complete a second encomium?

Reflective Teaching, Reflective Learning edited by McCann, Johannessen, Kahn, Smagorinsky, and Smith (Heinemann: Portsmouth, NH); © 2005.

References

BROWN, A. 1987. "Metacognition, Executive Control, Self-Regulation, and Other More Mysterious Mechanisms." In *Metacognition, Motivation, and Understanding,* edited by F. Weinert and R. Kluwe, 65–116. Hillsdale, NJ: Lawrence Erlbaum Associates.

CORLISS, R. 1998. "Bart Simpson." *Time,* June 8, 204–206.

COVEY, SEAN. 1998. *The Seven Habits of Highly Effective Teens.* New York: Simon and Schuster.

COVEY, STEPHEN. 1989. *The Seven Habits of Highly Effective People.* New York: Simon and Schuster.

FLAVELL, J. H., AND H. M. WELLMAN. 1977. "Metamemory." In *Perspectives on the Development of Memory and Cognition,* edited by J. R. V. Kail and W. Hagan, 3–33. Hillsdale, NJ: Lawrence Erlbaum Associates.

FOGARTY, R. 1994. *Teach for Metacognitive Reflection.* Palatine, IL: IRI/Skylight.

GORGIAS. 1990. "Encomium of Helen" (translated by G. A. Kennedy). In *The Rhetorical Tradition: Readings from Classical Times to the Present,* edited by P. Bizzell and B. Herzberg, 40–42. Boston: Bedford Books.

HACKER, D. 1998. "Definitions and Empirical Foundations." In *Metacognition in Educational Theory and Practice,* edited by D. Hacker, J. Dunlosky, and A. Graesser, 1–24. Mahweh, NJ: Erlbaum.

HILLOCKS, G., JR. 1986. *Research on Written Composition: New Directions for Teaching.* Urbana, IL: National Conference on Research in English/ERIC Clearninghouse on Reading and Communication Skills.

———. 1995. *Teaching Writing as Reflective Practice.* New York: Teachers College Press.

———. 1999. *Ways of Thinking, Ways of Teaching.* New York: Teachers College Press.

JOHANNESSEN, L., E. KAHN, AND C. WALTER. 1982. *Designing and Sequencing Prewriting Activities.* Urbana, IL: NCTE.

LUNSFORD, A., J. RUSZKIEWICZ, AND K. WALTERS. 2001. *Everything's an Argument.* Boston: Bedford/St. Martin's.

SITKO, B. 1998. "Knowing How to Write: Metacognition and Writing Instruction." In *Metacognition in Educational Theory and Practice,* edited by D. Hacker, J. Dunlosky, and A. Graesser, 93–116. Mahweh, NJ: Erlbaum.

SMAGORINSKY, P. 1991. "The Writer's Knowledge and the Writing Process: A Protocol Analysis." *Research in the Teaching of English* 2: 339–364.

SMAGORINSKY, P., T. MCCANN, AND S. KERN. 1987. *Explorations: Introductory Activities for Literature and Composition, 7–12.* Urban, IL: NCTE.

TOULMIN, S. E. 1958. *The Uses of Argument.* New York: Cambridge University Press.

14 Increase the Peace

Engaging Students in Authentic Discussion and Inquiry to Help Prevent School Violence

STEVEN GEVINSON

Oak Park and River Forest High School
Oak Park, Illinois

For three years, David Hammond, a writer and instructional designer; Phil Thompson, a commercial artist and digital media specialist; and I worked to design an instructional resource for adolescents that would decrease the incidence of violence in schools. In early 2001 when we, as fathers of children in the local public schools, began thinking about this project, we were tuned in to the growing alarm about school shootings and concerned that an apparent national epidemic of violence might come to our own hometown. We became convinced that we could create a teaching tool that would equip adolescents with decision-making skills and that might help minimize school violence. *Increase the Peace* (ITP) is our effort to make a resource for classroom use that is effective in preventing or reducing the likelihood of students committing violent acts. ITP contains six activities that invite learners to explore critical problems and to respond to them in a purposeful and constructive way. They are designed particularly for the classroom but appropriate for use in other settings as well. In designing the activities our thinking was informed deeply by some essential pedagogical principles fostered over the years by George Hillocks, Jr. Our interactive software requires access to a computer to display the program, but I describe here some of the activities that represent the goals and procedures of the CD-ROM[1] to give the reader a sense of the instructional possibilities.

Conceptual Underpinnings

Once we decided that our primary audience would be students in secondary-school classrooms, our intuitions suggested that the CD-ROM format would serve us best. It offers sophisticated, stimulating visual and audio possibilities as well as opportunities for interactivity. Further, our educational experiences, especially as influenced by Hillocks'

---

1   The CD-ROM referred to in this chapter will be available for purchase from Heinemann in 2006. Go to www.heinemann.com for details.

principles, suggested to us that the most effective teaching approach would be not to dispense advice didactically or simply to transmit information about violence prevention, but rather to engage students in critical thinking, focused imagining, and provocative discussion with peers about the live issues closely associated with school violence. To enhance our understanding, we read literature on school violence prevention, reviewed existing school violence prevention programs, and interviewed experts in the field of youth violence prevention.

The literature on youth violence prevention is consistent, its findings perhaps best digested and reflected in the pre-Columbine report issued jointly by the U.S. Departments of Education and Justice, *Early Warning, Timely Response: A Guide to Safe Schools* (Dwyer, Osher, and Wanger 1998). The report concludes that youth violence prevention is a communitywide effort to create an environment of safety and connectedness for young people, reaching out especially to those who are troubled and isolated. The report emphasizes the need for school policies, prevention programs, and response plans for dealing with violence. As the title suggests, a key to violence prevention is recognizing the early warning signs and intervening quickly and effectively. In addition to the need for effective communication between adults and young people around these issues, the report stresses how important it is for young people to share concerns with adults when something seems to be going wrong—personally or with a friend or peer.

In our survey of violence prevention programs targeting the school market, some quite extensive and expensive, we found a tendency to present information and provide advice rather than to emphasize putting students in situations in which they had to imaginatively confront complex circumstances and think, discuss, role-play, or analyze their way through to a solution or set of viable possibilities. Our Hillocks-influenced pedagogical predilections led us in the latter direction. As we designed our program and developed our activities, we attempted to incorporate the key research findings on recognizing early warning signs and the importance of effective communication into educational experiences in which students would be highly engaged and challenged to think authentically about the best ways to respond in specific, complex, threatening situations.

To test our predilections, we consulted subject-matter experts, professionals with direct experience in youth violence prevention and conflict resolution. The experts we consulted included a psychiatric social worker who had been brought into a school district to counsel and work with students following a deadly shooting spree in an elementary school; a psychiatrist with many years of experience in treating troubled, isolated, suicidal, violent young people; a township director of youth services with extensive experience in working with troubled youth and community-based violence prevention programs; a conflict resolution facilitator with substantial experience in working with parents, students, and educators; an experienced dean-counselor in a local high school; and a local chief of police.

To a person, the professionals agreed that our emphasis on bringing inquiry activities to students was a sound approach both psychologically and practically. No one could say, of course, to what extent our approach might prevent violent episodes; and the psychiatrist, in particular, voiced skepticism about whether a program like ours could have much of an impact on truly troubled children such as some of those he had treated over the years. But in judging the efficacy of this classroom intervention strategy, the clear preponderance of expert opinion reinforced our sense that highly engaged interaction involving realistic issues and situations would be most likely to bring students to a better understanding and to prepare them for effective action.

We also explored our concept in a focus group, with about ten thoughtful, socially conscious high school student activists in a group called Students for Peace and Justice. They offered many suggestions for improving the realism of our proposed scenarios and discussed quite thoughtfully the possibilities of actual learning about preventing school violence taking place in a classroom setting. Despite their past experiences with artificial programs that were "cheesy and stupid," their overall response to our approach was positive, and we came away increasingly encouraged that we were on to something that could work in significant ways.

It is no coincidence that the activities we designed conform in important ways to the profiles of activities incorporating the environmental mode and the inquiry focus of instruction as described by Hillocks (1984, 1986a, 1986b, 1995). Hillocks found environmental and inquiry instruction in writing to be by far the most powerful mode and focus of instruction in his landmark meta-analysis examining twenty years of experimental treatment studies of written composition instruction. We wanted the ITP activities to involve problem-centered discussions likely to engage students in active debate among themselves; Hillocks describes the environmental mode as characterized in part by "activities, such as small-group problem-centered discussions, conducive to high levels of peer interaction concerning specific tasks" (1986a, 122). We wanted the ITP activities to generate a kind of intellectual and emotional collision between students and facts, opinions, or concrete situations that would necessarily involve the students in reasoning or working through their complex responses to a specific resolution; Hillocks described the inquiry focus as presenting "students with sets of data . . . *and* . . . [requiring students to] develop skills or strategies for dealing with the data" (211). The results of Hillocks' meta-analysis suggest an inquiry-based approach—combining environmental mode with inquiry focus—as the most suitable means for encouraging young people to effectively confront and process the essential conditions and considerations that come into play in situations that may lead to violence.

In his meta-analysis, Hillocks discusses at length McCleary's 1979 study, which has clear implications for our purposes. McCleary's study involved college students in developing arguments in response to situations involving challenging ethical dilemmas. The students were presented with "concrete scenarios about actions in particular situations" (Hillocks 1986a, 183). For example, one scenario places a father and daughter in a conflict involving money and morality. The father promises to pay the daughter's college expenses if she maintains a C average. She carries a B average, but as a twenty-one-year-old junior, she moves into an apartment with her boyfriend—to the father's chagrin—paying her share of expenses with the money she receives from her father. He threatens to cut her off financially if she doesn't move. The students in the study had to decide whether the father was ethically justified in issuing his ultimatum and to develop a logical argument in support of their position.

Each of McCleary's treatment groups, whether they received instruction in formal logic or not, had pre-to-post effect sizes that exceeded 1.5 standard deviation points—among the largest gains in all the studies considered in Hillocks' meta-analysis (183). The key to success for McCleary's treatment groups seems to have been presenting students with compelling, concrete scenarios and providing them with specific instructions that defined their problem and clarified how the students were required to deal with it. As it will become apparent in the next section, in which I describe the various activities of *Increase the Peace*, we also took care to put students in situations requiring them to wrestle among themselves to solve morally complex problems and to explain how they did so.

Increase the Peace: The Whys and Wherefores of Six Activities

For our program we developed five core activities and one concluding activity. Although users of *Increase the Peace* may proceed through the program in any order (thanks to the flexibility of the CD-ROM format), we sequenced the activities as we did for pedagogical reasons.

We begin with two activities that call for relatively simple, direct responses, breaking the ice on the topic of violence prevention and activating students' prior knowledge on the subject as they engage in initial discussions of their opinions, assumptions, and preconceptions about various aspects of school violence. These activities introduce key issues, raise preliminary questions, explore untested opinions, and establish schematic context. They prepare students for the more complex, decision-requiring simulation, analysis, and application activities to follow.

The next three activities call on students to draw complex inferences in ambiguous but highly consequential and empathetically emotional scenarios, and to analyze psychological contingencies and moral responsibility in actual incidents. This set of activities is the heart of the ITP program, engaging students analytically and imaginatively in the highly charged, highly stressful intellectual, emotional, and even spiritual welter that young people may confront when violence erupts or threatens.

The final activity asks students to decompress and to apply what they have experienced and learned in the program to the actual world in which they live day to day. In completing the previous activities, the students in effect scale an essential scaffold to a height affording a clearer perspective on genuine possibilities. In reaching this concluding activity, they are ready to reflect responsibly, realistically, and purposefully on the roles they can constructively play in reducing violence in their world.

Activity 1: "Gut Reaction"

Everyone has an opinion about the causes of school violence, but we can be confident that those opinions are almost always wrong, or at least quite inadequate in accounting for the complexities of causation when it comes to violent behavior. Nevertheless, in a program attempting to engage students in productive reflection and discussion on the topic and to deepen their understanding and increase their capacity for effective action, it is useful to activate students' violence causation and prevention schemata, to break through what might be the thick ice between students' ideas and their eagerness to discuss them by eliciting their gut reactions to the provocative opinions of peers.

Our first ice-breaking activity presents thirty-second, "people-on-the-street" video clips of ordinary students responding pro and con to fundamental questions about school violence prevention, such as, "Would you report someone who brings a gun to school?" and "Could Columbine happen at your school?" Students see the question at the top of the screen with the words "YES" and "NO" flashing and moving, inviting a choice. The viewer may choose one response at a time.

For example, when the viewer clicks YES for the question "Would you report someone who brings a gun to school?" a young man appears on the screen saying, "I definitely would. I'm a pretty strong pacifist, and I think that gun threats, whether they are made seriously or nonseriously, they're still a serious issue and they should be reported." For the NO response the viewer sees a young man saying, "Personally, if I heard that a student would bring a gun to school, I wouldn't say anything, because if he's going to bring a gun to school and then I tell and he finds out that, oh, Damone told, then how do I know he's not going to come after me or something? And besides it's none of my business. If someone else gets hurt, I'll just have to pray for them" (see Figure 14–1).

FIGURE 14–1   *Screen capture from the NO response.*

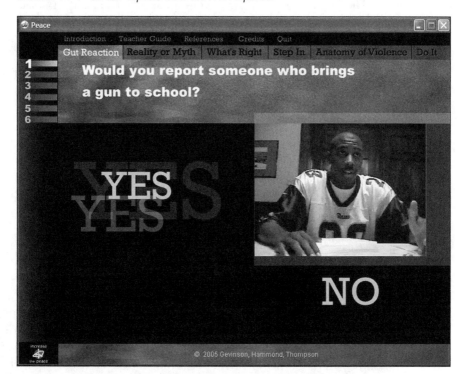

After viewing each pair of video responses, students in the classroom are asked to respond for themselves, yes or no. After students have responded to each question, the teacher tallies the number of yes and no responses for each question on the board and asks students on each side of the question to explain the reasoning behind their positions. This activity quickly involves students in taking controversial, even risky positions on seemingly simple questions and in justifying those positions and engaging in debate about them with classmates. The teacher clarifies that the object of "Gut Reaction" is not to delineate right and wrong answers to yes-or-no questions, but rather to engage students initially in dialogue about school violence prevention and to begin to explore the complexities involved in making schools as safe as they can be.

Activity 2: "Reality or Myth"

Just as it is useful to open students' eyes early, through debate and discussion, to complexities of causation and prevention efforts, it is also useful to challenge students to test common beliefs and intuitions about what's true when it comes to youth violence and preventing it. "Reality or Myth" brings students out of the world of opinion and belief and into the world of fact. We present students with five plausible truths about violence prevention (e.g., "Most students who bring a gun to school do not get caught" and "Watching a lot of violent television leads to more aggressive and violent behavior in children") and ask students to decide whether the statements represent reality or myth.

The "Reality or Myth" screen displays the statement at the top with the words "Reality" and "Myth" flashing and moving below. The viewer selects one and clicks. The correct answer pops up, accompanied by a noise indicating a successful or unsuccessful guess, as appropriate (see Figure 14–2).

As in "Gut Reaction," we suggest that students first respond individually to the question of whether each statement represents reality or a myth. The teacher then tallies the results on the board as a starting point for discussion. Students explain why they think each statement is reality or myth and what they find surprising or disturbing about the truth of the matter in each case. Further, students discuss the implications of each fact or set of facts for the issue of violence prevention. Students also brainstorm what actions social institutions in the larger society might take to deal with the problematic situations and trends that are the realities of our world.

Activity 3: "What's Right"

After the first two activities, with students beginning to think critically about many of the complexities of youth violence and the difficulties involved in preventing it, they are ready to engage productively in imagining realistic situations that they could encounter in their own world, situations that would call on them to make critical judgments about what is the right thing to do in such situations. In "What's Right" students see and hear three brief narratives in which they are participants or bystanders. As they listen to the voice-over narration, they view a series of line

FIGURE 14–2 *Screen capture of the correct response to the statement, "Most students who bring a gun to school do not get caught."*

drawings that suggest key moments in the scenario (see Figure 14–3). Students choose from several possible courses of action or propose their own ideas of what is the best thing to do to defuse a potentially explosive situation.

Again, the teacher may choose to tally the class results on the board for each of the scenarios to represent graphically where students stand, which can suggest how a teacher may decide to focus the discussion or arrange the debate. The class becomes a forum for a practical discussion of doing the right thing and presenting clear, thoughtful justifications—justifications that must convince classmates—for specific behavior.

An additional feature of this activity is that the program allows the teacher to bring expert opinion directly into the discussion. We have built in video clips of professionals in the field of violence prevention (a director of township youth services, a high school dean-counselor, a local police chief, and a conflict resolution facilitator) responding to the same scenarios discussed by the students. It is especially effective to carry out the student discussion before introducing the experts' opinions. After hearing from the experts, it is difficult to keep students from responding to those opinions and reflecting on their own, earlier choices and justifications. It is particularly interesting for students to discuss the ideas of the experts when they offer different solutions.

FIGURE 14–3 *Screen capture from the first scenario, "Conspiracy in the cafeteria?"*

Such a situation occurs strikingly in another scenario, "Bad Chemistry in the lab," in which a student tells the following story:

> One morning in science class we were combining chemicals for a lab, and this huge fight just broke out between two of these lab partners. Our teacher— she's this really small lady—she tried to get them separated, but that really wasn't going to happen. Then all these other kids in the class came in closer, and they started yelling at them and egging them on, and the kids started fighting, like, worse. I could see that someone was going to get really hurt if this fight wasn't going to get stopped fast.

After students listen to the voice-over and view the drawings, the screen poses a question and possible responses:

What would you do?

a. Run out of the room to find a security person or other adult.

b. Stay out of it.

c. Start yelling, "Break it up," encourage your classmates to help you stop it, and then step between the combatants to break up the fight.

d. Ask your teacher what you can do to help.

In this case, the experts disagree. Three of them recommend running out of the classroom to get adult help, while a fourth recommends taking directive action, telling one student to go get help, telling another to call 911, telling another to move students away from the combatants, and so on. The differences in expert opinion invite highly engaged, substantive debate among students over what is the best thing to do in such a situation and why.

Activity 4: "Step In"

The next activity, "Step In," takes students a step beyond critically reflecting on a what-if situation to gaining deeper imaginative insight by stepping into the shoes of a person in a threatening situation. The heart of this activity is serious role-play. A well-structured role-play activity engages students imaginatively, critically, and emotionally. In "Step In" students pair up, take the roles of people in dangerous situations that could easily happen in their world and could easily turn quite ugly and even violent, and play out the situation to a likely conclusion.

Viewers watch as a situation is briefly described by a series of still shots of Playmobil characters in suggestive positions. One scenario, "He's mine," involves two girls in a confrontation over a boy (see Figure 14–4). To give the students the imaginative experience from both sides, after they role-play the situation through to a conclusion, they switch roles and do it again. Depending on how the students

FIGURE 14–4   *Screen capture from "Step In" activity.*

talk to each other, the verbal confrontations may resolve themselves along a spectrum ranging from peaceful to violent.

After the role-playing in pairs, students share their various results with the class, either by describing them or acting them out. During discussion students explore the various paths that verbal confrontations may take, depending on how people talk to each other. Under the teacher's guidance they analyze how the situations played themselves out, looking for turning points and critical moments, trying to understand how decisions in the heat of high emotion are made, and discussing how thoughtful engagement can alter an outcome. An activity like "Step In" can bring young people closer to the truth of action and make their reflecting, imagining, feeling, and deciding more serious, genuine, and realistic.

Activity 5: "Anatomy of Violence"

The final core activity, "Anatomy of Violence," requires students to examine carefully an actual incident of school violence. As we know, unfortunately, there are many incidents from which to choose.

"Anatomy of Violence" is structured as a research assignment. The keys to a successful research project, both in assigning it and in carrying it out, are a high level of student interest in the research topic and a high level of analytical skill. At this stage in the ITP program, which elicits from students increasingly complex responses as they proceed through it, students should have a strong curiosity about how actual violent incidents have occurred as well as much critical insight into the conditions that can lead to violence and what can be done to prevent it.

For this activity we walk students through a straightforward rubric of analysis that they must apply on their own to a violent incident that they choose to research and analyze. Before turning students loose to pursue their research questions, the activity provides teachers with the opportunity to model and rehearse the thinking and questioning that students will be required to do. Students review the facts involved in a shooting in a San Diego high school and answer questions on what happened, who or what bears responsibility, and how the shooting could have been prevented. We provide sample answers with which students may compare their own analyses (see Figure 14–5).

Once students understand the rubric well and are given access to good sources of information, they are on their own to conduct independent research. "Anatomy of Violence" puts students in the position of applying the knowledge and skill they have gained in the classroom to an all-too-real sequence of events in the larger world, which can reinforce their understandings and increase their confidence in their capacity to make good independent decisions.

Activity 6: "Do It"

ITP closes with "Do It," which challenges students to consider and decide what action they can take to reduce violence and increase peace in their world. The idea behind this activity is that while ITP should put students in a better position to understand and act to prevent potential violence when they find themselves in its

FIGURE 14–5 *Screen capture displaying the central components of the "Anatomy of Violence" activity.*

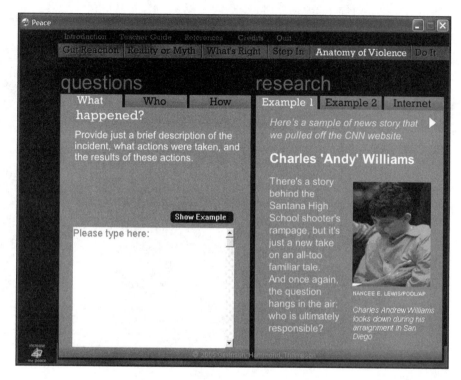

proximity, there is no reason for a young person to wait for violence to stare him or her in the face before taking effective action to prevent it.

First, the teacher reviews with students what they have done in the five core ITP activities (see Figure 14–6). After the review, each student reflects with a partner on what they can do to help prevent or reduce violence. After that, the teacher leads a class discussion on possible actions that students can take now. The teacher then reviews possibilities for actions suggested in ITP, which we have provided as bulleted lists under the verbs Be, Write, Join, Start, and Do (see Figure 14–7).

The following are the lists under each verb:

1. **BE** more peaceful and helpful in your daily interactions:

   - with siblings
   - with parents
   - with friends
   - with classmates
   - with relatives
   - in groups
   - when encountering strangers in public places

FIGURE 14–6 *Screen capture illustrating how the activity facilitates the review.*

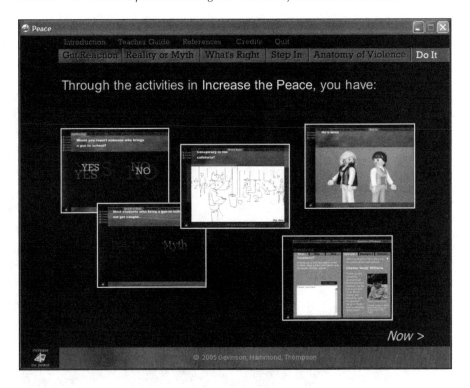

2. **WRITE** a letter to

   ▪ an editor

   ▪ a government official

   ▪ a manufacturer

   ▪ a media producer

3. **JOIN** an organization whose purpose it is to increase the peace:

   ▪ Stop the Violence (www.stv.net/)

   ▪ Student Pledge Against Gun Violence (www.pledge.org/)

   ▪ Coalition to Stop Gun Violence (www.gunfree.org/)

   ▪ Amnesty International (www.amnesty.org/)

   ▪ National Coalition Against Domestic Violence (www.webmerchants.com/ncadv/default.htm)

   ▪ Center for Study and Prevention of Violence (www.colorado.edu/cspv/)

4. **START** an antiviolence organization in your school, with a name such as:

- Students for Peace and Justice

- Students Organized Against Racism (SOAR)

- Give Peace a Chance

- Rules for Young Peace Radicals

5. **DO** some community outreach work:

- organize public hearings and forums

- participate in antiviolence youth rallies and awareness campaigns

- do gang-prevention work

- with permission, distribute antiviolence pamphlets at a concert

- organize a boycott of a gun manufacturer

- organize a memorial or vigil for a violence victim

FIGURE 14–7   *Screen capture illustrating how a viewer can access the lists.*

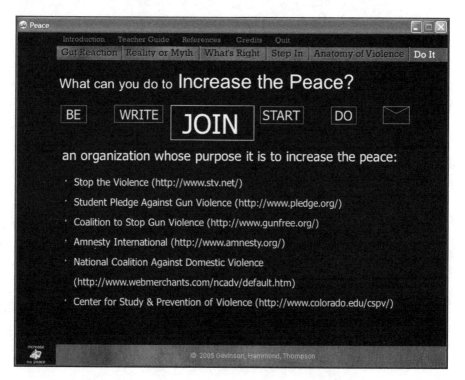

Finally, students write a letter to themselves, which the teacher will deliver to them in two or three months. The letter is a chance for students to memorialize their conviction and capitalize on their momentum, giving them a chance to remind themselves later of what they were thinking and feeling about increasing the peace as they finished the program.

Creating a program to help prevent school violence is an iffy proposition at best. But children do develop, and children do learn; and they learn and develop best, it seems, when they struggle genuinely and constructively with challenging tasks under excellent guidance and facilitation. Hillocks identified those most effective learning conditions in the field of composition instruction as the environmental mode and the inquiry focus of instruction. Hammond, Thompson, and I have reasoned that those conditions for learning apply in any field in which students must think critically, imagine creatively, feel empathetically, and communicate persuasively. We thus endeavored to create and exploit those conditions when we designed our program to help prevent youth violence. Because we have attempted to create the conditions for deep learning, we are hopeful that after young people have received a classroom treatment of *Increase the Peace*, they will have grown in such a way that they will be prepared to make important contributions to their dangerous world as true peacemakers.

Inquiry-based instruction is the best teacher, fostering better than any other approach the most important human learning. *Increase the Peace* is an effort to utilize the principles of inquiry-based instruction to make our schools safer for the best teaching and learning.

References

DWYER, K., D. OSHER, AND C. WANGER. 1998. *Early Warning, Timely Response: A Guide to Safe Schools.* Washington, DC: U.S. Department of Education.

HILLOCKS, G., JR. 1984. "What Works in Teaching Composition: A Meta-Analysis of Experimental Treatment Studies." *American Journal of Education* (November): 133–70.

———. 1986a. *Research on Written Composition: New Directions for Teaching.* Urbana IL: ERIC/NCRE.

———. 1986b. "The Writer's Knowledge: Theory, Research and Implications for Practice." In *The Teaching of Writing,* 85th Yearbook of the National Society for the Study of Education, Part II, edited by A. Petrosky and D. Bartholomae, 71–94. Chicago: National Society for the Study of Education.

———. 1995. *Teaching Writing as Reflective Practice.* New York: Teachers College Press.

MCCLEARY, W. J. 1979. Teaching Deductive Logic: A Test of the Toulmin and Aristotelian Models for Critical Thinking and College Composition. Unpublished doctoral dissertation, University of Texas.

CONTRIBUTORS

JULIANNA CUCCI enjoys teaching English at Maine West High School in Des Plaines, Illinois.

DECLAN FITZPATRICK teaches English and Reading at Ladue Horton Watkins High School in St. Louis, Missouri.

JOSEPH M. FLANAGAN teaches English and serves as the English department chair at York Community High School in Elmhurst, Illinois.

STEVEN GEVINSON is the English division chair at Oak Park and River Forest High School in Oak Park, Illinois, where he has taught English since 1978.

GEORGE HILLOCKS, JR. is professor emeritus, University of Chicago, where he was Director of the Master of Arts in Teaching English program for more than thirty years. His awards include the Russell Award for distinguished research in the teaching of English (for the book *Teaching Writing as Reflective Practice*) and the 2004 NCTE Distinguished Service Award.

LARRY R. JOHANNESSEN teaches at Northern Illinois University where he prepares secondary English teachers, and is the director of Undergraduate Studies in English. He is a coauthor of *In Case You Teach English: An Interactive Casebook for Prospective and Practicing Teachers* and *Supporting Beginning English Teachers: Research and Implications for Teacher Induction.*

ELIZABETH KAHN has been teaching English for twenty-eight years. She is currently chair of the English department at James B. Conant High School in Hoffman Estates, Illinois, and a National Board Certified teacher. She is coauthor of *Designing and Sequencing Prewriting Activities* and *Writing About Literature.*

JAMIE A. KOWALCZYK is a doctoral student at the University of Wisconsin in Madison, Wisconsin, where she currently teaches and supervises students at the undergraduate level in Curriculum and Instruction. After completing her MAT in English at the University of Chicago, she taught English in high schools in the Chicago area.

CAROL D. LEE is associate professor of Education and Social Policy as well as African American Studies at Northwestern University. She is past president of the National Conference of Research on Language and Literacy, author of *Signifying as a Scaffold for Literary Interpretation,* and coeditor of *Vygotskian Perspectives on Literacy Research.*

JEFFREY CONANT MARKHAM has taught English in Chicago area schools since 1992, and for the last eleven years, at New Trier High School in Winnetka, Illinois.

JOANNE M. MARSHALL is an assistant professor in educational leadership and policy studies at Iowa State University, where she studies religion and public schools.

THOMAS M. MCCANN is the assistant superintendent for Curriculum and Instruction for Elmhurst Public Schools, Elmhurst, Illinois, and an adjunct professor of English at Elmhurst College. He is a coauthor of *In Case You Teach English: An Interactive Casebook for Prospective and Practicing Teachers* and *Supporting Beginning English Teachers: Research and Implications for Teacher Induction.*

TIM PAPPAGEORGE has been teaching high school English since 1992 and now chairs the English department at Maine South High School in Park Ridge, Illinois.

KEVIN PERKS, a former language arts instructor, is a literacy specialist at Noble High School in North Berwick, Maine. He is also currently a PhD candidate at the University of New Hampshire.

DAVID A. RAGSDALE teaches English and journalism at Clarke Central High School in Athens, Georgia. He also is a participant in the Red Clay Writing Project, a National Writing Project affiliate, at the University of Georgia.

PETER SMAGORINSKY taught high school English in the Chicago area from 1976 to 1990 and is now professor of English Education at the University of Georgia. His recent books include *The Discourse of Character Education: Culture Wars in the Classroom* and *Research on Composition: Multiple Perspectives on Two Decades of Change.* He has been the recipient of the *English Journal*'s Edwin Hopkins Award, the *English Education*'s Janet Emig Award, and the Raymond B. Cattell Early Career Award for Programmatic Research presented by the American Educational Research Association.

MICHAEL W. SMITH is a professor at Temple University's College of Education. He joined the ranks of college teachers after eleven years of teaching high school. He has been chair of the Literature Special Interest Group of the American Educational Research Association, cochair of the National Council of Teachers of English Assembly for Research, and coeditor of *Research in the*

Teaching of English. He received the 2003 David H. Russell Award for Distinguished Research in the Teaching of English for his book, coauthored with Jeffrey Wilhelm, *"Reading Don't Fix No Chevys": Literacy in the Lives of Young Men.*

KIERSTIN THOMPSON teaches English at Downers Grove South High School in Downers Grove, Illinois.

JENNIFER ROLOFF WELCH, an MAT under George Hillocks' tutelage, taught middle school ESOL and high school English outside Chicago. Currently she is a doctoral student at Harvard's Graduate School of Education.

JEFFREY D. WILHELM is a professor of English Education at Boise State University and the founding director of the Boise State Writing Project. He is the author or coauthor of fourteen books about literacy education, including *You Gotta BE the Book* (winner of the NCTE Promising Research Award) and *"Reading Don't Fix No Chevys": Literacy in the Lives of Young Men* (winner of the David H. Russell Award for Distinguished Research in English Education).